An Introduction to

AS/400

System

Operations

By Patrice Gapen &
Heidi Rothenbuehler

A Division of
DUKE COMMUNICATIONS INTERNATIONAL

221 E. 29th Street • Loveland, CO 80538
(800) 621-1544 • (970) 663-4700 • www.dukepress.com

Library of Congress Cataloging-in-Publication Data

Gapen, Patrice.
   An introduction to AS/400 system operations / Patrice Gapen, Heidi
Rothenbuehler.
     p. cm.
   Includes bibliographical references and index.
   ISBN 1-882419-29-4
   1. IBM AS/400 (Computer) 2. Systems software. I. Rothenbuehler,
Heidi. II. Title.
QA76.8.I25919G355 1996
005.4'445—dc20   96-25318
                              CIP

Published by DUKE PRESS
DUKE COMMUNICATIONS INTERNATIONAL
Loveland, Colorado

It is the reader's responsibility to ensure procedures and techniques used from this
book are accurate and appropriate for the user's installation. No warranty is
implied or expressed.

This book was printed and bound in Canada.

ISBN 1-882419-29-4

3 4 5 6 7 WL 0 9 8

To Rod, Megan, and Robin: Who washed dishes, folded laundry, and did without my attention, so that I had time to write.
— *P.G.*

To John and Marcus: Thanks for your understanding.
— *H.R.*

Special thanks to Catherine Stoughton, Bob Yeager, Lisa Oedekoven, Luke Greene, Charlie McLean, and to Debbie Hendershot and Gale Shenefelt, for their time, effort, and resources in helping us complete this text.

Table of Contents

Preface

Preface to Instructors

A lucky few of you will have an AS/400 dedicated to instruction. Some of your institutions probably even grant extended system privileges and authorities to students studying system operations, and those students will be able to change system values, among other things. However, a great many of you are probably thrilled just to have permission to use your administration's AS/400 for a few courses. The majority of the schools that will be using this text probably have a core of courses taught on an AS/400 shared by the administration and the instructional departments, with limited levels of authority granted to the students.

To further complicate matters, the number of AS/400 models continues to increase, with all types and manner of hardware that may be attached to these various models. Open architecture and interconnection among non-IBM hardware will not simplify the AS/400's operating environment.

These greatly diverse situations explain the difficulty we experienced in producing a systems operations text that is versatile enough to be useful in your particular AS/400 scenario. With these constraints in mind, we have attempted to provide a text that covers typical daily AS/400 operational duties, as well as weekly and monthly tasks, using Version 3, Release 1, Modification 0 of OS/400, the AS/400's operating system. To ensure that the examples in the text will match your situation, we assume you are operating at a security level of 30 or higher. Even within those parameters, you may find that examples of screens we have included in this text may differ from screens you (and your students) will find on your system. This is because the screen view may vary depending on the security level at which your system is set, the authorities granted to the current user, and the assistance level at which the user is operating.

Preface to Students

When we set out to write an operations text, we were unsure what hardware, software, and authorities your school would be able to provide to you, the system operations student. Generally, we expect you to have some knowledge of the AS/400, probably in the form of an introductory course. We expect that you have learned how to sign on to the system, how to work with your particular keyboard to access the function keys, and how to access AS/400 on-line information. System operators typically help users resolve problems; separate printed output to be routed to the appropriate users; perform scheduled programs such as month-end procedures; and run the batch job queue. To facilitate your learning such functions, we assume you will have the appropriate authority to a task; and we expect the display of the AS/400 commands to be on your screen. We have provided descriptive text relating to how and when a task is done, to place this material in context. However, the figures in this text may vary from the display on your screen because your system may have a different security level. Even more likely, the figures may vary because your assistance level is not the same as that represented for a particular example.

As with other versions of OS/400, V3R1 generally places the keyboard in lowercase format. After the user or operator presses the Enter key, the text is converted into uppercase. The AS/400 operating system supports many types of keyboards, each capable of supporting different keyboard mapping schemes. To further increase the confusion, displays produced by the AS/400 are shown in both uppercase and lowercase, depending on the command submitted. In this text, all commands to be keyed from the text material are printed in uppercase. At the keyboard, you may enter the commands in uppercase or lowercase, whichever is easier for the keyboard type you are using and its mapping defaults.

Chapter 1

Introduction to the AS/400

Objectives

To understand

✓ the basic AS/400 architecture, including
    single-level storage (memory)
    the function of licensed internal code

✓ the differences between versions, releases, and modification levels of OS/400 operating systems, including
    the difference between batch and interactive subsystems

✓ the function of system values

✓ the purpose of Control Language (CL)

✓ AS/400 objects, libraries, and queues

AS/400 Architecture

The AS/400 has a highly complex architecture that includes hardware, software, security, and other components. To effectively manage this complex system and the daily tasks it performs, system operators must understand the AS/400's basic architectural concepts and related terminology. The AS/400 supports a great variety of hardware devices and software, but in this text we will discuss only the most commonly used components and those that a system operator typically needs to know about or work with.

Concepts and terms we will discuss in this chapter include the system's single-level storage approach to memory, licensed internal code, how IBM keeps the system's operating system (OS/400) current, subsystems (batch and interactive), system values, the AS/400's Control Language, objects, libraries, and queues.

Storage Management Concepts

One of the unique characteristics of the AS/400 is its use of the single-level storage concept. Other hardware manufacturers separate storage management into two separate hardware components: main memory, which is also called RAM (random access memory), and disk (more correctly called DASD, for direct access storage devices). With single-level storage, these two hardware devices are combined into a logical unit, because they are inseparable. To help you understand this concept, consider your car. The transmission and the engine are two separate, physical pieces of hardware; but if either one is not functioning, the car doesn't run. Single-level storage (or storage management) applies the same principle. Both components of memory must be functioning and be properly integrated, or the user will not be able to access the data (s)he needs.

Another storage management concept that is designed into the AS/400 is the non-traditional method of storing data on the disk drives and disk platters. Traditionally, a file is stored contiguously. If a part of the disk is unused but too small for a particular file, the operating system will bypass the small space in preference for a larger space. This approach causes gaps on the disk platter and results in the need for the system to "compress" these unused spaces.

On the AS/400, for improved performance, a single database object is usually spread over several disk drives and multiple disk platters. This approach allows for several users' data to be retrieved (seemingly) simultaneously and quickly displayed on multiple display station screens. The disk drives actually retrieve data at the same speed as before; but data retrieval appears faster to the user. This method not only improves performance but also eliminates the need to compress unused disk space. Having data distributed in this way does, however, make comprehensive backup mandatory.

Licensed Internal Code

Licensed Internal Code (LIC), also called system licensed internal code, is software that relates directly to the AS/400 hardware. LIC typically performs the following functions: storage management, pointer and address management, program management, expectation and event management, data management, I/O management, and security management. To support specific hardware models and processors of the AS/400, IBM also issues Model Unique Licensed Internal Code (MULIC) or, for some models, Feature Unique Licensed Internal Code (FULIC). MULIC/FULIC programs are model or processor dependent and change as more models are added and others are upgraded. You as the system operator may be required to install Program Temporary Fixes (PTFs) for Licensed Internal Code. A new release of LIC may be required when a new machine is being installed if the IPL disk has crashed, or if you are restoring your system after a complete system loss. We discuss installing LIC PTFs in the next section and in greater depth in Chapter 7.   *Patches*

OS/400 Versions, Releases, Modifications, and PTFs

The AS/400 is not a static, unchanging combination of hardware and software. IBM provides continuous repairs to address reported problems and make improvements to OS/400 software so the system remains at top efficiency for its users. These repairs and improvements take the form of versions,

Baby Blue = Version 4

always load PTF's as temp fix.
(Patches)

releases, modifications, and Program Temporary Fixes (PTFs). A new *version* of OS/400 contains significant new code or functions for the OS/400 operating system. A new *release* represents a major improvement to the operating system (see the Preface for the version and release being used for this text). A release is a new product, or new functions or PTFs made permanent, for an existing version of the operating system. A release can take the form of a smaller upgrade than a version. A *modification level* is frequently a collection of PTFs issued since the previous modification, release, or version; this collection of PTFs may be shipped as a single package. A change in modification level does not add new functions to the release.

IBM may ship a new release with a modification level of zero. When the release is shipped with one or more additional changes incorporated, the modification level is incremented accordingly (i.e., for Version 3, you might receive Release 2, Modification 3). PTFs are generally small corrections to a specific device or to pieces of software. PTFs are used to correct problems or potential problems found within a particular IBM licensed software product; for example, RPG/400, COBOL/400, PC Support/400, Client Access for OS/400, and RUMBA. PTF lists are updated daily and should be reviewed regularly for applicability to your hardware and software. PTF lists are available via IBM's Electronic Customer Support, which gives on-line access to IBM service facilities, technical information, and marketing support information.

electronic Customer Support.

work Management

Subsystems

The AS/400 hardware and software join together to make a secure and efficient platform for jobs performed on the system and the work management concepts associated with these jobs. One management tool available on the AS/400 is the capability to divide the system into separate work groups, called subsystems. All work on the AS/400 is done within a subsystem. The AS/400 can be divided into a myriad of subsystems for more efficient processing of different types of jobs. The subsystem description (*SBSD) is an object used to describe a subsystem and to control what tasks the subsystem performs. The subsystem and subsystem description allocate resources and manipulate system objects for the most efficient use of the different hardware and tasks the system has been designed to perform.

Priority   QINTER
QBATCH

Batch vs. Interactive Subsystems

Subsystems may run either interactive jobs or batch jobs. Interactive jobs begin when a person signs on to the terminal, and they usually have a higher priority than other tasks. Generally, interactive jobs require the user to type a command, wait for the machine to display the requested material, type another command, and so on. While waiting for the user to enter the next instruction, the operating system is either checking (polling) to see whether other users have completed a command, or it is executing tasks for another user.

A batch job generally runs with minimal (or no) interaction with the user. Batch jobs usually run on a lower priority than interactive tasks; consequently, they usually run when the AS/400 has time available. An example of a batch job might be posting all the detail journals to the general ledger. Batch jobs may also be held until a certain time of day. For example, a given batch job may be automatically run each night at 11:00 p.m. An example of such a batch job would be the nightly deletion of work files before a system backup.

System Values

System values, *SYSVAL, are AS/400 attributes that allow each installation to customize the machine to the organization's own needs and specifications. Consider, for example, the differing needs of an AS/400 installed in China and one installed in Holland. Each machine would need different alphabet characters, different displays of the time and date, and probably different security levels and hardware.

A user must have proper authority to change a system value; in many installations only the security officer has sufficient authority to make these changes. However, operators must be aware of many of the nearly 100 system values, because these values provide a convenient method for modifying small portions of the operating system — they control how a given command, or even the entire system, will perform. Particular system values control system performance; others define the security levels; yet others simply provide defaults to command options that were unspecified. System values can be divided into eight categories: Date/time, editing, system control items, library lists, allocations, message logging, storage values, and security values.

Consider the date system value QDATE, which may be either a 5-digit or 6-digit field. A 6-digit field could hold a date such as 11-28-96, while a 5-digit field would be used for a Julian date. Julian dates have no days or months; instead, they contain a single value for the day of the year. For example, the first day of January expressed as a Julian date is 1, while December 31 is 365 (or 366 in a leap year). Another system value is QYEAR, which would hold only the year value — in this example, 96. QDATFMT (an editing system value) defines how your machine will use the date value. Several options are available for this, including mm-dd-yy, used for most reports; yy/mm/dd, convenient for sorting; or dd:mm:yy, used in military format, and in many European countries. You can also customize the type of separators; the previous examples show three such options — the hyphen, the dash, and the colon.

The time value, QTIME, represents the system time of day. It comprises three other system values, QHOUR, QMINUTE, and QSECOND. QHOUR is based on a 24-hour clock. For example, 1:00 p.m. is 13. The system value QCURSYM determines the currency symbol, which is country dependent; for example, the yen, lira, franc, and dollar use different symbols.

Other system control values of interest are shown in Figure 1.1.

Figure 1.1
Commonly Used AS/400
System Values

System Control Values	Description
QABNORMSW	Indicates how the system last ended (0=normal and 1=abnormal).
QATNPGM	Contains the name of the attention program.
QAUTOCFG	Turns the auto configuration feature on (1) or off (0).
QCTLSBSD	Specifies which subsystem is to be in control when the system starts. This usually is QCTL or QBASE; can be modified.
QDEVNAMING	Defines how to name devices, using either S/36 or AS/400 standards.
QDSCJOBITV	Contains the time interval that an interactive job can remain disconnected before it is ended.
QINACTITV	Contains the time interval that an interactive job can remain inactive before the system disconnects it, ends it, or takes some other action.
QIPLDATTIM	Contains the date and time to automatically IPL.
QIPLSTS	Contain the IPL status indicator, which indicates what form of IPL last occurred.
QPWRRSTIPL	Specifies whether an automatic IPL should be started when power is restored following a power failure.
QIPLTYPE	Specifies type of IPL to perform when the system is powered on manually, with the key in the normal position. 0=unattended IPL, 1=attended IPL, 2=for problem resolution.
QKBDTYPE	Specifies a language character set for the keyboard.
QKBDBUF	Indicates whether keyboard buffering is allowed. Keyboard buffering allows the user or operator to type into a storage buffer before the key strokes are requested.
QMODEL	Holds the system model number and cannot be modified.
QPRTDEV	The name for the system's default printer, usually PRT01. This can be modified.
QRMTSIGN	Specifies whether a remote sign-on is allowed, and how to handle the remote sign-on.
QSFWERRLOG	Turns software error logging on or off.
QSTRPRTWTR	A 1 means that all print writers should be started automatically after IPL; a 0 requires the operator to manually start print writers.
QSRLNBR	Contains the pre-loaded serial number.
QTOTJOB	Indicates the total number of jobs that can be started. Affects performance.
QURPSDYTIM	If the system has an uninterruptible power supply (UPS), specifies how long the batteries are designed to supply power to the system in the event of a power failure.

Figure 1.1 continued

Figure 1.1
Continued

System Control Values	Description
QUPSMSGQ	Designates to which message queue the UPS will send messages.
QASTLVL	Contains the user assistance level.

Library List Values	Description
QUSRLIBL	A default list of up to 25 libraries for the user portion of the library list.
QSYSLIBL	A default list of up to 15 libraries for the system portion of the library list.

Allocation Control Values	Description
QACTJOB	Specifies the initial number of active jobs that will have space allocated.
QADLACTJ	When the number of jobs in QACTJOB is exceeded, specifies the additional number of active jobs that will have space allocated.
QJOBSPLA	Specifies how large to allocate a spooling area for a job.
QRCLSPLSTG	Specifies how many days to keep empty spool database members.

Message System Values	Description
QACGLVL	Indicates what job accounting level is in use; *NONE is the default.
QHSTLOGSIZ	Specifies how many records are to be stored in each version of the history log.
QPRBHLDITV	Specifies how many days a problem in the problem log should be retained.

Storage System Values	Description
QBASACTLVL	Specifies how many jobs can compete concurrently for the memory in the base storage pool.
QBASPOOL	Defines the minimum for the base storage pool size (in kilobytes).
QMAXACTLVL	Specifies the maximum number of active jobs allowed on the system.
QMCHPOOL	Specifies the machine storage pool size (in kilobytes).

Figure 1.1 continued

Figure 1.1 Continued	Security System Values	Description
	QALWOBJRST	Provides multiple choices to restore security-sensitive objects.
	QALWUSRDMN	Specifies which libraries allow user domain objects to be located in them.
	QAUDCLT	Provides choices to control how security auditing is performed.
	QAUDENDACN	Specifies action to take when security auditing cannot be performed.
	QAUDFRCLVL	Specifies how often to write security auditing journal to disk.
	QAUDLVL	Lists which security-related actions to journal.
	QAUTORMT	Turns on (1) or off (0) automatic configuration of remote controllers.
	QAUTOVRT	Indicates how many (0-9999) virtual devices to allow to be automatically configured in a remote communications environment.
	QCRTAUT	Sets the system-wide default public authority for new objects created on the system. This can be overridden by the create command.
	QCRTOBJAUD	Defines default auditing level for a newly created object.
	QDSPSGNINF	Controls the display of sign-on information.
	QINACTMSGQ	Specifies what action to take when a job is inactive for the time specified in the QINACTITV system value
	QLMTSECOFR	Specifies whether to limit the security officer from certain device access.
	QMAXSIGN	Specifies how many invalid sign-on attempts are allowed.
	QMAXSGNACN	Specifies the action to be taken after the QMAXSIGN limits have been reached.
	QPWDEXPITV	Defines the number of days a password is valid before it expires. *NOMAX is a valid option.
	QPWDMINLEN	Defines the minimum number of characters required in a password.
	QPWDRQDDIF	Controls duplicate passwords, and limits how often a user can reuse a password.
	QSECURITY	Indicates the security level; valid levels are 10, 20, 30, 40, and 50.

Control Language

Control Language (CL), an integral part of OS/400, is a set of commands by which users control operations and request system-related functions on the AS/400. A CL command usually is made up of three-character words; up to 10 characters (usually three words) can be merged together to form commands. For example, in CL, work is abbreviated as WRK, system is abbreviated as SYS, and status is abbreviated as STS. The command WRKSYSSTS, therefore, is translated as Work with the System Status. CL commands can be entered on the command line or executed from within a program. When commands are entered via a program or menu, the user selects options that are displayed in more friendly, English-type format. The program then translates the selected option into the appropriate CL command or commands. We will discuss CL commands further in Chapter 3.

Objects and Libraries

Every item stored on the AS/400 is considered to be an *object*. Because every stored item is an object, backup and restore procedures become more manageable. Objects are categorized by type, which allows the user to specify what types of objects are required for a given task or backup procedure. Objects include data files, user profiles, job queues, message queues, print queues, compiled programs, word processing documents, menus, and so on. Some file objects may contain other items, called *members*, depending on the characteristics of the main file object.

Each object is assigned an owner when it is created. The owner is either the user or the group profile that created the object. When the object is created, the owner is given all the object and data authorities to that object. If ownership of the object is given to another user profile, the original owner has the option to keep all the object and data authorities the same, or to remove all authority to the object. If the creating user has specified that the group profile should be the owner of the object, then all members of the group profile have authority to the object. If the owner of an object is a group profile, then any user assigned to the group may add, modify, or delete records in the object, assuming all data authorities are provided. This feature is helpful when data sharing is necessary. Consider a company that takes orders by telephone. Each clerk taking orders would need to access all the customer records, so each clerk must be a member of a group profile that includes authority to the object containing customer records. We will present additional information about group profiles in Chapter 2.

Objects on the AS/400 exist within a special object called a *library*. A library acts as a holding area for related objects. The AS/400 uses a library in much the same way that personal computers use directories. Libraries and directories are holding areas for related material. For example, one library might be dedicated to payroll programs, another to inventory control. Libraries generally contain many other objects. Unlike directories, however, libraries cannot contain other libraries (with one exception — library

QSYS, discussed below). To find an AS/400 object requires the name of the library and the name of the object. The AS/400 identifies objects by their *qualified name*, which takes the form LIBRARY/OBJECT. For example, to reference the EMPMASTER file in the PAYROLL library, you'd usually refer to PAYROLL/EMPMASTER.

IBM supplies several libraries with the AS/400; some of these libraries contain the objects that make up the operating system; others hold the programs, data files, and other objects that make up licensed program products, such as language compilers, or OfficeVision. Independent software vendors also supply their own libraries with the objects that make up their applications. You can also create libraries to hold your own organization's programs and data files. Most IBM-supplied library names begin with the letter Q. Therefore, you generally should avoid creating libraries with a first letter of Q. Figure 1.2 lists the common AS/400 libraries.

Figure 1.2
Common AS/400
Libraries

Library Name	Typical Contents

QSYS	System library
	    Operating system code
	    User profiles
	    I/O configuration objects
	    References to other libraries

QDCT	Language dictionaries for OfficeVision
QDOC	Documents, shared folders

QGPL	General-purpose library
	    Job queue descriptions
	    Printer output queue descriptions
	    Miscellaneous installation-specific descriptions

QHLPSYS	System help screens
QOFC	OfficeVision/400

QPDA	Application Development Toolset
	    Program Development Manager (PDM)
	    Source Entry Utility (SEU)
	    Screen Design Aid (SDA)

QPFR	Performance measurement tools
QPWXALIB	Client Access base programs
QPWXCLIB	Client Access for Windows 3.1
QRPG	RPG/400 compiler
QRPGLE	ILE RPG/400 compiler
QSPL	Spool library for printed reports, etc.
QSQL	DB2/400 Query Manager and SQL Development Kit

Figure 1.2 continued

Figure 1.2	Library Name	Typical Contents
Continued	QTEMP	Library to hold temporary objects Work files Temporary data areas
	QUSRSYS	System library for installation-specific information System journals, journal receivers Database cross references Files used by system commands Message queues Character translation tables

QSYS is the system library for the AS/400. It contains the programs and other objects that make up the operating system. QSYS must exist on an AS/400 for the system to work. Other libraries on the AS/400 exist within the context of the QSYS library; it is the only library that can "contain" other libraries. A few special objects, such as user profiles and I/O configurations, can exist only within QSYS. You should never modify or delete any object within the QSYS library, because the operating system might stop working if you do. Only in unusual circumstances would you ever add an object to QSYS; you would normally create objects only within a user-defined library.

QUSRSYS is a library where user objects can exist and also be available to the system. QUSRSYS is frequently used to hold message queues for individual users and to hold a common message file for an application's error messages.

QHLPSYS contains the on-line help information that is displayed when the Help key or the extended help function keys are pressed.

QGPL is the general-purpose library that contains IBM-provided objects. The system places newly created objects that are not specifically placed in a distinct library in QGPL. User objects that are inadvertently placed in QGPL should be moved to the appropriate user library.

QSPL holds the spooled, printed output pages that have not yet been printed. As system operator, you should not manipulate the QSPL program or command files.

OfficeVision for OS/400 and Client Access for OS/400, both licensed IBM products, use **QDOC** to contain folders and documents. OfficeVision for OS/400, PC Support/400, and Client Access for OS/400 use folders and documents to store the users' work. You can also use PC Support and Client Access to upload/download or convert files from the AS/400 EBCDIC format to DOS (ASCII) format.

QTEMP is a library that is created for each job. Each time a user signs on, the system creates a QTEMP library for this interactive job. If the user submits a job to the batch queue, another QTEMP library is created for the batch job. The QTEMP library is deleted when the job ends. QTEMP is used to store temporary objects, such as work files, that a job might need.

Because each job's QTEMP is deleted at the end of a job, any objects in QTEMP will also be deleted. QTEMP objects are private to a job. A job can access only those QTEMP objects in its own QTEMP, not those in any other jobs' QTEMP libraries.

Most AS/400s contain the QSYS, QUSRSYS, QHLPSYS, QGPL, QSPL, and QDOC libraries. These libraries are usually required to run the system and support common user needs. With the introduction of OS/400 Version 3, Release 1, multiple new system libraries and directories are included for the integrated file and system programs. You can generate other IBM libraries, depending on the IBM products your organization purchases. Product libraries contain IBM licensed program products that are self-contained software packages, and each product resides in a separate library. For example, the RPG/400 compiler and RPG/400 support programs are loaded into the QRPG library.

In most installations, the system administrator creates user libraries. User libraries are commonly created to hold one individual's work; for example, each programmer should have his or her own user library. The administrator can create as many user libraries as are convenient; the only limit is the amount of disk space available in DASD.

Queues
Objects that are of special importance to operators are queues. Queues are holding areas for messages, printed reports, batch jobs, and other work that is waiting to be received, released to the CPU, or accessed by a specific user. For example, when a message is generated and sent, it is then retained in the user's message queue.

Message Queue, *MSGQ, is an area for holding messages. Users may choose to delete unneeded messages after they have read them. The system automatically creates message queues when the user profile is created.

Output Queue, *OUTQ, is a holding area for reports that are waiting to be printed. We will discuss output handling in detail in Chapter 5.

Other Objects
A message file has an object type of *MSGF. Message files hold predefined message texts and their corresponding message numbers. When a program detects an error, rather than display a message number, the system shows a predefined message text to the user. The text may suggest appropriate actions to correct the error or it may direct the user to contact the computer center. The system message files include QCPFMSG and many more in the QSYS library. Some program products have their own message files; for example, the RPG compiler holds messages in the QRPGMSG message file in library QRPG. All together, there are more than 26,000 predefined messages. A common example of a predefined message is "Device STAT1 is no longer communicating."

Documents, which are object type *DOC, must be stored in the QDOC library. Documents typically are word processing letters, memos, and other types of text files, including files in PC formats. Document library objects can be processed by OfficeVision for OS/400, PC Support/400, or Client Access for OS/400.

Folders, with object type *FLR, are objects similar to paper folders in the respect that they are a container of other documents. All folders have a name and reside in a library. Folders are processed by OfficeVision for OS/400, PC Support/400, and Client Access for OS/400.

Journal and the Journal Receiver, with object types *JRN and *JRNRCV, are objects that record events that have happened in the system. Any file may use journaling; but generally database file operations such as adding, deleting, or changing records are tracked automatically whenever the journaling system is active. Changes are recorded in a journal object to provide an audit trail of modifications.

Menus, which have an object type *MENU, are objects used to list a choice of predefined or related activities. Each activity is displayed on the screen and the user chooses an option. The menu program then runs the user's choices by calling the appropriate CL commands and other programs. Generally, menus have message files associated with them to explain any errors or problems to the users.

Programs, having an object type *PGM, are objects stored in machine language for faster execution. The *PGM object is not a displayable file but has a source file object linked to it. The source is written in languages such as RPG/400, COBOL/400, or CL; the source file is displayable.

Key Terms

Control Language (CL)
data files
file descriptions
libraries
Licensed Internal Code (LIC)
machine executable code
members
menus

objects
Program Temporary Fix (PTF)
programs
    compiled programs
queues
    job queues
    message queues
    output queues

single-level storage
subsystems
    batch
    interactive
system values
user profiles

Review Questions

1. What is single-level storage?

2. What is licensed internal code? What functions does it perform?

3. What is the difference between a release and a modification?

4. What is the purpose of Program Temporary Fixes? Why are they important?

5. Think about interactive and batch jobs. Which has the highest priority? Why?

6. What functions do the system values perform?

7. What types of information can be stored in an object? List several types of objects.

8. How are libraries different from directories? What library is the exception to this difference? Why?

9. What library is required for the AS/400 to operate?

10. What is the purpose of a queue? List several types of queues.

Exercises

1. Access the user profile by typing DSPUSRPRF on any command line. A screen showing the fields User Profile, Type of Information, and Output will be displayed. Type your user profile on the User Profile line and press <Enter>, then press the <Print Screen> key to copy the user profile to your queue. Print the user profile, write your name on the printed list, and turn the results in to your instructor.

2. Access the system values by typing DSPSYSVAL on any command line. A screen that includes the options of System Value and Output will be displayed. Place the cursor on the System Value field and use the prompt function <F4> to get a list of system values that can be displayed. Type QACTJOB and press <Enter>. Use the <Print Screen> key to copy the QACTJOB screen to your queue. Press <Enter> to return to the command line. Print the screen, write your name on the printed screen, and turn the results in to your instructor.

Exercises Continued

Exercises continued

3. Press the <F9> key (Retrieve) to display the last command that was executed. Arrow over to QACTJOB and change this to QBASPOOL. Press <Enter> to display the system values. Use the <Print Screen> key to copy the QBASPOOL screen to your queue. Press <Enter> to return to the command line. Print the screen, write your name on the printed screen, and turn the results in to your instructor.

Chapter 2

Security

Objectives

To understand

- ✓ how system values can be used
- ✓ the various security levels
- ✓ the use of assistance levels
- ✓ how user profiles and user-specific object authorities affect security
- ✓ how group profiles can be interfaced with the user profile
- ✓ user classes and object authorities
- ✓ job descriptions
- ✓ library lists
- ✓ authorization lists
- ✓ object authority issues
- ✓ how to use the object authority command
- ✓ the authority search path

Security

Information is one of a company's most valuable assets. Imagine attempting to process an order with only the customer's credit card slip, while the file with the customer's name, address, and product order numbers were lost. What if the company's inventory was in multiple warehouses throughout the country and the inventory file was destroyed? Imagine trying to pay suppliers if the accounts payable file had been corrupted. Realistically, loss of the corporate database may cause a business to fail. Security isn't just a matter of proper backups; rather, it requires comprehensive thinking. Envision a jeweler putting the gold and diamonds into a vault at night. The next morning, the jeweler can open the vault, look around and determine whether any items were stolen. Now picture the computer center manager, looking at the disk drives. Unlike the jeweler, the manager can't be sure that the data files weren't copied and sold to a competitor. Keeping the corporate data confidential and accurate is of utmost concern in maintaining a successful business.

Security has three separate aspects: physical security of the hardware, backup of the data files, and prevention of unauthorized access to the data files. Physical security of the system unit, display stations, and printers must be part of any security considerations. The AS/400 includes a key lock to help prevent unauthorized access to the functions on the control panel of the system unit. Data-file backup media should be stored off site to avoid damage or loss of information in the event of disaster (flood or fire) to the system unit, or any event that involves data loss. Backup and restore are such important topics that we devote Chapter 7 to the subject. But in today's world of connectivity, fire and floods pale when they are compared to the risk of corporate data being accessed by unauthorized outside users. Security violations within the corporation are often unintentional incursions by employees; nonetheless, such violations can cause many problems.

The AS/400 security system allows a wide range of configurations to control and monitor authorized user access both on-site and via outside connectivity. The AS/400 security system is built into the operating system, allowing for consistent security between the operating system and other licensed programs. This configuration ensures that an application program cannot easily bypass security, because the security features are integrated into the operating system.

The AS/400's operating system provides several methods using many different tools to create a secure environment. System values, security levels, assistance levels, user profiles, group profiles, and authorization lists work together to allow the manipulation and control of data on the AS/400. Higher security levels require a user to sign on with a predefined, unique user ID and a password. The user ID can be defined in a user profile created for each user. System values work with the user profile by supplying default values for assistance-level and group-profile parameters when a user profile is created.

System Values

As we discussed in Chapter 1, system values are attributes that can change how the entire computer system functions. Some system values can be used within other commands if *SYSVAL is specified as the parameter's value. The operating system uses the contents of the corresponding system value to execute the command. For example, the security audit journal, QAUDJRN, is provided with the operating system. The system value that determines what is logged in the audit journal is QAUDLVL, the audit level system value. Some of the values that can be specified within QAUDLVL are *NONE to inactivate the auditing function, *AUTFAIL to log authority failure events, *CREATE to log when objects are created, *DELETE to log when objects are deleted, *JOBDTA to log job start, stop, and disposition information, *OBJMGT to log when objects are moved or renamed, *PGMFAIL to log system integrity violations, *SAVRST to track restore operations, and *SECURITY to log security changes and related functions. There are also a number of other options that provide a full range of security auditing.

The QCRTAUT (System Default Create Authority) system value determines the public authority of a new object. This system value usually works in conjunction with the CRTAUT (Create Authority) parameter of the library description where the new object is being placed. The public authority values consist of *CHANGE, *ALL, *USE, and *EXCLUDE. The "public" is considered any valid AS/400 user who did not create the object. Those users with public authority can change newly created objects if the authority value is *CHANGE, but they can only view objects if they have been granted the *USE authority value. These users are not allowed to view or change an object with the *EXCLUDE value. If you create an object with *ALL public authority, public users have complete control of the object. The *CHANGE value is recommended for this system value, because several IBM-supplied libraries' CRTAUT parameter value is *SYSVAL, and *CHANGE is required for some operations. Additionally, some objects located in the IBM-supplied libraries must be accessed before users are allowed to sign on. Certain system value changes will be effective immediately; more frequently, however, the change will become effective only after the next system IPL.

To monitor a user's profile and password, the system value QDSPSGNINF (Display Sign-on Information) can be activated. This system value lets you show the user additional sign-on information each time s(he) signs on to the system. The sign-on information includes the date of last sign-on, the number of any sign-on attempts that were not valid, and (if there are fewer than seven days remaining) the number of days until the password will expire. A value of 0 for this parameter specifies that the sign-on information is not to be displayed. A value of 1 specifies that the sign-on information is to be displayed when the user signs on to the system.

To foil unauthorized users from attempting to sign on to the system, the maximum sign-on attempts system value, QMAXSIGN, can be used. The maximum number of consecutive invalid sign-on attempts allowed is stored in the QMAXSIGN system value. When the specified value is reached, an action specified in the QMAZSGNACN system value is executed. The possible actions are to disable the device, disable the user profile, or disable both the device and the user profile. Valid entries for the QMAXSIGN system value are 1 through 25 and *NOMAX. Three sign-on attempts are recommended to allow authorized users enough attempts to correct typing errors before the system disables the device. See Appendix A for information about how to reactivate the device.

Limiting users to signing on to a single workstation concurrently promotes unauthorized password awareness, and limits the possibility of users leaving a device available to unauthorized persons. The QLMTDEVSSN (Limit Device Sessions) system value, set to 1, limits users to one device session at a time. The value of 0 allows an unlimited number of sessions.

System values also determine what action the system should take if a user forgets to sign off a workstation. The QINACTITV (Inactive Job Time-Out Interval) system value specifies how long an interactive job can be inactive before the system should intervene. The QINACTMSGQ (Inactive Job Message Queue) system value dictates what action the system should take when the QINACTITV parameter's value has been reached. If the QINACTMSGQ value is *ENDJOB, the job is terminated. If the QINACTMSGQ system value is *DSCJOB, the job is suspended and the workstation returns to the sign-on screen. The suspended job can be resumed if the same user signs on to the same workstation. The QDSCJOBITV (Disconnected Job Time-out Interval) system value determines how long a job can remain suspended before the system ends it.

System values control how the system reacts during a power failure. The system value QUPSMSGQ (Uninterruptable Power Source Message Queue) determines the queue to which power-related messages will be sent. The system value QUPSDLYTIM (Uninterruptable Power Source Delay Time) specifies how long to wait on standby power before powering down the system. The system value QPWRRSTIPL (Power Restart Initial Program Load) determines whether the system should begin an automatic IPL when power returns. To help clarify the QUPSMSGQ and QUPSDLYTIM system values, the Uninterruptible Power Supply (UPS) referenced in each value is a battery pack. You can purchase a UPS with enough batteries to keep your system running for 30 minutes and longer. For example, a hospital or police dispatch that runs on an AS/400 may require a UPS with battery packs for 48 hours. Therefore, the UPS-related system values must be defined according to the UPS your company has purchased. Let's assume that your company's UPS has 12 hours' worth of power and that shutting down the machine takes 90 minutes. In this case, it might be wise to set the QUPSDLYTIM system value to begin the shut-down after 10 hours on the UPS battery packs.

Security Levels

OS/400 supports five security levels. Each level has varying degrees of security support (see Figure 2.1). Each increase in the security level increases the safety of objects, but it also makes sharing objects more difficult. The system value that activates the security level on the AS/400 is QSECURITY. A summary of security level descriptions, based on the system value QSECURITY, is shown in Figure 2.1.

Figure 2.1
Security Level
Descriptions

Security Level	Security Activities
10	No pre-existing user profile or password is required to sign on, and there is no resource security. Anyone who signs on can use any file, library, or device if special authorities specified in the user profile use the default values. The system will create a user profile for anyone who signs on. The system is set at level 10 when it is shipped by IBM.

Figure 2.1 continued

Figure 2.1
Continued

Security Level	Security Activities
20	A user profile and a password are required to sign on, but there is no resource security. When there is no resource security, any user who can sign on has authority to all objects on the system and can therefore modify or delete any object.
30	Password and resource security are enforced. When a user requests an object, multiple levels of object authority go into effect.
40	There is additional security-checking during program execution. For example, users submitting jobs using a job description containing a user profile name must have *USE authority.
50	Levels 40 and 50 are similar. Level 50 security provides the additional function of the C-2 Federal government standard for audit trails.

You can find out the security level of the system you are working on by using the DSPSYSVAL (Display System Value) command. For example, to display the screen shown in Figure 2.2, perform the following sequence of steps:

Type	DSPSYSVAL	on the command line
Press	F4	to prompt
Type	QSECURITY	
Press	Enter	

Figure 2.2
Display System
Value Screen

```
                           Display System Value

System value . . . . . . . :  QSECURITY

Description. . . . . . . . :  System security level


System security level  . . :  30      10=Physical security only
                                       20=Password security only
                                       30=Password and object security
                                       40=Password, object, and
                                          operating system integrity
                                       50=Password, object, and enhanced
                                          operating system integrity




Press Enter to continue.

F3=Exit        F12=Cancel
```

As you can see, this system operates with level 30 security, meaning passwords and object authority are verified for each request.

To exit the Display System Value screen,

Press   F3   to "Exit"

Assistance Levels

You can minimize user mistakes by eliminating menu items and function key options that do not relate to the user's job. The system's assistance levels customize the user's view of the displays with additional information or with information in less technical terms. Three assistance levels are supported on the AS/400. The basic assistance level, *BASIC, provides an Operational Assistant interface for beginners using friendly, non-technical language. Intermediate assistance level, *INTERMED, uses the system interface with more functions available; *INTERMED is for users more accustomed to technical computer terms. Advanced assistance level, *ADVANCED, uses the expert system interface. Frequently, the *ADVANCED level does not display the option numbers and the function keys. The advanced assistance level is for sophisticated users familiar with commands and function key activities. The system value for assistance level is QASTLVL.

The assistance level can be changed on any display that allows the use of the F21 function key, or with the commands that have the assistance-level parameter. Not all displays have more than one assistance level. The Operational Assistant interface retains different assistance level values for the following groups of displays: Printer Output, Printers, Jobs, Handling Messages, Device Status, User Enrollment, and System Status. If the user signs off the system, the current assistance level for each display remains stored until the user signs on and changes it. If the assistance level's system value is not suitable for a user's needs, the user profile can be modified to override the system value.

User Profiles and User-Specific Objects

The user profile is an object that defines system access for the user: what objects can be accessed, what libraries can be used, what authorities are assigned, and to what special groups the user belongs. When your system is set at security level 20 or higher, the user profile must be created before the user can sign on. The user profile's User ID value can be up to 10 characters in length, but it cannot begin with a number. OS/400 is not case sensitive, and it will display user profile listings in alphabetical order regardless of whether the entries are uppercase or lowercase. Several IBM licensed programs, including Client Access for OS/400, suggest limiting the User ID to eight characters. This limitation is mandatory when you are linking to certain communications networks.

A user profile must be generated for each user before a user can access the system. Security level 10 automatically generates the user profile before a new user finishes the sign-on process. A problem with how security level 10 generates the user profile, however, is that the new user profile will be generated even if the user misspells his or her sign-on name. Systems using security levels 20, 30, 40, and 50 must have the user profile completed by the Security Officer or System Administrator before the user's first sign-on.

The user ID and password are combined to complete the sign-on process. User IDs and passwords should be kept private. For security reasons, it is recommended that passwords should exceed several digits in length, because longer passwords are harder to guess. The password length is determined by two system values, QPWDMAXLEN (Password Maximum Length), and QPWDMINLEN (Password Minimum Length). A value from 1 to 10 is allowed, but a minimum of five characters is recommended. Like the user ID, the password may not begin with a number. A user's password cannot be displayed on the AS/400. If the user has forgotten his or her password, the Security Officer or System Administrator can modify the user ID, giving it a new password. For convenience in this situation, the password is generally changed to the same characters as the user ID value; the user should then choose a new password when (s)he next signs on. See Appendix A for more information about how to modify a user's password.

To display your operator profile information,

Type	DSPUSRPRF	on a command line
Press	F4	to prompt
Type	your user ID	
Press	Enter	

The user profile information will be displayed, as shown in Figure 2.3 and Figure 2.6. These figures are the first and second pages of the Display User

Figure 2.3
Display User Profile
Screen at the Basic
Assistance Level

```
                    Display User Profile - Basic

User profile . . . . . . . . . . . . . . . . . .:   QSYSOPR

Previous sign-on  . . . . . . . . . . . . . . :   09/15/06  10:16:44
Sign-on attempts not valid. . . . . . . . . :   0
Status. . . . . . . . . . . . . . . . . . . :   *ENABLED
Date password last changed. . . . . . . . . :   04/25/96
Password expiration interval. . . . . . . . :   *SYSVAL
Set password to expired . . . . . . . . . . :   *NO
User Class. . . . . . . . . . . . . . . . . :   *SYSOPR
Special authority . . . . . . . . . . . . . :   *IOSYSCFG
                                                 *JOBCTL
                                                 *SAVSYS
Group profile . . . . . . . . . . . . . . . :   *NONE
Owner . . . . . . . . . . . . . . . . . . . :   *USRPRF
Group authority . . . . . . . . . . . . . . :   *NONE
Group authority type. . . . . . . . . . . . :   *PRIVATE
Supplemental groups . . . . . . . . . . . . :   *NONE


                                                          More...

Press Enter to continue

F3=Exit    F12=Cancel
```

Profile screen generated by the DSPUSRPRF command. We will discuss only the entries in these figures that are of concern to the system operator.

The DSPUSRPF (Display User Profile) command provides such information as the date and time of the previous sign-on, and sign-on attempts that were not valid. This information could assist in verifying unauthorized access. For example, this field may show sign-on attempts during a time period when a user was on vacation or otherwise not available to use the system. To monitor whether an unauthorized person has been attempting to gain access to the system, the number of invalid sign-on attempts is included in the information retrieved by the DSPUSRPF command.

The "Status" field determines whether the user profile is valid for sign-on. Possible parameter values are *ENABLED and *DISABLED. The profile must be enabled to allow the user to sign on. To enhance security, a user's profile may be disabled while (s)he is on vacation or for whatever reason is not using the system for a period of time.

The "Date password last changed" field and the "Password expiration interval" field help determine whether users should change their passwords. If the password is not modified before the preset interval, the operating system will display the Change Password screen. The "Password expiration interval'" field can use *NOMAX if no change is required, *SYSVAL to use the predefined value from the QPWDEXPITV system value, or any number from 1 to 366 to denote the number of days a password will remain valid.

The "Set password to expired" field can be defined as *YES to force the user to change his or her password. You use this field in conjunction with the "Set password to expired" parameter when you are creating a new user profile. When the "Set password to expired" system value is *NO, the user is not prompted to change his or her password and may continue to use the current password indefinitely.

User Classes and Object Authorities

Assuming that the system security is at level 30 or higher, there are five user profile classes: security officer (*SECOFR), security administrator (*SECADM), programmers (*PGMR), system operator (*SYSOPR), and system users (*USER). Each user profile class has special default authorities based on the security level. Unless users specifically need to use other system functions, their user class should be set to *USER. The *USER user profile class results in a modified view of the menu and limits the use of certain commands. Reducing options and commands for most users should not, however, be considered detrimental or punitive; rather, such management allows users to focus on their actual job functions.

With the *SYSOPR user class, the system operator can perform tasks such as backing up libraries and objects, restoring objects from tape, or powering down the system. Usually, a system operator will monitor a special message queue, named QSYSOPR. The QSYSOPR message queue receives the system error messages, and informational messages about the batch jobs that are running or about jobs that have special needs. For example, a job may request that invoice forms be loaded into the printer. This type of message will be sent to the QSYSOPR message queue. Because batch jobs are disconnected from the interactive user who started the job, batch jobs also are handled by the system operator. If a batch job requires additional information or has special instructions, the request is sent to the QSYSOPR message queue.

Each object, whether it is a library, a menu, or a queue, has authorities attached to the object. These authorities are the normal authorities and can be *ALL, *CHANGE, *USE, or *EXCLUDE. *ALL authority gives the user the ability to create, delete, or modify the object. *CHANGE authority lets the user modify the object but does not allow the user to delete the object. *USE authority gives the user the right to view the object, but nothing more. *EXCLUDE authority removes all rights to the object, including the authority to view the object.

The "Special authority" field in Figure 2.3 extends the actions a user can be authorized to perform on the system resources or on groups of objects. These authorities include saving the system, controlling other users' jobs, using the system service tools, controlling spooled output files, and creating user profiles.

Multiple values are possible for the "Special authority" field. The system value *USRCLS (user class) can be used to grant a user the authorities that correspond to that individual's user profile. The *SECADM special authority name can also be used in this parameter. If the user needs no special authority, you can use the value of *NONE. (*NONE is normally used with a group profile to define the group's authorities.)

Individual authority values can be entered in the "Special authority" field. The various authorities and their associated actions are shown in Figure 2.4. The "User Class" column lists the user classes that include a special authority by default (at security level 30).

Figure 2.4
Special Authorities and
Associated Actions

Authorities	Actions	User Class
*ALLOBJ	Allows a user access to all system resources.	*SECOFR
*AUDIT	Allows the user to change the auditing attributes with the commands CHGOBJAUD, CHGDLOAUD, and CHGUSRAUD. Use of the *AUDIT special authority can cause considerable risk to the system and should be allowed infrequently.	*SECOFR
*IOSYSCFG	Allows the user to change the system's configuration. The *IOSYSCFG authority is required for setting up things such as TCP/IP, OSI commands, and other communications requirements.	*SECOFR

Figure 2.4 continued

	Authorities	Actions	User Class
Figure 2.4 Continued	*JOBCTL	Allows a user to change, cancel, hold, or release all files on output queues; or to hold, release, and clear job queues; or to hold, release, change, and cancel other users' jobs; or to start print writers; or to change the attributes of a job, such as the printer forms; or to stop/start subsystems; or to perform an IPL.	All user classes except *USER
	*NONE	Special authorities are not granted for this user.	As needed
	*SAVSYS	Allows a user to do save and restore operations for all resources.	All user classes except *USER
	*SECADM	Allows the person to add user IDs; or to change, delete, or display authority for those users in OfficeVision/400; or to add and remove access codes; or to give and remove a user's access code authority; or to change security items for a user; or to modify certain system values.	*SECADM *SECOFR
	*SERVICE	Allows a user to perform the display and alter service functions.	*SECOFR
	*SPLCTL	Allows a user to control spool functions, such as cancel, delete, display, hold, and release other users' spooled output files.	*SECOFR

Group Profile Concerns

A group profile is similar to a user's profile except it gives the same set of authorities to multiple users. A user whose profile is a member of a group profile generally has the same authorities as the group. In rare instances, a user profile may be defined to override the authority of the group profile. Group profiles are frequently created to provide every user in the department with the same authority to the same objects. When a group profile is connected to a user profile, the user is automatically granted object management — *OBJMGT and *CHANGE — authorities to the group profile's objects.

When an individual user creates an object, ownership of the object is clearly defined. However, when a member of a group creates an object, the ownership can be confusing. The "Owner" parameter in the user profile is employed to aid in defining ownership of any objects the user creates.

Ownership values can be *USRPRF (when the individual user owns any newly created objects) or *GRPPRF (when the group profile is considered to be the owner of all newly created objects).

The "Group authority" field in the user profile works in conjunction with the "Owner" field in the group profile to further define ownership of newly created objects. See Figure 2.5 for further explanation.

Figure 2.5
Group Authority and
Owner Consideration

User Profile's "Group authority" Field	Group Profile's "Owner" Field	Results
*All, *USE, *CHANGE, or *EXCLUDE	*USRPRF	The user profile gains the authority over the new object. The authority may be one of the four choices: *ALL, *USE, *CHANGE, or *EXCLUDE.
*NONE	*GRPPRF	The group profile gains the authority over a newly created object. Because the group has all the authority, the user profile must be specified as *NONE.

As Figure 2.5 suggests, using the group profile allows more flexibility in the security scheme and is less complicated for the security officer or system administrator responsible for managing a large number of profiles.

To view the next page of the User Profile,

Press   Page Down

As we discussed earlier in the chapter, the ASTLVL (Assistance level) parameter defines the assistance level for the user profile, and it can be *SYSVAL (as shown in Figure 2.6), basic, intermediate, or advanced. The ASTLVL parameter initiates control at sign-on and functions for all commands executed from the command line. The *SYSVAL entry refers the user profile back to the QASTLVL system value. If the QASTLVL value contains the basic assistance level, the user profile will be set at the basic assistance level. A menu may have a separate assistance level value. Operational Assistant has a predetermined value, but the user can override the initial value by requesting a different assistance level.

Figure 2.6
Display User Profile
Screen at the Basic
Assistance Level

```
                        Display User Profile - Basic

User profile . . . . . . . . . . . . . . . . . :   QSYSOPR

Assistance level . . . . . . . . . . . . . :       *SYSVAL
Current library . . . . . . . . . . . . . :        QSYSOPR
Initial program . . . . . . . . . . . . . :        *NONE
  Library . . . . . . . . . . . . . . . . :
Initial menu . . . . . . . . . . . . . . :         SYSTEM
  Library . . . . . . . . . . . . . . . . :          QSYS
Limit capabilities . . . . . . . . . . . :         *NO
Text . . . . . . . . . . . . . . . . . . :         System Operator

Display sign-on information . . . . . . . :        *SYSVAL
Limit device sessions . . . . . . . . . . :        *SYSVAL
Keyboard buffering . . . . . . . . . . . :         *SYSVAL
Maximum storage allowed . . . . . . . . . :        6348
  Storage used . . . . . . . . . . . . . :            256
Highest scheduling priority . . . . . . . :        0

                                                              More...

Press Enter to continue

F3=Exit      F12=Cancel
```

HINT

In Figure 2.6, the current library is listed as QSYSOPR. This library is not shipped with the computer, but the authors have found that creating a common library for the operators on the various shifts can be quite helpful. The shared library also provides a single location for custom-built programs or menus that make the operator's functions easier.

The "Current library" value specifies the name of the current library for the user. The current library is where any new objects that the user creates reside by default. The system will search the current library before it looks for information in any other user libraries. The *CURLIB value is used in many other commands. *CURLIB is accessed from the user profile's "Current library" value. The CRTDFT (Create default) command specifies that the user has no current library. If the *CURLIB value is used with the CRTDFT command, the QGPL library becomes the current library. As we discussed in Chapter 1, QGPL should be reserved for IBM needs. Therefore, you should avoid using *CRTDFT. Specifying a library name for this parameter helps users save new objects in the proper library. Any library can be specified as the current library. You can use the current library to enhance system organization; however a user can place new objects into any library to which (s)he is authorized. Before you can specify a current library for a user, you must have already created the library.

The "Initial program" field determines the program to be executed immediately after sign-on is completed. Any valid program name can be used. The "Library" value is the library that contains the program. For example, consider the accounting staff at a hospital. The bookkeepers may prefer that when they complete sign-on, the billing program is displayed automatically.

The "Initial menu" field determines the menu displayed after sign-on. The available options include MAIN, the AS/400 system's main menu; SYSTEM, the menu for operational tasks; or any valid menu name. If the value of *SIGNOFF is entered, the user is automatically signed off the system after the initial program completes. *SIGNOFF can be used to lock a user into only one program, thus enhancing security. OfficeVision/400 users can use this field to go directly to OfficeVision/400 and bypass the initial menus.

To exit the User Profile screen,

Press   F3   to "Exit"

The User Profile screen includes many other parameters you can make use of; the few items we have discussed here only introduce you to the power of the AS/400's security system and the user profile's place in that system.

Job Descriptions

A user's job description is another aspect of security. A job description can be attached to a single user or it can be assigned to a group of users sharing the same authorities and job requirements. Job descriptions should be set up for batch jobs to control how those jobs will enter the operating system.

A job description includes attributes such as where the job is executed, the priority of the job, the printer to be used (if printer output is part of the job), and how message logging is to be handled. The use of job descriptions provides flexibility and control over the job's execution. IBM supplies some job descriptions, such as QBATCH or QPGMR; you can also create your own job descriptions.

HINT

A job description should be created for any user who can submit a batch job. Creation of the job description will prevent future batch job problems.

Two Control Language (CL) commands relate to batch jobs: The BCHJOB (batch job) and SBMJOB (submit job) commands can override the values in the job description. A user profile name, usually that of an interactive user, is required to start a batch job. However, in a batch job situation, the user who scheduled or started the batch job is disconnected from the job once the job is submitted.

To display your job description information,

Type   DSPJOBD   on any command line
Press   F4   to prompt
Type   your user ID
Press   Enter

(If there is no job description named after your user ID, you may use an IBM-supplied job description, such as QBATCH.)

Figure 2.7
Display Job
Description Screen

```
                         Display Job Description
                                                      System XXXXXXX
Job description:    QSYSOPR        Library:   QSYSOPR

User profile . . . . . . . . . . . . . . :    *RQD
CL syntax check. . . . . . . . . . . . :      *NOCHK
Hold on job queue  . . . . . . . . . :        *NO
End severity . . . . . . . . . . . . . :      3Ø
Job date . . . . . . . . . . . . . . . :      *SYSVAL
Job switches . . . . . . . . . . . . . :      ØØØØØØØØ
Inquiry message reply. . . . . . . . . :      *RQD
Job priority (on job queue). . . . . . :      5
Job queue. . . . . . . . . . . . . . . :      QBATCH
  Library. . . . . . . . . . . . . . . :      QGPL
Output priority (on output queue)  . . . :    5
Printer device . . . . . . . . . . . . :      *USRPRF
Output queue . . . . . . . . . . . . . :      *USRPRF
  Library. . . . . . . . . . . . . . . :

                                                         More...

Press Enter to continue

F3=Exit    F12=Cancel
```

The job description information will be displayed, as shown in Figure 2.7. As with the User Profile information, we will discuss only the entries that are of concern to the system operator.

On the Display Job Description screen, the name of the job description and the associated library are displayed. The "User profile" parameter is shown as *RQD, indicating that a valid user ID must be associated with the job description.

The "CL syntax check" parameter allows you to check the syntax of CL commands as you submit the job, rather than when the job actually runs. In Figure 2.7, no checking will occur until the job runs. By specifying an option here, a job description can provide for early diagnosis of syntax errors. The CL syntax check program assigns numeric values to an error based on the severity of the error. Values of 00 through 99 are possible, with zero indicating the least serious error. By specifying a value 00-99 in this job description parameter, you can control how serious a syntax error must be before it ends the processing of the job. In most instances, the "End severity" level of 30 is appropriate.

A job will automatically be held on the job queue if the value of the parameter "Hold on job queue" is *YES. If a job is held on the job queue, the batch job will not be run until it is released by an authorized user or operator who has *JOBCTL authority. This is a valuable option when you are submitting large batch jobs and holding them until a later (and probably less busy) time. The default for this value is *NO and informs the operating system to process the job when it reaches the top of the job queue.

The "Job date" parameter is the date on which the job was started. If *SYSVAL is the value of this parameter, the date stored in the QDATE system value is used.

The "Job switches" parameter specifies the initial settings for a group of eight job switches. You can use these switches to control the flow of programs. The initial setting for the "Job switches" parameter is all zeros (or all off). Programmers can modify these switches to call CL or other high-level programs, depending on the circumstances. Job switches are a remnant from the punch-card era of computing and are rarely used in today's processing.

An inquiry message is a message that requires a response from the user or operator. The "Inquiry message reply" parameter determines how inquiry messages are to be answered. The options for this parameter are *RQD (require a reply), *DFT (reply with the message's predefined default reply), or *SYSRPYL (reply with a reply stored in the system reply list). Normally, *RQD is used so that the inquiry messages are displayed with the various answer choices. If *RQD is specified, the messages must be answered before the job continues running. The *SYSRPYL value tells the operating system to check the system reply list for an answer. If a reply is located, the system uses the reply just as if the operator had entered it. The reply list commonly is used when the system is retrying a failing device or restarting a communications line that has gone down. These conditions do not necessarily require an operator to input the answer.

When a job is submitted to batch, the "Job priority" parameter determines the scheduling priority for this job on the job queue (i.e., its relative position in the line of jobs waiting to execute). The highest job priority is a 1, with the lowest priority being a 9. If two batch jobs are submitted to the job queue at nearly the same time, the "job priority" parameter will determine which job will be executed first. If the two batch jobs have the same job priority, the job received on the queue first will be processed first, assuming that no higher priority job is in the queue.

The "Output priority" parameter determines the priority for spooled files to be printed. As with job priorities, the highest priority is a 1 and the lowest priority a 9. If a spooled output file with priority 3 is received at the same time as a spooled output file with priority 6, the spooled output file with priority 3 will be sent to the printer first. If two job descriptions have the same priority specified, the first job on the queue will be printed first.

Most computer centers use various printers for different reports. The "Printer device" parameter in the job description specifies which printer will receive the spooled output from a job. If the *USRPRF value is used, the printer specified in the user's profile will receive the output. This parameter allows a user to change printers as needs and conditions vary.

The "Output queue" and "Library" parameters determine where the spooled output files will be stored until the files are sent to a printer. Allowing multiple output queues to hold spooled files helps keep both the user and the operator organized. If the parameter value *USRPRF is entered, the value specified in the user's profile will determine the output queue that will receive the spooled files.

To exit the Job Description screen,

Press   F3   to "Exit"

Library List

The library list provides an effective method to help programs locate objects on the system. If a program or a user doesn't specify an object by qualified name (library/object), the system will search the library list to locate the object. Standardized library lists can be specified by name, or the QUSRLIBL and QSYSLIBL system values can be used. The system searches only the libraries included in the library list on the Display Library List screen to locate objects the user has requested. The libraries are searched in the sequence in which they are listed.

To display the Library List Screen,

Type   DSPLIBL   on the command line
Press Enter

Figure 2.8
Display Library
List Screen

```
                          Display Library List
                                              System:  XXXXXXX
  Type options, press Enter.
    5=Display objects in library

  Opt    Library      Type     Text
   _     USRSYS       SYS      User changes to IBM supplied objects
   _     QSYS         SYS      System Library
   _     QSYS2        SYS      System Library for CPI's
   _     QUSRSYS      SYS      SYSTEM LIBRARY FOR USERS
   _     QHLDSYS      SYS
   _     QSYSOPR      CUR      QSYSOPR production library
   _     QTEMP        USR
   _     QGPL         USR      General Purpose Library




                                                            Bottom
   F3=Exit     F12=Cancel    F17=Top    F18=Bottom
```

The Display Library List screen, as shown in Figure 2.8, lists the library search path. The library name, text description, and the library type are displayed. The operating system uses standard abbreviations for library types. A system library is identified by SYS. A production library is identified by PRD. A user's current library is identified by CUR, and other user libraries are identified by USR.

Option 5 offers an easy way to determine whether an object is located within a user's library. When you specify this option for a particular library, a list of all the objects in the library and the library name will be displayed. This display is functionally similar to the DOS directory list. If two objects share the same name but are located in different libraries (and both libraries are included in the library list), when the first object is located from the library placed highest in the library list, the search will be concluded.

To exit the Library List screen,

Press   F3   to "Exit"

Using the library list does not prevent a user from accessing objects in libraries not included in their library list. If a user has authorization and specifies the correct name of any library, the operating system will search the library for the listed object. To prevent unauthorized use of a library or other objects, object authority must be limited for each object that requires protection.

Authorization Lists

OS/400 offers great flexibility in creating an environment where users can access the same library but have individual limitations to the objects within that library. For example, the payroll administrator should have access to all payroll information, yet another user with the same group authority as the payroll administrator might only need access to monthly totals for reports. The payroll administrator should be given all rights to the objects within the payroll library. On the other hand, the user should be given read-only authority to payroll objects and perhaps no authority to salary items. Authorization lists facilitate establishing differing access for multiple users to the same object. Authorization list authority can be granted to the public, to a group of users, or to an individual user. An authorization list must exist in QSYS and can be attached to any number of objects.

For example, consider a group of users — in this case, all members of the same department. The security administrator can create an authorization list for the members of the department to have access to their department's data. By generating one authorization list, it is easier for the security administrator to add and delete authorized employees to and from this list.

Authorization lists also are helpful when objects need to be set at different levels of authority for a specific group of users. Consider the following situation: The company president has approved a new procedure for the accounts receivable department. This object needs to have *PUBLIC access, but other departments should not be bothered with the new procedure. In this case, the authorization list can provide the *PUBLIC authority to the group profile of the users in the accounts receivable department. The authorization list provides access to the accounts receivable department — but only this department, thus solving many issues with one authorization list.

To access the Display Authorization List screen,

Type	DSPAUTL	on any command line
Press	F4	to prompt
Type	the name of a valid authorization list	
Press	Enter	

(Ask your instructor to provide the name of a valid authorization list.)

Authorization lists (*AUTL) are objects created to simplify security access to other objects, as shown in Figure 2.9. The authority listed for a user in the "Object Authority" column indicates a user's authority to an object secured by this authorization list. An X located in the "List Mgt" column denotes that the user has been granted authority to manage the authorization list. Management includes adding and deleting users authorized to the list.

Figure 2.9
Display Authorization
List Screen

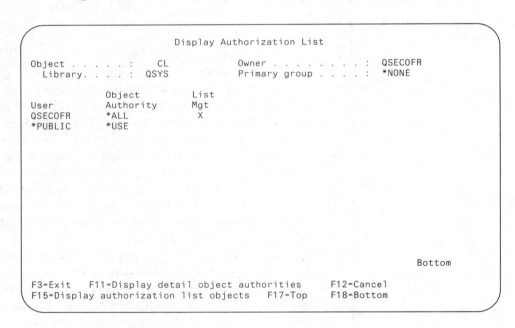

To see more details from this screen,

    Press   F11   to "Display detail object authorities"

The Display Authorization List screen (Figure 2.10) shows the further details about authorities allowed for each user included in this particular list.

As shown in Figure 2.10, the right side of the screen relates specifically to the objects controlled by the authorization list. There are five types of authorities. Object operational (Opr) authority allows users to access the object as specified by the object's data authorities; we discuss these authorities further in Figure 2.11. Object management (Mgt) authority allows the object to be moved and renamed, and it allows members to be added to the object. Object

Figure 2.10
Display Authorization List
Screen, Detailed

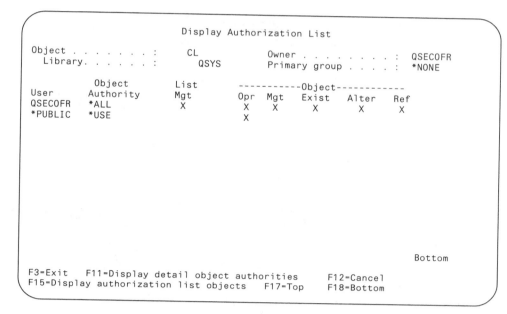

```
                          Display Authorization List
Object . . . . . . . . :    CL          Owner . . . . . . . . . :  QSECOFR
   Library. . . . . . :       QSYS      Primary group . . . . . :  *NONE

            Object        List        ----------Object-----------
User        Authority     Mgt         Opr  Mgt  Exist  Alter   Ref
QSECOFR     *ALL          X           X    X    X      X       X
*PUBLIC     *USE                      X




                                                                  Bottom
F3=Exit    F11=Display detail object authorities      F12=Cancel
F15=Display authorization list objects    F17=Top     F18=Bottom
```

existence (Exist) authority allows the object to be deleted, or removed from existence. Alter (Alter) authority allows changes to the attributes of an object, such as adding or removing triggers for a database file. Object reference (Ref) authority allows for modification of how the object is related to other objects.

OS/400 supplies predefined object authority values to use for individuals or for groups. All authority, *ALL, allows users full authority to operations on an object. Change authority, *CHANGE, allows the user to change, modify, or view an object. Use authority, *USE, allows the user to only view information in the object or execute a program object. The *EXCLUDE value grants no authority to or use of the object.

Authority to an object is divided into two categories: object authority and data authority. Object authority determines what specific functions can be applied to the entire object. Data authority usually applies to the operations (generally read, add, change, or delete) allowed on the contents of an object that contains data. A user's authority can also be custom defined with object and data authority classifications, such as those listed in Figure 2.11. Data authority, as shown in Figure 2.11, has five classifications.

To exit the Display Authorization List screen,

Press   F3   to "Exit"

Figure 2.11
Data Authority
Classifications

Data Authorities	Description
*READ	Read authority allows the user to view the contents of an object.
*ADD	Add authority allows the user to add entries to an object. A user must have *ADD authority to add records to a file or jobs to a queue.
*UPD	Update authority allows the user to change the items in an object.
*DLT	Delete authority allows the user to delete items contained in an object.
*EXECUTE	Execute authority allows the user to run a program, or to locate an object in a library.

Display Object Authority Command

The DSPOBJAUT (Display Object Authority) command allows the operator to view the authorized users for an object. This approach is the reverse of that for viewing the user profile, group profile, or authorization list. In the previous material, the operator always viewed access from the user at the top to the data object at the bottom. With the DSPOBJAUT command, the operator is looking from the bottom upward. Assume that a user is receiving an error message saying that the user does not have access, or is unauthorized, to the object. The operator would likely find it helpful to review the object's authorities. The operator must have the authority to use the DSPOBJAUT command.

To view the Display Object Authority screen,

Type	DSPOBJAUT	on the command line
Press	F4	to prompt

You must specify the name of the object, along with the library in which the object is located, and the object type. There is an option to view on-screen or to print the output. *TO DISK*

> **HINT**
>
> Position the cursor on a field you may have questions about, then press the F4 function key. A list of the available options will be displayed.

To access the Display Object Authority screen,

Type	the name of a valid library	for name of the object
Type	*LIBL	for the name of library
Type	*LIB	for the type of object
Press	Enter	

(Ask your instructor for the name of a valid library, or you may use QGPL.)

The Display Object Authority screen, as shown in Figure 2.12, displays the authorities allowed for the user.

HINT

X Press the F11 function key to view details of the screen (similar to the detail shown in Figure 2.10 on page 33).

If a user owns an object, the user should have all authorities to that object. If the operator wishes to see all users and their authorities to an object, the operator must have object management authority. The security administrator can use the DSPOBJAUT (Display Object Authority) command to list all users and their authorities to an existing object.

Figure 2.12
Display Object Authority
Screen, Detailed

```
                              Display Object Authority

Object . . . . . . . . :    QSYSOPR      Owner . . . . . . . . . :    QSECOFR
    Library . . . . . :       QSYS       Primary group . . . . . :    *NONE
Object type . . . . . :     *LIB

Object secured by authorization list . . . . . . . . . . . . . . :    *NONE


                 Object       List    ----------Object-----------
User             Authority    Mgt     Opr   Mgt   Exist   Alter   Ref
*PUBLIC          *USE                  X





                                                                    Bottom
Press Enter to continue.

F3=Exit  F11=Display data authorities  F12=Cancel  F17=Top  F18=Bottom
```

Authority Search Path

Any time access to an object is requested, the operating system examines authorities in a specific sequence. It is important to understand this sequence, because the system will discontinue the search if sufficient authority is given at any level of examination. The search path is shown in Figure 2.13.

Figure 2.13
Authority Search Path

The search path for authority is

A. Ownership of program
1. The owner's special authority specified in the owner's user profile
2. The owner's specific authority attached to the object
3. Authorization lists attached to the object

B. User profile
1. The user's special authority specified in the user profile
2. The user's specific authority attached to the object
3. Authorization lists attached to the object

C. Group profile
1. The group's special authority specified in the group's profile
2. The group's specific authority attached to the object
3. Authorization lists attached to the object

D. Public authority to the object

Your AS/400's security should be configured according to the search path, or a security risk may be involved. For example, if a user's special authority (item B1) to an object is *EXCLUDE, but the user is also included in an authorization list (item A3) with authority of *CHANGE, the user *will* have change authority.

To exit the Display Object Authority screen,

Press   F3   to "Exit"

Security on the AS/400 supports many different needs for diverse organizations. Because of the AS/400's provisions for assistance levels, library lists, and the user profile's first menu option, unauthorized users can be limited to a narrow view of the system, should they gain access. Through the use of group profiles and authorization lists, security becomes easier to maintain. The user profile and job description combine to control both interactive and batch jobs by enforcing the security of the object authorities. A major advantage of the AS/400 is its capability to let you combine the various objects to create customized security configurations to meet the differing needs of users.

Key Terms

Assistance Levels
    Basic
    Intermediate
    Advanced
Authorization Lists
Authority Search Path
Current Library
Group Profiles
Job Description
Library List
Data Authorities
    *ADD
    *DLT
    *READ

*UPD
*EXECUTE
Object Authorities
    *ALL
    *CHANGE
    *EXCLUDE
    *USE
System Values
Security Level
    Level 10
    Level 20
    Level 30
    Level 40
    Level 50

Uninterruptible
    Power Supply (UPS)
User Classes
    Security Officer
    Security Administrator
    Programmers
    System Operator
    Users
User Profile
    User ID
    Password

Review Questions

1. What system value determines the default public authority of a new object?   *USE* [handwritten]

2. A user profile exists and a password is required at what security level(s)?   *20 30* [handwritten]

3. What parameter in the user profile works with the user class to limit users' access?   *ID PASSWORD* [handwritten]

4. Explain the difference between a group profile and an authorization list. → *Determines who is authorized for use. group profile determines group which can use but don't give out to all aspects of DTA* [handwritten]

5. How does a job description affect security?   *needs valid USRID controlling of Batch jobs.* [handwritten]

Exercises

1. Display the system values that determine how the system reacts during a power failure.

2. Display your user profile and determine whether you are attached to a group profile.   *A Star** [handwritten]

3. Display object authority for your library and determine the public's authority for it.

Chapter 3

The User Interface

Objectives

To understand

✓ AS/400 General System Tasks

✓ the AS/400's Operational Assistant

✓ the purpose and use of Command Language (CL)

✓ the F9 Retrieval function

✓ use of CL keyword and positional notation

✓ how to use AS/400 help and extended help

✓ how to use the AS/400 InfoSeeker function

General System Tasks

The AS/400's General System Tasks menu does not apply to the majority of users; it is commonly displayed as the first screen to those with a user class of *SYSOPR. This menu, as shown in Figure 3.1, usually will appear as soon as the system operator signs on. Because many of the same tasks are available through the General System Tasks menu and the Operational Assistant, this text will concentrate on the more friendly Operational Assistant. Other users on the system are generally shown the AS/400 Main Menu.

The General System Tasks screen allows you as the operator to accomplish tasks from among the following options: Jobs; Status; Display system operator messages; Messages; Files, libraries, and folders; Save; Restore; Device operations; Communications; and other system tasks. You frequently are the initial contact point for resolving user problems. Therefore, you also need to be familiar with the AS/400 Main Menu, shown in Figure 3.2.

Figure 3.1
General System
Tasks Menu

```
SYSTEM                          General System Tasks
                                                    System:   xxxxxxx

Select one of the following:

          1. Jobs
          2. Status
          3. Display system operator messages
          4. Messages
          5. Files, libraries, and folders
          6. Save
          7. Restore
          8. Device operations
          9. Communications

         60. More system task options




Selection or command
===>_____
F3=Exit   F4=Prompt   F9=Retrieve   F12=Cancel   F13=Information Assistant
F16=AS/400 Main menu
```

Figure 3.2
AS/400 Main Menu

```
Main                            AS/400 Main Menu
                                                    System:   XXXXXXXX
Select one of the following:

          1.  User tasks
          2.  Office tasks
          3.  General system tasks
          4.  Files, libraries, and folders

          6.  Communications
          7.  Define or change the system
          8.  Problem handling
          9.  Display a menu
         10.  Information Assistant options
         11.  Client Access tasks

         90.  Sign off




Selection or command
===>_____
F3=Exit    F4= Prompt  F9=Retrieve   F12=Cancel   F13=Information Assistant
F23=Set Initial menu
```

To access the AS/400 Main Menu from the General System Tasks menu,

Press   F16   for "AS/400 Main Menu"

HINT

If there is a name in the top left corner of any menu, you may go directly to the menu by typing **GO (menu name)** on any command line; for example, GO MAIN.

After a careful review of the various menu options, you might be concerned that the average user may have access to areas that do not seem appropriate. But any option the user selects will activate the security system, and unauthorized users will be denied further access.

To return to the General System Tasks menu,

Press   F3

Operational Assistant

Operational Assistant consists of a series of user-friendly menus that aid the operator in performing routine tasks: controlling jobs, printer output, message handling, power on/off tasks, and system backups. You can access the Operational Assistant menu (Figure 3.3) by pressing the Attention key (if the system value QATNPGM is set to *ASSIST), or by typing GO ASSIST on any command line:

Type   GO ASSIST   on any command line
Press   Enter

Figure 3.3
AS/400 Operational
Assistant Menu

```
ASSIST                 AS/400 Operational Assistant(TM) Menu
                                                      System:    XXXXXXX
To select one of the following, type its number below and press Enter:

        1. Work with printer output
        2. Work with jobs
        3. Work with messages
        4. Send messages
        5. Change your password

       10. Manage your system, users, and devices
       11. Customize your system, users, and devices

       75. Information and problem handling

       80. Temporary sign-off




   Type a menu option below
   __
F1=Help   F3=Exit   F9=Command line   F12=Cancel
```

Option 1 of the Operational Assistant menu gives you access to the Work with Printer Output display. You will be able to view and control all the spooled output printer files for output that has not been printed. The printing options are covered in greater depth in Chapter 5.

Option 2, "Work with jobs," lets you hold, delete, release, display messages, or work with printer output from the jobs that are running within the system. Chapter 4, "Working with Jobs and Message Handling," covers these topics in greater depth.

Option 3, "Work with messages," displays all the messages in the system operator message queue (if your user profile has been assigned the QSYSOPR message queue). As the system operator, you receive all messages concerning batch jobs and jobs requiring special attention. Chapter 4, "Working with Jobs and Message Handling," covers these topics in greater depth.

Option 4, "Send messages," allows you to send a message to any single user or group of users, whether or not they are currently signed on to the system.

Option 5 lets you "Change your password," permitting a new password to be entered. This option is limited to changing the password for the user ID that is currently signed on.

Option 10, which lets you "Manage your system, users, and devices," is quite versatile. You can display the system status; run a backup; work with system operator messages, printer output, jobs, signed-on users, device status tasks; and customize the system, users, and devices. Chapter 6, "Device Configuration," covers this topic in more depth.

Option 11 is used to customize the AS/400 configuration. This option will lead the Security Officer to other menus to create new user IDs or to edit existing functions. Menus for creating new devices or changing configurations for existing devices are accessed through this menu option.

Option 75 provides tools for accessing valuable information about procedures to assist in problem resolution.

Option 80 provides the user or operator with a temporary sign-off. This option is valuable when a user is required to leave his or her workstation unattended for a period of time when (s)he is in the middle of an activity or program. A temporary sign-off allows the user to suspend the application, thus saving the user's time because (s)he does not have to pass through all the menus to return to his or her activity, and system security is maintained. When the user returns to the system, the AS/400 will automatically return to the application screen that was displayed at the time of temporary sign-off.

If you are in the middle of an application and want to temporarily sign off the system, you must access the AS/400 Operational Assistant menu. From this menu,

Type   80   to sign off temporarily
Press   Enter

The sign-on screen, as shown in Figure 3.4, will be displayed.
To sign back on to the system,

Type   your user ID
Type   your password
Press   Enter

To return to the application that was in use before you accessed the AS/400 Operational Assistant menu, you must press F3.

Figure 3.4
Sign-On Screen

```
                                    Sign On


                                                System: .  .  .  .  .  .  :    XXXXXXX
                                                Subsystem .  .  .  .  :    XXXXX
                                                Display .  .  .  .  .  .  :    XXXXXXX

                    User .  .  .  .  .  .  .  .  .  .  .  .  .    _____
                    Password .  .  .  .  .  .  .  .  .  .  .    _____
                    Program/procedure  .  .  .  .  .  .  .    _____
                    Menu .  .  .  .  .  .  .  .  .  .  .  .  .    _____
                    Current library  .  .  .  .  .  .  .  .    _____
```

CL Commands

The first five Operational Assistant menu options have corresponding AS/400 Control Language (CL) commands that execute the same programs triggered by the menu options. The table shown in Figure 3.5 displays the commands that correspond to the menu items.

Figure 3.5
Operational Assistant
Menu Options and
Associated CL Commands

Operational Assistant Menu Options	CL Commands
Work with printer output	WRKSPLF
Work with jobs	WRKUSRJOB
Work with messages	WRKMSG
Send messages	SNDMSG (See note)
Change your password	CHGPWD

(Note: The Operational Assistant Menu does not actually use any CL command to perform its task, but the SNDMSG command accomplishes a similar function.)

CL consists of more than 1,000 commands that execute OS/400 functions. The naming structure IBM uses to create CL commands is English-like in nature, which makes the commands easy to comprehend. CL commands can consist of a verb and a noun, or a verb, an adjective, and a noun. Figure 3.6 shows an example of the CL command WRKSPLF (Work with Spooled File), which consists of a verb, an adjective, and a noun.

Figure 3.6
Sample CL Command
Structure

CL Abbreviation	English Word
WRK	work
SPL	spooled
F	file

As you can see, abbreviations are used to construct CL commands. Vowels are rarely used in a CL command. Figure 3.7 shows a table of the most frequently used command abbreviations.

Figure 3.7
Most Frequently Used CL
Command Abbreviations

WRK	work
CHG	change
DSP	display
CRT	create
DLT	delete
CPY	copy
OBJ	object
STR	start
STS	status
SYS	system
WTR	writer
PTR	printer

Many experienced AS/400 users prefer to use commands rather than menus, because this allows them to access the tasks directly without traveling through the menu layers. In this text we will attempt to provide both the menu options and the CL commands as appropriate. To enter CL commands, you must use a command line. If a command line is not visible when you are displaying the Operational Assistant Menu,

Press   F9   to get a command line

Whenever you enter a CL command, at least three function keys are available to you as the operator or user. These function keys are F4=prompt, F9=Retrieve, and F12=Cancel.

The F4 function key provides prompting help to view the CL command groups. To access the Major Command Groups menu,

Press   F4   to prompt the command

Figure 3.8 shows the major CL command groups (e.g., object management commands, file commands, print commands). By choosing a certain command group, you can narrow the search for a specific command. For example, operators are frequently interested in verb commands because of all the actions they need to perform on the system.

Figure 3.8
Major CL Command
Groups

```
MAJOR                  Major Command Groups
                                                    System: xxxxxxx
Select one of the following:

           1.   Select Command by Name          SLTCMD
           2.   Verb Commands                    VERB
           3.   Subject Commands                 SUBJECT
           4.   Object Management Commands       CMDOBJMGT
           5.   File Commands                    CMDFILE
           6.   Save and Restore Commands        CMDSAVRST
           7.   Work Management Commands         CMDWRKMGT
           8.   Data Management Commands         CMDDTAMGT
           9.   Security Commands                CMDSEC
          10.   Print Commands                   CMDPRT
          11.   Spooling Commands                CMDSPL
          12.   System Control Commands          CMDSYSCTL
          13.   Program Commands                 CMDPGM



                                                          More...
Selection or command
===>
F3=Exit    F4=Prompt    F9=Retrieve    F12=Cancel   F13=Informational Assistant
F16=AS/400 Main Menu
```

To access the first screen of a list of verb commands from the Major Command Groups menu,

Type   2   for "Verb Commands"
Press   Enter

The Verb Command menu, shown in Figure 3.9, which displays all possible subcategories for verb commands, requires you to further narrow the search for the appropriate command.

Figure 3.9
Verb Command
List Screen

```
VERB                        Verb Commands

Select one of the following:

           1.   Add Commands                     CMDADD
           2.   Allocate Commands                CMDALC
           3.   Answer Commands                  CMDANS
           4.   Analyze Commands                 CMDANZ
           5.   Apply Commands                   CMDAPY
           6.   Ask Commands                     CMDASK
           7.   Auditing Commands                CMDAUD
           8.   Call Commands                    CMDCALL
           9.   Configure Commands               CMDCFG
          10.   Change Commands                  CMDCHG
          11.   Check Commands                   CMDCHK
          12.   Close Commands                   CMDCLO
          13.   Cleanup Commands                 CMDCLNUP
          14.   Clear Commands                   CMDCLR



                                                          More...
Selection or command
===>
F3=Exit    F4=Prompt    F9=Retrieve    F12=Cancel   F13=Informational Assistant
```

You can continue, pressing the Page Down key to see more verb commands. Let's work through an example using the Display Commands that operators use quite frequently. Continue scrolling through the Verb Command menu until you come to item 31, Display commands.

Press   Page Down   to continue through list
Press   Page Down   again, to view item 31
Type   31   to select "Display Commands"
Press   Enter

You will now be viewing all the various display commands, as shown in Figure 3.10. You can choose a command by selecting the corresponding number from this menu.

Figure 3.10
Display Commands Menu

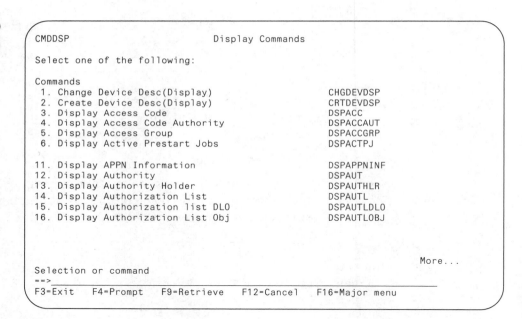

```
CMDDSP                        Display Commands

Select one of the following:

Commands
  1. Change Device Desc(Display)            CHGDEVDSP
  2. Create Device Desc(Display)            CRTDEVDSP
  3. Display Access Code                    DSPACC
  4. Display Access Code Authority          DSPACCAUT
  5. Display Access Group                   DSPACCGRP
  6. Display Active Prestart Jobs           DSPACTPJ

 11. Display APPN Information               DSPAPPNINF
 12. Display Authority                      DSPAUT
 13. Display Authority Holder               DSPAUTHLR
 14. Display Authorization List             DSPAUTL
 15. Display Authorization list DLO         DSPAUTLDLO
 16. Display Authorization List Obj         DSPAUTLOBJ


                                                           More...
Selection or command
==>
F3=Exit    F4=Prompt    F9=Retrieve    F12=Cancel    F16=Major menu
```

When you are ready to exit the command-prompting menus,

Press   F3   to cancel the display

CL commands do not always need to be typed on a command line. CL commands can be incorporated into a CL program and programmers can actually create new CL commands. CL programs are similar to batch files on a PC, but CL programs are much more flexible and sophisticated.

Most CL commands have additional parameters that can be specified if the default values are not applicable to the job at hand. In fact, some CL commands require that additional parameters be specified. The Display Command screen (Figure 3.11) lets you view optional and required parameters for

any CL command. To access the Display Command (DSPCMD) screen and
see these additional parameters,

Type   DSPCMD   on the command line
Press   Enter

Figure 3.11
Display Command
(DSPCMD) Screen

```
                          Display Command (DSPCMD)
  Type choices, press Enter.

  Command . . . . . . . . . . . . . :                    Name
    Library . . . . . . . . . . . . :    *LIBL           Name, *LIBL, *CURLIB
  Output  . . . . . . . . . . . . . :    *               *, *PRINT










                                                                    Bottom
  F3=Exit    F4=Prompt    F5=Refresh    F12=Cancel  F13=Information Assistant
  F24=More keys
```

The Display Command screen requires that you enter the name of the
command you want to view. Optional parameters are the library name and
the output device. The library name is required if the library is not contained
in the library list. The default output device option (*) lets you view the
information on your workstation screen. If you want a printed copy, change
the output option to *PRINT. If, for example, you wanted to view parameters
for the DSPMSG command, you would

Type   DSPMSG   as the command parameter
Press   Enter

All the current assigned parameter values for the DSPMSG command would
be shown in the Display Command Information screen (Figure 3.12).

The parameter values listed on the Display Command prompting screen
(Figure 3.11) are defaults or assigned values. When you type a command on
the command line and press the Enter key, the command will be executed
according to the command parameter default values, assuming the command
has required parameters associated with it.

Many times, however, the defaults are not suitable for the task at hand.
Pressing the F4 function key while the cursor is located on a parameter will
provide you with more parameter values that you can choose instead of using

Figure 3.12
Display Command
Information Screen

```
                        Display Command Information

Command  . . . . . . . :    DSPMSG      Library  . . . . . . . . :    QSYS

Program to process command . . . . . . :    QMHDSMSS
  Library  . . . . . . . . . . . . . :      QSYS
  State used to call program . . . . . :      *SYSTEM
Source file  . . . . . . . . . . . . :
  Library  . . . . . . . . . . . . . :
Source file member . . . . . . . . . :
Validity checking program  . . . . . . :    *NONE
Mode(s) in which valid . . . . . . . . :    *PROD
                                             *DEBUG
                                             *SERVICE
Where allowed to run . . . . . . . . . :    *IMOD       *BMOD        *IREXX
                                             *BREXX      *BPGM        *IPGM
                                             *EXEC       *INTERACT    *BATCH
Allow limited user . . . . . . . . . . :    *YES
Maximum positional parameters  . . . . :    1

                                                                     More...

Press Enter to continue.


F3=Exit   F12=Cancel
```

the default values. The parameters listed will depend on which CL command is displayed. Some CL commands have pages of required parameters, and others have none — for example, the Signoff command, which needs no parameters.

To exit the Display Command Information screen,

Press   F3   to "Exit"

For example, let's use a value other than the default message queue value on the Work with Messages (WRKMSG) screen (Figure 3.13). To access the Work with Messages (WRKMSG) screen,

Type   WRKMSG   on the command line
Press   F4   to prompt the command

HINT

Typing a question mark before the command name on the command line has the same effect as pressing the F4 (Prompt) key after the command is entered. This is an alternative when you are accessing a system with a modified keyboard mapping program and the F4 key has another purpose.

Figure 3.13
Work with Messages
(WRKMSG) Screen

```
                        Work with Messages (WRKMSG)
 Type choices, press Enter.

 Message queue  . . . . . . . . .    *WRKUSR        Name, *WRKUSR, *SYSOPR...
   Library  . . . . . . . . . .                    Name, *LIBL, *CURLIB
 Output . . . . . . . . . . . .      *             *, *PRINT
















 F3=Exit    F4=Prompt    F5=Refresh    F10=Additional parameters  F12=Cancel
 F13=How to use this display        F24=More keys
```

Now, in place of the *WRKUSR default,

Type   your user ID   for the message queue
Type   your library name
Type   *   for the output parameter

To see keywords associated with the WRKMSG command's parameters,

Press   F24   for more function keys
Press   F11   for keywords

HINT

You can press the F11 key even if it is not one of the keys shown at the bottom of the screen. You may press any valid key, whether or not it is shown. As you become more familiar with the keys, you can skip pressing F24.

Figure 3.14
Work with Messages
(WRKMSG) Screen with
Keywords Displayed

```
                          Work with Messages (WRKMSG)

Type choices, press Enter.
Message queue  . . . . . . . . .  MSGQ        *WRKUSR
  Library  . . . . . . . . . .                _____
Output . . . . . . . . . . . .  OUTPUT        *_____








                                                                  Bottom

F9=All parameters   F11=Choices   F14=Command string   F24=More keys
```

Press   F3   to return to the Operational Assistant

The F9 Retrieval Function

When you are viewing a command screen that has been prompted, the keyword and the values are shown in an English-like format. However, when the
command is sent to the operating system for execution, it is restructured into
CL syntax. To redisplay the previous CL command syntax,

Press   F9   to retrieve

In this case, the command line should return the following:

```
WRKMSG MSGQ(your library/your message queue) OUTPUT (*)
```

In this example, there are two parameters: the message queue name and the
output method.

Advanced users frequently wish to type their command on the command line and specify the values for the parameters, rather than prompting
the command. To practice entering CL keyword notation, type the previous
CL command on the command line:

Type   WRKMSG MSGQ(userlib/userid) OUTPUT(*)
Press   Enter

Although we specified a value for the OUTPUT parameter, the default is to
view the output on screen.

As you have worked through this chapter, you have seen how the help
functions and the CL commands insert keywords and the appropriate values
to complete a CL command. If you or other users must perform the same

task more than once, the F9 function key minimizes the typing that would otherwise be required. The F9 function key will display the previous CL command that was typed, along with the related keywords. The previous command is saved in a buffer for the user's current session. Each time you press F9, the system will back up an additional command, so you can browse through previous commands until you find the one you want to repeat. During sign-off, the buffer is cleared.

CL Keyword Notation

A CL command can be broken down into parts. In a simplified form, the command name is followed by the parameters. Each parameter has two parts: the keyword and the value. Keywords help you learn the CL commands and their options. Each CL command has a general structure as follows:

COMMAND NAME   KEYWORD(VALUE)   KEYWORD(VALUE)   KEYWORD(VALUE) ...

Parameter 1   Parameter 2   Parameter 3

Any CL command that has parameters will be structured this way. Each parameter shown in Figure 3.13, for example, has a keyword associated with it.

In Figure 3.14, the corresponding keywords for each parameter are listed in the center column, with the default values in the right column. The message queue keyword is MSGQ. The library does not show an associated keyword and is indented two spaces under the message queue name because it is part of the MSGQ keyword. The message queue is a qualified name with two parts; first is the name of the message queue, next is the name of the library. If the library value is not specified, the library list, *LIBL, will be searched.

When you are using keyword notation, the parameters can be in any order. Therefore, the message command above can also be entered as

```
WRKMSG OUTPUT(*) MSGQ (userlib/userid)
```

Notice that the value for the MSGQ parameter is listed with two parts, the library name and the message queue name. For technical reasons, when you are using keyword notation, the order of the values within a qualified name is the reverse of the order for the same qualified name on the command prompting screen (Figure 3.14).

Now let's cancel the Work with Messages (WRKMSG) screen,

Press   F12   to "Cancel"

CL Positional Notation

Three methods exist to execute CL commands. The easiest approach is to use the command line and the F4 prompt function. Another method some operators prefer is to type the commands on the command line using keyword notation. Finally, as you become more familiar with the CL command parameters, you might use positional notation. When parameter values are entered by position, they must be entered in the order in which they are specified within the command syntax. The F4 prompt function lists the parameters in sequence. Positional notation saves typing, but entries must be accurate. You should reserve this method for commands with brief parameter lists until you have more experience using CL commands.

As an example of using positional notation to enter a CL command, the WRKMSG (Work with Messages) command would be typed as

```
WRKMSG userlib/userid   *
```

Most commands limit the number of parameters that you can enter using positional notation.

You can also use a combination of keyword notation and positional notation. For example, the WRKMSG command can be typed as

```
WRKMSG userlib/userid OUTPUT(*)
```

When you use a combination of keyword and positional notation, the positional parameters must occur first; once keyword notation is used, positional notation is no longer valid, and any additional parameters must be specified in keyword notation.

To cancel the command line in the above example(s),

Press   F12   to "Cancel"

AS/400 Help

AS/400 Help provides users with several levels of Help functions. The AS/400 supports on-line help for menus, entry screens, and prompt functions. The user also can search the Help database for information while (s)he is using an index. For example, if you press the Help key while the cursor is located on a menu (or a menu option), the system will retrieve a description and instructions about how to use the menu (or option).

HINT

If the cursor is still located on the command line, you will receive help information for the command line instead of the Help menu.

To display the Operational Assistant help, you may have to first type GO ASSIST on any command line, then

Move   cursor   to the title line
Press   Help   to display the Operational Assistant's help information

The Help screen, as shown in Figure 3.15, overlays the Operational Assistant menu with information about the Operational Assistant. This is general information relating to the menu. The information included in the Help

Figure 3.15
AS/400 Operational
Assistant Menu with Help
Screen Overlay

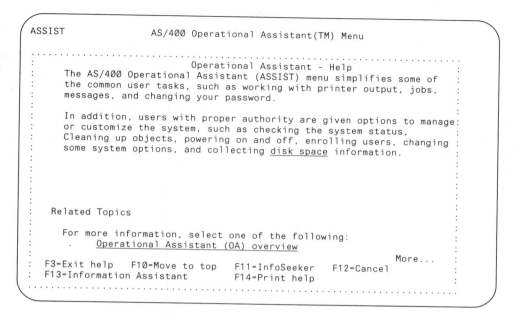

```
 ASSIST                 AS/400 Operational Assistant(TM) Menu
 .........................................................................
 :                      Operational Assistant - Help                     :
 :   The AS/400 Operational Assistant (ASSIST) menu simplifies some of   :
 :   the common user tasks, such as working with printer output, jobs,   :
 :   messages, and changing your password.                               :
 :                                                                       :
 :   In addition, users with proper authority are given options to manage:
 :   or customize the system, such as checking the system status,        :
 :   Cleaning up objects, powering on and off, enrolling users, changing :
 :   some system options, and collecting disk space information.         :
 :                                                                       :
 :                                                                       :
 :                                                                       :
 :   Related Topics                                                      :
 :                                                                       :
 :     For more information, select one of the following:                :
 :      .   Operational Assistant (OA) overview                          :
 :                                                            More...     :
 :   F3=Exit help    F10=Move to top    F11=InfoSeeker    F12=Cancel     :
 :   F13=Information Assistant           F14=Print help                  :
 .........................................................................
```

function will vary depending upon the current AS/400 display and the position of the cursor on that display. The on-line Help lets you and other users successfully use the appropriate parameters to accomplish your tasks without having to reference a manual printed on paper.

To further explore the on-line help capabilities, let's experiment with the help information covering the GO command. First, it is necessary to cancel the information on the Operational Assistant — Help screen. Then we will be able to start the on-line help functions.

Press	F12	to "Cancel" the Help screen overlay
Press	F9	to access a command line
Type	GO	on the command line
Press	F4	to prompt

You will now see the Go to Menu (GO) screen, as shown in Figure 3.16.

To gain further information about a parameter, position the cursor somewhere within the parameter, then press the Help key. Information specific to the parameter will be overlaid on the existing display.

To access the screen shown in Figure 3.17,

Press	arrow keys	to position the cursor somewhere on the "Return point" line
Press	Help	to activate the overlay

As shown in Figure 3.17, the F2=Extended help option is located within the help area so users can access the information relating to the entire screen. When parameters are listed for an entry, the cursor must be

Figure 3.16
Go to Menu (GO) Screen

```
                          Go to Menu (GO)

Type choices, press Enter.

Menu . . . . . . . . . . . .   _____   Name, generic*, *ALL
  Library . . . . . . . . . .   *LIBL        Name, *LIBL, *CURLIB...
  Return point. . . . . . . .   *YES         *YES, *NO




                                                           Bottom
F3=Exit  F4=Prompt  F5=Refresh  F12=Cancel  F13=How to use this display
F24=More keys
```

Figure 3.17
Go to Menu (GO) Screen
with Return Point
Help Overlay

```
                          Go to Menu (GO)

Type choices, press Enter.

Menu . . . . . . . . . . . .   _____   Name, generic*, *ALL
  Library . . . . . . . . . .   *LIBL        Name, *LIBL, *CURLIB...
Return point . . . . . . . . .  *YES         *YES, *NO
    ..................................................................
    :               Return point (RTNPNT) - help                     :
    :                                                                 :
    :  Specifies whether to return to the display where the          :
    :  command is entered when the Exit key is pressed.              :
    :                                                                 :
    :  The possible values are:                                      :
    :                                                                 :
    :  *YES  The display where the command is entered is             :
    :        returned to when the Exit key is pressed.               :
    :                                                                 :
    :  *NO   The display where the command is entered is             :
    :        not returned to when the Exit key is pressed.           :
    :                                                                 :
    :  F2=Extended help   F10=Move to top   F11=InfoSeeker           :
F3=Exit F4=P: F12=Cancel        F20=Enlarge       F24=More keys      :
F24=More key:....................................................:
```

positioned on an entry field. To access the extended help, a user must first access the Help function.

To retrieve Extended help,

Press F2 for "Extended help"

Figure 3.18 represents a sample of an extended help screen. The extended help information was selected for the GO command.

Figure 3.18
The GO (Go to Menu)
Command Screen

```
                              Go to Menu (GO)
..................................................................................
:                           Go to Menu - Help                                   :
:                                                                               :
:   The GO (Go to Menu) command shows the menu requested. This command          :
:   lets you specify either a particular menu or a generic menu                 :
:   name. You can optionally specify whether or not to return to the            :
:   menu from which the command is entered after showing the menu               :
:   specified.                                                                  :
:                                                                               :
:     Note: Do not precede an entry with an asterisk unless that                :
:     entry is a "special value" that is shown (on the display itself           :
:     or in the help information) with an asterisk.                             :
:                                                                               :
: Menu (MENU)                                                                   :
:                                                                               :
:   Specifies the name and library of the menu to be shown.                     :
:                                                                               :
:   This is a required parameter.                                               :
:                                                                               :
:                                                                   More...     :
:   F3=Exit help  F10=Move to top  F11=InfoSeeker  F12=Cancel                   :
:   F13=Information Assistant      F14=Print help                               :
:                                                                               :
..................................................................................
```

To return to the General System Tasks screen in preparation for the exercises at the end of this chapter,

Press   F3   repeatedly to "Exit help" and the other menus

InfoSeeker Function

The InfoSeeker function on the AS/400 lets you and other users obtain information by searching on-line documentation stored on the AS/400. When InfoSeeker is active, you can press F11 to show the InfoSeeker display, which contains a list of on-line bookshelves and books. You can open one of these, or type in keywords to begin a search to look for specific information. To use InfoSeeker, your machine must have the documentation stored on-line. Otherwise, the function will not be available. The AS/400 user interface is designed to provide all levels of users multiple methods to accomplish their tasks. All techniques for interacting with the system are interchangeable, allowing advanced users to fall back to the "easy to use" menus and beginners to progress as their own needs dictate. It is important to remember to always read the screen for options, function keys, and other information. The on-line help available on the AS/400 is a valuable, time-saving tool that lets you obtain information quickly.

Key Terms

CL commands
    Command structure
    Command groups
    Command information

Keyword notation
Positional notation
Extended help
InfoSeeker

Main menu
Operational Assistant menu
On-line help

Review Questions

1. How do you access the Operational Assistant?

2. Why should a user sign off from his or her terminal when (s)he is going to lunch?

3. How would a user access a list of commands related to jobs?

4. Is the following a valid command?
   WRKMSG MSGQ(userid) *PRINT

5. What help function lets the user browse on-line documentation?

Exercises

1. Display the system operator's messages using Operational Assistant.

2. Display the system operator's messages using the keyword method, not Operational Assistant.

3. Display the system operator's messages using the positional method, not Operational Assistant.

4. Use the proper Help function to find out how to temporarily sign off the system from within an application.

5. Temporarily sign off the system.

Chapter 4

Working with Jobs and Message Handling

Objectives

To understand

- ✓ how jobs are submitted
- ✓ how to use the Submit Job command
- ✓ job scheduling entries
- ✓ how to work with batch jobs
- ✓ how to work with jobs by status
- ✓ how to work with job queues
- ✓ the difference between batch and interactive jobs
- ✓ how to work with interactive users
- ✓ how to answer messages
- ✓ where messages are derived from
- ✓ how to get message details
- ✓ message queues
- ✓ how to change a message queue

How Jobs Are Submitted and Scheduled

AS/400 users and operators accomplish their tasks by executing jobs. A job can be one short, simple function or it can be a series of programs working together to complete a complex task.

The two basic types of jobs are interactive jobs and batch jobs. During an interactive session, the user types a request (and presses Enter or a function key) and the system responds to the request. These sessions, called interactive jobs, begin when a user signs on to a display station and end when the user signs off.

When constant system interaction with the user is not required, the job can be run as a batch job. Once submitted, a batch job disconnects from the workstation, allowing the workstation to be available for further interactive tasks or for additional batch jobs. Two common examples of jobs that are run in batch mode are printed Query reports and month-end data posting.

A batch job is submitted to a job queue, as shown in Figure 4.1. A job queue is a waiting area for pending batch jobs. Assuming that the job priorities are the same among batch jobs, each new batch job is entered at the bottom of the job queue. The subsystem will retrieve these jobs in order of receipt and execute them. Jobs can be held; or if the subsystem is inactive, the batch jobs will be postponed indefinitely. Jobs may be intentionally submitted to an inactive job queue to control scheduling for an unattended night shift. The operator starts the subsystem at the end of the work day and job processing will begin automatically.

Figure 4.1
Representation
of a Job Queue

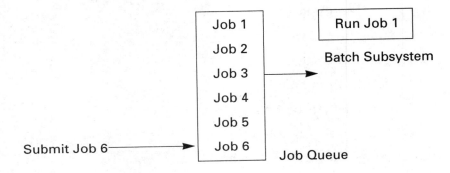

Submit Job Command

Another method to control scheduling on a one-time basis is to use the SBMJOB (Submit Job) command. The Submit Job screen, shown in Figure 4.2, has many options and parameters available. If the job to be submitted is a program, type the word CALL and the name of the program for the "Command to run" parameter; for example, CALL PAYROLL. A CL command can be executed in the same way by typing the command as it would be entered on a command line. To access the Submit Job screen,

Type	SBMJOB	on any command line
Press	F4	to prompt

HINT

To access additional information, from the Submit Job (SBMJOB) screen, position the cursor and press the Help key to view the possible parameter values.

Job Names

Each job on the AS/400 has a unique, qualified job name that incorporates three parts: job name, user name, and job number. When a user submits a job to batch, (s)he can either specify his or her own job name or accept the system default value. The system default value, *JOBD, uses the name of the job

Figure 4.2
Submit Job
(SBMJOB) Screen

```
                          Submit Job (SBMJOB)

 Type choices, press Enter.

 Command to run . . . . . . . _____
 _____
 _____
 _____


 Job name. . . . . . . . . . . .     *JOBD        Name, *JOBD
 Job description . . . . . . . . .   *USRPRF      Name, *USRPRF
   Library . . . . . . . . . . . .   _____      Name, *LIBL, *CURLIB
 Job queue . . . . . . . . . . . .   *JOBD        Name, *JOBD
   Library . . . . . . . . . . . .   _____      Name, *LIBL, *CURLIB
 Job priority (on JOBQ). . . . . .   *JOBD        1-9, *JOBD
 Output priority (on OUTQ) . . . .   *JOBD        1-9, *JOBD
 Print device  . . . . . . . . . .   *CURRENT     Name, *CURRENT,*USRPRF...



                                                          More...
 F3=Exit F4=Prompt F5=Refresh F10=Additional parameters F12=Cancel
 F13=How to use this display        F24=More keys
```

description indicated on the Job description parameter. The user name included in the qualified job name is the name of the user profile for the job that is executing. The job number is assigned by the system. Examples of valid qualified job names might be 000667/QSYSOPR/PAYROLL for a submitted batch job, or 135792/QSYSOPR/DSP01 for an interactive workstation session.

Schedule Date and Time Parameters

The next options related to the Submit Job (SBMJOB) screen that are of interest to the operator are the "Schedule date" (SCDDATE) and "Schedule time" (SCDTIME) parameters; but these options are not displayed on the initial screen. To display these and other additional parameters, use the F10 function key:

Press   F10

Press   Page Down   twice

The resulting screen is shown in Figure 4.3.

The SCDDATE parameter specifies the day the job is to be released to the job queue. The SCDTIME parameter specifies the time of day the job will be released to the job queue. To release the job immediately to the job queue, you can use the *CURRENT value for both the SCDDATE and SCDTIME parameters.

The SBMJOB command allows for many types of jobs, including programs and CL commands, to be submitted at a convenient time and have a delayed execution.

Figure 4.3
Submit Job (SBMJOB)
Screen, Further Options

```
                              Submit Job (SBMJOB)

Type choices, press Enter.

System library list . . . .   *CURRENT      *CURRENT, *SYSVAL
Current library . . . . . .   *CURRENT      Name, *CURRENT, *USRPRF...
Initial library list. . . .   *CURRENT      Name, *CURRENT, *JOBD...
      + for more values       _____
Message logging:
   Level . . . . . . . . .    *JOBD         0-4, *JOBD
   Severity . . . . . . . .   *JOBD         0-99, *JOBD
   Text. . . . . . . . . .    *JOBD         *JOBD, *MSG, *SECLVL, *NOLIST
Log CL program commands       *JOBD         *JOBD, *NO, *YES
Inquiry message reply . . .   *JOBD         *JOBD, *RQD, *DFT, *SYSRPYL
Hold on job queue . . . . .   *JOBD         *JOBD, *NO, *YES
Schedule date . . . . . . .   *CURRENT      Date, *CURRENT, *MONTHSTR...
Schedule time . . . . . . .   *CURRENT      Time, *CURRENT
Job date . . . . . . . . .    *JOBD         Date, *JOBD, *SYSVAL
Job switches  . . . . . .     *JOBD         Character value, *JOBD
Allow display by WRKSBMJOB    *YES          *YES, *NO

                                                              More...

F3=Exit  F4=Prompt  F5=Refresh  F12=Cancel F13=How to use this display
F24=More keys
```

To experiment using the SBMJOB command, use the Page Up key so that the initial Submit Job screen is displayed. Then send a message to yourself with a three-minute delay. Use Figures 4.2 and 4.3 for reference.

Press	Page Up	twice to return to the Submit Job screen
Type	SNDMSG	for the "Command to run" parameter
Press	F4	to prompt and fill in the message command
Type	your user ID	as the receiving user ID
Press	Page Down	twice
Type	a time value	that is three minutes later than the current time of day on the "Schedule time" entry (SCDTIME) to specify your message to appear in your own message queue.
Press	Enter	to send the message to yourself

Working with Job Schedule Entries

Another job scheduling tool that is available on the AS/400 is the WRKJOBSCDE (Work with Job Schedule Entries) command. This command contains the information you need to submit a batch job at regular intervals. This tool also has an easy-to-use interface that lets you submit any type of job or command at specified times. Adding a job schedule entry will cause a job to be submitted at the specified time. Removing a job schedule entry will stop the job from being submitted. Other types of changes in job schedule entries are allowed, such as holding and releasing entries in the job scheduler. Each job schedule entry has a unique job name and entry number.

To access the WRKJOBSCDE command screen,

Type   WRKJOBSCDE on any command line

Press   Enter

To schedule a job once, weekly, or monthly, use F6=Add on the Work with Job Schedule Entries screen, as shown in Figure 4.4. The job scheduler submits the job automatically at the specified time.

Figure 4.4
Work with Job Schedule
Entries Screen

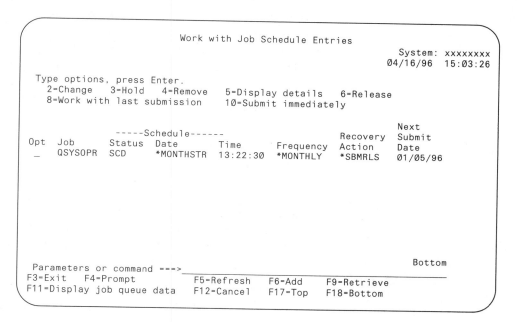

```
                        Work with Job Schedule Entries
                                                     System: xxxxxxxx
                                                     04/16/96  15:03:26

   Type options, press Enter.
    2=Change   3=Hold   4=Remove   5=Display details   6=Release
    8=Work with last submission     10=Submit immediately


                     -----Schedule------             Next
                                              Recovery  Submit
   Opt  Job      Status  Date      Time     Frequency  Action  Date
    _   QSYSOPR  SCD     *MONTHSTR 13:22:30 *MONTHLY   *SBMRLS  01/05/96










                                                        Bottom
   Parameters or command ===> _____
   F3=Exit   F4=Prompt        F5=Refresh   F6=Add    F9=Retrieve
   F11=Display job queue data  F12=Cancel  F17=Top   F18=Bottom
```

Commonly used options on the Work with Job Schedule Entries screen are shown in Figure 4.5.

Figure 4.5
Commonly Used
WRKJOBSCDE
Command Options

Work with Job Options	Description
2=Change	Option 2 modifies the job schedule entry for the selected job but does not affect any jobs already submitted.
4=Remove	This option will permanently delete a job schedule entry so that the job is not executed on the schedule.
3=Hold	Holding a job schedule entry will result in the job entry being bypassed if the scheduled time occurs while the job is held.
6=Release	This option releases a held job schedule entry. If the scheduled time has not passed, the job will be submitted for execution. If the scheduled time has passed, a warning message is displayed indicating that job was missed. As operator, you can submit the job manually or use Option 10 to submit it immediately.

Figure 4.5 continued

Figure 4.5
Continued

Work with Job Options	Description
10=Submit immediately	The "Submit immediately" option can be used when a held job's scheduled time has passed. This option is also helpful for clean-up activities; occasionally, it is necessary to run these functions immediately, usually because of problems.

Verifying the Status of Batch Jobs

Whenever you have changed the status of a batch job, you should verify the change. To check the status of batch jobs, use the Operational Assistant (GO ASSIST) menu to access the Work with Jobs screen:

Type	GO ASSIST	on any command line
Press	Enter	
Type	2	for the "Work with jobs" option
Press	Enter	

An example of the Work with Jobs screen is shown in Figure 4.6.

HINT

Job Schedule Entry jobs do not appear on this display until they are submitted to the batch job queue.

Figure 4.6
Work with Jobs Screen

```
                              Work with Jobs
                                                         System: XXXXXXX
User . . . . .  _____        Name, *ALL, F4 for list
Type options below, then press Enter.

  3=Hold   4=Delete (End)   6=Release    7=Display message
  8=Work with printer output
      Job Queue/
Opt    Job          Status
  _    QBATCH
  _      BONUS2       Message waiting (use opt 7)
  _      BONUS        Running
  _      NOBONUS      Running job held (use opt 6)
  _      PAYCODE      Ending
  _      PAYROLL      Waiting to run (2 of 4)
  _      OVERTIME     Scheduled 11/30/96 12:00:00
  _      TIMECARD     Held (use opt 6)
  _      HOLIDAY      Held (use opt 6)


                                                            Bottom
F5=Refresh   F9=Command line   F11=Display dates/times
F12=Cancel   F14=Select other jobs   F22=Work with job queues
```

HINT

To view or manage the jobs of other users, including batch jobs, you must have job control (*JOBCTL) authority.

HINT

To display the status of a single user, you can type the user's ID in the user parameter. If you forget the user ID, you can press F4 to prompt for a list of all user IDs.

To see all batch jobs (you must have *JOBCTL authority), type *ALL in the user parameter on the Work with Jobs screen and press the Enter key. You can enter a generic name; for example, D* shows all the jobs for all users whose names start with a D, such as David, Diana, or Duke. You can enter a generic name on the Select Other Jobs display.

Type   *ALL   in the user parameter

Press   Enter

The Work with Jobs screen is displayed with the User parameter (see Figure 4.7). Accessing this screen provides a convenient method to determine which user submitted each job. The default on the Work with Jobs screen is to sort by job queue and within each job queue by status.

Figure 4.7
Work with Jobs Screen

```
                              Work with Jobs
                                                      System: XXXXXXX
 User . . . . . .     *ALL_____    Name, *ALL, F4 for list

 Type options below, then press Enter.
   3=Hold   4=Delete (End)   6=Release   7=Display message
   8=Work with printer output

      Job Queue/
 Opt     Job         User        Status
         QBATCH
 _        BONUS       SMITH       Message waiting (use opt 7)
 _        MYJOB       HARRY       Running
 _        BONUS2      SHEMP       Ending
         QS36EVOKE
 _        PAYROLL     DUNNJ2      Waiting to run (1 of 4)
 _        INVOICES    MAHONEY     Waiting to run (2 of 4)
 _        INVOICES2   MONTEY      Waiting to run (3 of 4)
 _        INVOICES3   GEORGE      Scheduled 12/15/96 22:00:00


                                                           Bottom
 F1=Help  F3=Exit  F5=Refresh   F9=Command line  F11=Display dates/times
 F12=Cancel F14=Select other jobs F22=Work with job queues F24=More keys
```

Work with Jobs by Status

Most AS/400 systems have great quantities of jobs in the batch queue. Generally, the system operator is responsible for ensuring that the queued jobs are progressing quickly and efficiently. To help you process jobs, you may find it useful to obtain the status of jobs by category. For example, you may be concerned with jobs that have a status of "hold" because of an unanswered message. To view the various choices (Figure 4.8),

Press   F14   to "Select other jobs" on the Work with Jobs screen

Figure 4.8
Work with Jobs Screen,
Select Other Jobs Option

```
                          Work with Jobs

                        Select Other Jobs

Select the following jobs for the list.

Type choices below, then press Enter.

  User . . . . . . . . . . . .  *ALL_____   Name, *ALL, F4 for list
  Status:
    Message waiting. . . . . . . . . .  Y          Y=Yes, N=No
    Running. . . . . . . . . . . . .  Y          Y=Yes, N=No
    Running job held . . . . . . . .  Y          Y=Yes, N=No
    Ending . . . . . . . . . . . . .  Y          Y=Yes, N=No
    Waiting to run/Scheduled . . . . .  Y          Y=Yes, N=No
    Held . . . . . . . . . . . . . .  Y          Y=Yes, N=No
    Job queue held . . . . . . . . .  Y          Y=Yes, N=No
    Queue not assigned . . . . . . .  Y          Y=Yes, N=No
    Printer output . . . . . . . . .  N          Y=Yes, N=No




  F1=Help   F5=Refresh   F12=Cancel
```

The default on this display is to select *ALL for the User parameter and to include all jobs in any status except "Printer output." Excluding the finished jobs with printer output waiting helps to reduce the volume of the display. To clear specific job types from this display, type N for no next to each job status you're not interested in. After you press the Enter key, only the selected jobs will be displayed. To return jobs to the display, change the status column to Y for yes.

To see when jobs were submitted, press F11 on the Work with Jobs screen to "Display dates/times." The operator can view the lag time on the job queue to attempt to predict waiting times until a job has begun to execute.

Press Enter to return to the Work with Jobs updated display

Changing Job Sequence

Occasionally, a batch job is submitted that must run immediately. To expedite the critical job, you as operator will have to hold all currently running jobs, all batch jobs that have a higher priority, and any jobs that are in the queue before the critical job. To hold the executing job, use option 3 from the Work with Jobs screen. The status of the job(s) will be changed to Running job held, or to Held. Press the F5 key to refresh the screen and ensure the job status has changed.

After the critical job has been completed, all the held jobs must be released. To release a batch job on the Work with Jobs screen, select option 6, Release, for the job or jobs you want released. The status of the jobs should be changed to Released. Again, press the F5 key to refresh the screen and ensure the job status has changed. The status of the released jobs should be changed to Running, Waiting to run, or Scheduled.

Occasionally, a job is submitted at an inappropriate time or by accident. To remove a batch job, use option 4 on the Work with Jobs screen to Delete, or End, the job. The Confirm Delete message will be shown. Press the Enter key to confirm the end of the job, or press F12 to cancel and to keep the job.

When you delete the batch job, it no longer appears on the display. However, the ended job will still be displayed if the job had printer output waiting, and you had specified a status of Yes for the "Printer output" parameter on the Select Other Jobs display.

Working with Job Queues

Most system operators are required to monitor other job queues, as they do the batch queue. You can accomplish this easily using the Work with Job Queues screen:

Press   F9   to get a command line
Type   WRKJOBQ   on the command line
Press   Enter

You can now view job queue activity information, as shown in Figure 4.9.

Figure 4.9
Work with Job
Queues Screen

```
                        Work with Job Queues
                                                    System: XXXXXXX
User . . . . . :     *ALL
Type options below, then press Enter.
  3=Hold    6=Release

       Job Queue/
 Opt     Job            Status
  _      HILGEREL       Job queue not assigned
  _      MHJOBQ         Job queue not assigned
  _      NORBERT        Held (use Opt 6)
  _      NORBERT2       Ready
  _      NOBELL         Job queue not assigned
  _      QBATCH         Ready
  _      QCTL           Ready
  _      QSNADS         Ready
  _      QXFPCS         Ready
  _      SCHMALL        Job queue not assigned
  _      TLMJOBQ        Job queue not assigned



                                                          More...
 F1=Help      F3=Exit   F5=Refresh   F11=Display libraries/descriptions
 F12=Cancel   F14=Include jobs on job queue
```

On the Work with Job Queues screen, you can hold or release any job queue. Individually holding every job submitted to the job queue prevents those jobs from actually running, but it does not prevent newly submitted jobs from running. Using this display to inactivate the entire queue at once is faster and more error-free, because no jobs in the queue will run.

To hold a job queue using the Work with Job Queues screen, use option 3, "Hold," for the job queue that must be held. The status of the job queue will change to "Job queue held." The Work with Job Queues screen shows only job queues that have "waiting" or "running" jobs. If there are no active jobs associated with a job queue, the Work with Job Queues screen appears empty.

HINT

Always use the F5 function key to refresh your display to ensure that you are viewing the most current display.

Option 6, "Release," releases a job queue. The status of the job queue changes to "*Job queue released."

To return to the Operational Assistant,

Press   F12   twice

Working with Signed-On Users

Another system operator function is to monitor the subsystem QINTER that runs interactive user jobs. Interactive users may not use the largest share of AS/400 resources, but these users frequently have the highest priority for system use. Therefore, smooth functioning of interactive users' jobs is paramount. To display all users who are currently signed on the system and what they are working on, select option 12 from the "Manage Your System, Users, and Devices" menu.

Type   10   to "Manage your system, users, and devices"
Press   Enter
Type   12   to select the "Work with signed-on users" option
Press   Enter

The Work with Signed-On Users display, shown in Figure 4.10, allows messages to be sent to all the users currently signed on; it also allows the operator to display details about interactive jobs. This display can also be used to sign off users who have forgotten to sign off.

HINT

Signing off a user stops his or her interactive job regardless of any processing that may be active. Therefore, it is important to use caution when signing a user off the system. Ending a user's interactive job that is performing a file update can cause the file to be updated incorrectly.

If you are sure that a user must be signed off the system, use option 4, "End," on the Work with Signed-On Users screen. Press the Enter key to confirm the sign-off, or press F12, "Cancel," to leave the user signed on. The Work with Signed-On Users screen will no longer show the User ID(s) of the user(s) who have been signed off the system.

Figure 4.10
Work with Signed-On
Users Screen

```
                          Work with Signed-On Users
                                                      System: XXXXXXX
 Find display station .  .  .  .  .  _____   Starting characters

 Type options below, then press Enter.
   3=Send message  4=Sign off 5=Display details  7=Display message

                   Display
 Opt  User         Station      Activity
  _   BRUNS        BRUNSS3      ASSIST menu
  _   EVERLY       EVERLYS2     INVENTORY program
  _   GOETZ        QPADEV0004   Command entry
  _   JACK         JACKS4       Message waiting (use Opt 7)
  _   SMITH        SMITHS1      WRKUSRJOB command
  _   TELLY        QPADEV0008   MAIN menu
  _   TUBER        QPADEV0002   WRKSPLF command




                                                             Bottom
 F1=Help     F3=Exit     F5=Refresh     F10=Send message to all
 F11=Display additional information  F13=Sort list  F24=More keys
```

Assume that the operator needs to send a message to a user but can't remember the correct spelling of the user's ID. The user's profile name is required for the SNDMSG command but this name is not readily available when many users are signed on to the system. To display a signed-off user's name, enter the first few characters of the user's name in the "Find user" area. The display will begin at the first user profile name that matches the supplied characters. The list is initially sorted by user profile name and it shows each user's activities.

To sort the list by user profile name or display station name,

Press	F13	to "Sort list"
Type	1	to sort by user name
or	2	to sort by display station name
Press	Enter	

You can also include on the display those users who are temporary signed off:

Press	F24	to view more function key options
Press	F14	to display a window that allows you to select other users

Users who are temporarily signed off are not initially included in this list. To include these users, type a Y in the "Include temporarily signed off users..." field in the Select Other Users and Display Stations display.

There are two ways to display additional information about the users currently signed on to the system. For a single user listed on the Work with Signed-On Users screen, select option 5, "Display details." The Display

Details screen presents the user, the display station description, and the current activities.

To get additional information for all users shown on the Work with Signed-On Users screen, use the "Display additional information" function key. This displays a pop-up window, shown in Figure 4.11, where you can select the type of information you want. The selections are "Activities," "Display station descriptions," or "User descriptions."

Figure 4.11
Display Additional
Information Pop-Up
Screen

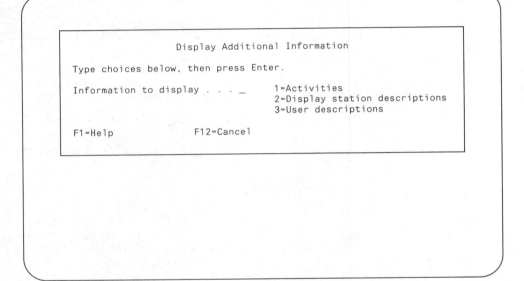

```
                    Display Additional Information

  Type choices below, then press Enter.

  Information to display . . . _      1=Activities
                                      2=Display station descriptions
                                      3=User descriptions

  F1=Help                 F12=Cancel
```

To return to the Operational Assistant.

Press   F3   repeatedly

Message Handling

Messages provide the means for you to communicate with the system and with the users of the system. When you as the operator, or when the user, asks the system to do something, the system may respond with messages indicating the status of that request. In addition, you can communicate with other users of the system through messages that are sent via the system.

As the system operator, you receive messages from system users and programs that communicate conditions you must respond to and indicate actions you need to take. As a system user, you receive messages in response to your actions at a workstation. These messages are placed in message queues.

The system sends informational or inquiry messages for certain system events. Informational messages are generated by the system and give a status report about what the system is doing. Inquiry messages request a reply. These messages are sent to either the system operator's message queue (QSYSOPR), to a user's message queue, or to the workstation's message queue.

HINT

The Send Message display is set to interrupt users who are working. If you do not want to disturb them, change the "Interrupt user" field to N.

You can find out more about messages on the Work with Messages screen from the Operational Assistant menu. Then use the "Display details and reply" option:

Type	GO ASSIST	if necessary
Type	3	for the "Work with Messages" option
Type	5	on any available message needing a reply
Press	Enter	

Usually, one of the causes listed on this screen will help you to identify the problem. See Figure 4.12 for a sample of the Additional Message Information screen. Occasionally, these message explanations may be misleading and the suggested solutions might not correct the problem; the listed causes are only *probable* explanations for what might be causing an error.

HINT

If you select option 5, "Display details and reply," for a message that does not need a reply, the additional information is about the message. If the message requires a reply, type the answer in the field provided at the bottom of the Additional Message Information screen you see when your system is set at the Basic Assistance level.

Figure 4.12
Additional Message
Information Screen

```
                        Additional Message Information
 Message ID . . :    CPA57EF
 Date sent  . . :    11/18/96    Time sent . . . . .    15:43:02

 Message . . . . :   Controller SYSTEM01 contact not successful. Probable remote
                     station problem. (C R)
 Cause . . . . . :   The system was trying to exchange identifiers with the
      station when an error occurred. The probable causes are:
         -- The controller description on the remote system is not varied on.
         -- A configuration problem.
         -- A remote hardware problem.
         -- A local hardware problem or network problem if on an Ethernet network.
         -- A timing or performance problem.
 Recovery . . . :    Do the following:
         -- Contact the remote operator to verify the remote system.



                                                                        More...
 Type reply below, then press Enter.
 Reply  . . . . _____

 F1=Help   F3=Exit    F6=Print    F11=Display message details    F12=Cancel
 F21=Select assistance level
```

Press the Page Down key to see the remaining information about the message. When you have read the information, type an answer in the Reply field and press the Enter key.

The Additional Message Information screen includes the message ID. The system uses the message ID to keep track of its messages. Programmers use these identifiers to handle error messages within their programs.

The error message is accompanied by a letter and number code, as shown in Figure 4.12. This is the "message identifier," or message ID, that distinguishes one message from another in the message file. The first three letters indicate the message category. Some typical message categories are shown in Figure 4.13.

Figure 4.13
Typical AS/400
Message Categories

Category	Explanation
CPA through CPZ	Messages from the operating system
CBE through CBX	COBOL messages
CSC	COBOL language syntax checker messages
LBE through LSC	COBOL messages
MCH	Licensed Internal Code messages
QRG	RPG language messages
RPG through RXT	RPG language messages
SBX through SSC	COBOL messages
SQL	Structured Query Language (SQL) messages

The remaining four digits in an error message (which may include hexadecimal values) indicate the sequence number of the message. In Figure 4.12, the message ID indicates this is a message from the operating system (CPA) and the message is numbered 57EF. A message ID is shown when you use the Help key to request the Display Additional Message screen.

The lower right corner of the screen includes the "More..." notation, and a second page includes details about the message, as shown in Figure 4.14. To view these additional details,

Press   F11   on the Display Message Details screen

HINT

To see all the information about a message on one display, switch to the Intermediate Assistance level using the F21 key while you are on the Additional Message Information screen.

To return to the Additional Message Information screen,

Press   Enter

Figure 4.14
Display Message Details
Screen, Page 2

```
                        Display Message Details
Message ID . . . . . :    CPA57EF    Severity . . . . . . :    99
Date sent . . . . . :    11/18/96    Time sent. . . . . . :    15:43:02
Message type. . . . :    Inquiry

From job. . . . . . . . . . . . . . :    QSYSARB
  User  . . . . . . . . . . . . . . :    QSYS
  Number . . . . . . . . . . . . . :    009302

From program. . . . . . . . . . . . :    QSWCDCR
To message queue. . . . . . . . . . :    QSYSOPR
  Library  . . . . . . . . . . . . :    QSYS




                                                              Bottom
Press Enter to continue.

F1=Help  F3=Exit  F12=Cancel
```

To print an individual message, use the F6=Print option on the Additional Message Information screen. This prints all the information about the message shown on both screens of the display. The output is sent to a spooled file named QSYSPRT; the output can be viewed or printed from the output queue.

Press   F6   on the Additional Message Information screen

Occasionally, a problem seems to grow as efforts are made to correct it. When problem resolution becomes lengthy, printing out the sequence of error messages is one of the best things you can do to help resolve the problem. Rather than print each individual message, you may find it is easier to print the entire message queue.

Press	F12	several times until the Operation Assistant menu is shown
Press	F9	to get a command line
Type	WRKMSG	on any command line
Press	F4	to prompt the command
Type	MSGQNAME	your message queue name
Type	*PRINT	for the output parameter value
Press	Enter	

When you specify the *PRINT parameter on the Work with Messages command, the output will be placed in your output queue, where you can display it or send it to the printer of your choice.

Message Queues

Previously in this chapter, we discussed messages generated by the system in response to a problem or as a request for action by the operator, such as changing paper forms. The QBATCH subsystem usually sends all system operator messages to the message queue named QSYSOPR. During an interactive session, messages sent from other users and messages sent by the system are typically placed in the interactive user's message queue.

A message queue is like a mail box. Each workstation has a message queue with the same name as the workstation ID and each user has a message queue with the same name as the user ID. To view the setup of your message queue, use the "Display list details" option on the Work with Messages screen, as shown in Figure 4.15:

Figure 4.15
Display List
Details Options

```
                        Display List Details

Message queue . . . . . . . :   SMITHS1
   Library . . . . . . . . :     QSYS
Delivery  . . . . . . . . . :   *NOTIFY
Program . . . . . . . . . . :   *DSPMSG
Severity  . . . . . . . . . :   0
Description . . . . . . . . :   Work Station Message Queue

Message queue . . . . . . . :   SMITH
   Library . . . . . . . . :     QUSRSYS
Delivery  . . . . . . . . . :   *NOTIFY
Program . . . . . . . . . . :   *DSPMSG
Severity  . . . . . . . . . :   0
Description . . . . . . . . :   Jim Smith's message queue




Press Enter to continue.

F1=Help  F3=Exit  F12=Cancel
```

A discussion of the various portions of the Display List Details screen follows. This display shows details about both the workstation message queue and the user message queue. This discussion applies to the most commonly used parameters for both message queues.

The Message queue value is the name of the message queue that contains the messages. This is generally the same name as the display station name or the user ID.

Press   F22   on the Work with Messages display

The Library parameter is the library that stores the message queue. The library values should be included in the user's library list.

The Delivery value is the method by which messages are delivered — the message either will interrupt the user at the time of delivery, sound an alarm, hold until answered, or automatically send a default reply.

The Program entry is more appropriately called the "break message handling program." This entry names a program that the system will call if a message of sufficient severity arrives at a message queue that is in *BREAK (interrupt) mode. The program may activate an error-correction sequence, stop the job stream, or call a message program. The severity value is usually defined by a programmer. The default value is *DSPMSG, to use the system-supplied message display program.

The "Severity" parameter determines whether a message has a level equal to or greater than the severity value that has been established. If so, the operating system will either interrupt the user or turn on the message-waiting light, depending upon the designated Delivery value.

The "Description" entry is the description of the message queue; this information is commonly entered when the message queue is created. When message queues become overly full, it is helpful to have both the name and phone extension of the message queue owner included in this description.

When an interactive user signs on to the system, his or her message queue is put into the delivery mode specified in the user's profile. The system operator using the user profile QSYSOPR is assigned the message queue QSYSOPR. Message queues can be changed to customize the values listed in the above text. To change the information displayed on the Display List Details display, use the CHGMSGQ (Change Message Queue) command, as shown in Figure 4.16.

Press	F12	repeatedly to return to the Operational Assistant
Press	F9	to display a command line
Type	CHGMSGQ	on any command line
Press	F4	to prompt for parameters

As the operator, you will frequently be selecting and modifying the delivery mode, DLVRY. You can select one of four values: *BREAK, *NOTIFY, *HOLD, and *DFT. The *BREAK value specifies that when a message is received, the user's work is interrupted and a message is displayed on his or her screen. This value can be overridden if a program was specified to handle the message condition. For example, the *BREAK value can be used when you as the system operator need to shut down the system. The "shut down" message would interrupt all interactive users and allow them time to close their jobs and sign off their workstations.

The *NOTIFY value specifies that when a message is received, the user's work is not interrupted. The message turns on the workstation attention light (or message-waiting symbol), and an alarm may sound. Not all workstations are equipped with an alarm. To display the message, use either the

Figure 4.16
Change Message Queue
(CHGMSGQ) Screen

```
                        Change Message Queue (CHGMSGQ)

 Type choices, press Enter.

 Message queue  . . . . . . .   _____      Name, *USRPRF, *WRKSTN
   Library  . . . . . . . . .     *LIBL         Name, *LIBL, *CURLIB
 Delivery . . . . . . . . . .   *SAME           *SAME, *HOLD, *BREAK...
 Severity code filter . . . .   59              0-99, *SAME
 Text 'description' . . . . .   Sandra Smith at Ext 485








                                                                   Bottom
 F3=Exit   F4=Prompt   F5=Refresh   F10=Additional Parameters   F12=Cancel
 F13=How to use this display        F24=More keys
```

DSPMSG (Display Messages) command or the WRKMSG (Work with Messages) command.

The *HOLD value acts as a silencer. The user is not notified in any way when a new message arrives. The message queue retains the messages until the user requests his or her messages, using the DSPMSG (Display Messages) command or the WRKMSG (Work with Messages) command.

The *DFT value can potentially cause problems and should be used with caution. When you use the *DFT value, all informational messages are ignored. Messages requiring a reply are sent a system-supplied default reply. Messages may be sent to other users or workstation message queues, but none of the messages are kept in the receiving queue if the receiving queue is in *DFT delivery mode. The system operator's message queue, QSYSOPR, is treated differently — these messages are kept in the queue and logged in the history log, QHST. For unattended operations, you can use the *DFT value.

The next value of interest is the severity code. You can use the severity code in *BREAK mode to filter out messages that interrupt the user's work. For example, if a message severity code of 59 is defined, the system will "break" into the user's work only if messages with codes of 59 or greater are detected. Any message with a severity code of less than 59 will be sent to the message queue and the "Display message" symbol will be lit. (This is assuming that the Program value is *DSPMSG).

Now assume we have the same message severity code of 59 but that the message queue is in *NOTIFY mode. In this case, the system notifies the user of any messages received that have a severity code of 59 or greater by lighting the "Message waiting" symbol and/or sounding the alarm, if the display station has one. Any message with a severity code of less than 59 will be sent to the message queue, but the "Display message" symbol will not light. The message will be saved until the user reads and deletes it.

The "Text 'description'" value should be a description of the message queue. As an aid in trouble shooting, the authors recommend that for message queues assigned to users, the "Text 'description'" contain users' names and phone extensions, as shown in Figure 4.16.

To access additional parameters from the Change Message Queue (CHGMSGQ) Screen,

Press   F10

This will take you to the screen represented in Figure 4.17.

Figure 4.17
Change Message Queue
(CHGMSGQ) Screen,
Additional Parameters

```
                      Change Message Queue (CHGMSGQ)

 Type choices, press Enter.

 Message queue  . . . . . . . . . . .  _____    Name, *USRPRF, *WRKSTN
   Library  . . . . . . . . . . . .    *LIBL       Name, *LIBL, *CURLIB
 Delivery . . . . . . . . . . . . . .  *SAME       *SAME, *HOLD,*BREAK...
 Severity code filter . . . . . . . .  *SAME       0-99, *SAME
 Text 'description' . . . . . . . . .  *SAME

                       Additional Parameters

 Break handling program . . . . . . .  *SAME       Name, *SAME, *DSPMSG
   Library  . . . . . . . . . . . .    _____    Name, *LIBL, *CURLIB
 Reset old messages . . . . . . . . .  *NO         *NO, *YES
 Force to auxiliary storage . . . . .  *SAME       *SAME, *NO, *YES




                                                                  Bottom
 F3=Exit   F4=Prompt   F5=Refresh   F12=Cancel   F13=How to use this display
 F24=More keys
```

The "Break handling program" (PGM) parameter is more frequently called the Break message-handling program. This program specifies the program name and library location for a program to be executed if the normal default, *DSPMSG, is not desired.

Specify *NO for the "Reset old messages" parameter to prevent a message you have already read and viewed from being redisplayed in your message queue. Specifying *YES to the "Reset old messages" parameter makes the operator review the messages again and again until the messages are deleted.

The "Force to auxiliary storage" parameter is usually specified as *SAME, to use the value specified in the message queue. The message queue will usually have this parameter specified as *NO to indicate that changes made to the message queue, including its messages, are not immediately forced into auxiliary storage. When *YES is specified, then all changes made to the message queue description and each new message in the queue are immediately forced to auxiliary storage and duplicated in DASD. The *YES option is an important message-queue recovery tool that provides communications between programs, but it slows down system performance and uses additional disk space.

Key Terms

Delivery mode
Job queue
Job name

Job schedule entry
Message ID
Message queue

Severity code

Review Questions

1. What are the two basic types of jobs that an AS/400 operator commonly deals with?

2. What is the purpose of the Submit Job command?

3. What is the purpose of the Job Scheduling Entry?

4. What happens to a Job Scheduling Entry that has a "Held" status when it is released to the job queue?

5. What are the three parts of the qualified job name?

6. What is a job queue?

7. How can the operator change the sequence of the jobs on the job queue?

8. How do you find a specific user signed on to the system?

9. What command allows changes to message queues?

10. What do the first three letters of the message identifier indicate?

Exercises

1. Change your message queue to interrupt you whenever you receive a message.

2. Print a message that you have received.

3. Schedule a batch job to send a message to your instructor at a certain time.

4. Using the Work with Jobs screen from the Go Assist menu, display all the jobs that are running and all the running jobs that are held. Use the <Print Screen> key to capture the results; print these results and turn them in.

Chapter 5

Managing Print Functions

Objectives

To understand

- ✓ how to work with queued printer output
- ✓ how to access the Operational Assistant's printer output screens at the Basic Assistance level
- ✓ spooled output file status
- ✓ how to modify the status of the various spooled output files
- ✓ how to work with spooled output files at the Intermediate Assistance level
- ✓ the function of print writers
- ✓ how to change printer output quickly
- ✓ how to work with printer messages
- ✓ how to work with printers
- ✓ default output queues and default message queues
- ✓ the function of completed printer output

Printing

AS/400 programs generally do not send data directly to printers. While the AS/400 does support direct printing, which may be suitable for PCs with one workstation and one printer, this approach is generally unacceptable in a multitasking environment. Consider that interactive jobs are not completed until the user signs off, possibly at the end of the work day. And when direct printing is used, the printer is dedicated to one job and is unavailable to any other jobs until that one job is completed.

Programs create images of printer output; these images are called spooled file members in AS/400 terminology. On the AS/400, spooled file members are placed on output queues until a printer is available to print them. Like other queues, an output queue is a holding area — in this case, of spooled file members waiting to print. A single output queue may have spooled file members from many different jobs and many different users. In some cases, a single job might place spooled file members on more than one output queue. This would mean that each user who requires the job output must have his or her own copy within an output queue that (s)he can access. Many times, however, users do not need to print the entire job; within a large output report, a user may need only a small portion of the job. In that case, the user can then print only the pages (s)he requires, or (s)he may be able to view the data and not even require a printed report.

As operator, you should encourage users to review their reports at the terminal before they print. Then hopefully, if an error occurs, they can delete the spooled file, correct the input that caused the error, and rerun the job — without requiring that you be involved in the process at all.

Instructions from application programs or system-supplied programs combine with data to create the spooled files. The software and the printer device file further interact to determine how printed reports can be formatted. Format information is usually stored separately from the program that creates the report. Certain aspects of a report format can be changed before the report is printed, such as the number of lines to be printed on a page, what type of form to use, and whether to use large or small font types. Printer formatting capabilities are stored in a printer device file. Before you switch a spooled print file to another printer, it is important to know the formatting capabilities of the printers. For further information about printer formatting, see Appendix A.

The Operational Assistant lets you as the operator work with queued printer output in many different ways (e.g., by user, printer, job, job status, or output name). A series of menus helps you perform these routine tasks of controlling jobs and printer output. Often, much of your job involves directing and controlling the printing process. This is particularly true in a multitasking, multiple-printer environment. To access the Operational Assistant Menu,

Type   GO ASSIST   on any command line

Press   Enter

The Operational Assistant Menu is shown in Figure 5.1.

If you select Operational Assistant's option 1, "Work with printer output," you will be shown the Work with Printer Output screen, which offers you a user-friendly interface by which you can work with all types of printer output. As the system operator (with QSYSOPR authority), you will be able to view and control all the printer output files for all users who have unprinted reports.

To access the Work with Printer Output screen,

Type   1   to "Work with printer output"

Press   Enter

Figure 5.1
AS/400 Operational
Assistant Menu

```
ASSIST                 AS/400 Operational Assistant (TM) Menu
                                                       System: XXXXXXX
To select one of the following, type its number below and press Enter:

        1. Work with printer output
        2. Work with jobs
        3. Work with messages
        4. Send messages
        5. Change your password

       10. Manage your system, users, and devices
       11. Customize your system, users, and devices

       75. Information and problem handling

       80. Temporary sign-off

    Type a menu option below
       __



F1=Help    F3=Exit    F9=Command line    F12=Cancel
```

HINT

You can substitute the CL command WRKSPLF for the GO ASSIST command and option 1, "Work with printer output." At the Basic Assistance level, both of these methods will show the same display.

Working with Printer Output at the Basic Assistance Level

The assistance level at which a user is operating causes different screens to be displayed from Option 1 on the Operational Assistant menu. To ensure that your work and the text are in agreement, check to be sure your assistance level is set to *BASIC:

Press   F21   to "Select assistance level"

Type   1   for Basic Assistance level

As the operator, you will use the Work with Printer Output screen shown in Figure 5.2 to inspect the flow of spooled print jobs as they proceed to the printer. Spooled output reports that are assigned to a printer (assuming that everything else is prepared) will be printed according to their output priority. Jobs are assigned an output priority by a programmer or administrator before the jobs are run.

Let's assume that all the jobs in a queue have the same output priority level. When another job adds a spooled file with the same priority to the queue, the AS/400 operating system will place the new spooled file at the bottom of the queue. However, if the new job has the highest output priority, the spooled file will be placed in the queue above all the other jobs' files and thereby be printed next. The operating system will not stop a lower priority file in the middle of the printing process to allow a higher priority file access to the printer. If it is necessary to interrupt the spooling program to print a higher priority report, you as the operator must hold the spooled output. We discuss this process in the next section.

Figure 5.2
Work with Printer
Output Screen

```
                        Work with Printer Output
                                              System:  XXXXXXXX
User . . . . . :   QSYSOPR      Name, *ALL, F4 for list

Type options below, then press Enter.  To work with printers, press F22.
  2=Change   3=Hold   4=Delete   5=Display   6=Release   7=Message
  9=Work with printing status    10=Start printing       11=Restart printing


     Printer/
Opt   Output      Status
     PRTMFG
__     INVENTORY  Printer stopped (use opt 10)
__     ORDENTRY   Printer stopped (use opt 10)
     PRTACT
__     PAYROLL    Printing page 3 of 1549
     Not Assigned
__     TIMECRD    Not assigned to printer (use opt 10)



                                                            Bottom
F1=Help    F3=Exit      F5=Refresh   F6=Completed printer output
F11=Dates/pages/forms   F20=Include system output    F24=More keys
```

Typing the user profile ID in the User field will display only one individual's spooled output. The screen will be displayed as shown in Figure 5.2, with the name of the user (in this case, QSYSOPR) to limit the number of queued reports on the display. The Work with Printer Output screen divides the spooled output by printer name. Spooled output with a status of "Not assigned to a printer" will appear last on the display. To view all the printer output, type *ALL in the User field. The queued printer output in Figure 5.2 is sorted by printer name.

HINT

If you do not know the user ID, press F4 to display a complete list of users.

HINT

A partial name can be entered in the User field together with the asterisk wild-card character. For example, if you want to see output that starts with AR, type AR* in the User field.

Working with Printer Output Options and Function Keys at the Basic Assistance Level

The following material is a discussion of the options and commonly used function keys you will be working with as you direct and control the printing process in a multiple-printer environment via the Work with Printer Output screen. Several of the options display additional screens for review or for modification.

Option 2, "Change," lets you modify the print attributes. To practice with this option,

Type   2   in the option column

Press Enter

The attributes of a spooled print job, as shown in Figure 5.3, include, among other items, the printer device, the number of copies to be printed, and the type of forms to be placed in the printer. You may specify the device name of a printer to use to print a report. Use this field to assign a printer to a report that has not been assigned, or to move a report from one printer to another.

HINT

If you do not know which printer to use, press F4 to see the "Select printer" list.

To change the number of copies to be printed, type the desired number in the "Number of copies" field. To specify the page number that this printer output should begin printing on, type the page number in the "First page to print" field. If it is unnecessary to print the entire report, type a page number in the "Last page to print" field. These two fields can be used together if, for example, part of the report was damaged by a paper jam or you want to print only a portion of a report.

To change the form type, key the desired name of the form in the "Type of forms" field. This can be useful during application testing — for example, to verify check or invoice alignment by printing the spooled output on plain paper.

To change when printer output prints and to move printer output to the front of the queue for printing, type a Y in the "Print this output next" field. The user who owns the spooled printer output has authority to make this change. As operator you can also make these changes if you have been granted *SPLCTL authority (the user profile defines the highest print priority allowed for this profile). The printer output is placed with other reports with the same priority and forms type. Higher priority print jobs will be printed first.

To save the printer output after printing, type a Y in the "Save printer output" field. Normally, you would delete printer output to avoid cluttering up the system. However, for output that prints on special forms, it may be helpful to save the spooled output. If alignment problems are discovered after the output has printed, you can reprint without having to rerun the program (which may be impossible to do without a great amount of effort). If the printer output is currently printing, you can change the "Number of copies" and "Save printer output" fields. If it is necessary to modify other options, first hold the printer output, make the change, and then release the printer output. This sequence will provide you with all the print options.

Figure 5.3
Change Printer
Output Screen

```
                         Change Printer Output
User . . . . . . . . :  JCHARLES        Date . . . . . . . . :  10/21/96
Printer output . . . :  ACCTPAY         Time. . . . . . . . :  13:40:01

Pages . . . . . . . :  10
Status . . . . . . . :  Waiting to print
Type choices below, then press Enter.
Printer to use . . . .      PRTACT        Name, F4 for list

        Copies and pages:
          Number of copies . . . .  1           1-255
          First page to print  . .  1           Number
          Last page to print . . .  *LAST       Number, *LAST
          Type of forms  . . . .    *STD        Form type, *STD

          Print this output next    N           Y=Yes, N=No
          Save printer output  . . . N          Y=Yes, N=No




F1=Help   F3=Exit   F5=Refresh   F12=Cancel
```

To return to the Work with Printer Output screen,

Press　　F3　　to "Exit"

You use option 3, "Hold," to specify the spooled output to be held. When spooled output is held, the status will change to Held and the spooled file will not be printed until an operator releases it. Once released, the job will be sequenced according to its priority. Select option 6, "Release," for the spooled output to be released, and note that the status of the spooled output changes to Released.

Use option 4, "Delete," to permanently remove spooled output from the Work with Printer Output screen, and press Enter. Press Enter again to confirm the delete. The spooled output that was deleted should no longer appear on the Work with Printer Output screen. If the spooled output remains visible, press F5 to refresh the display.

As operator, you should use extreme caution when deleting jobs from the output queue, because it may not be possible to regenerate spooled output. For example, some print jobs simply report on the contents of the user's database files and these can be deleted and rerun with no long-term consequences. However, you should not delete any reports that serve as an audit trail for a database file update. These output reports frequently cannot be regenerated without restoring a previous version of the file and re-entering the file updates. In rare cases, a user who deletes audit trail reports may actually be committing fraud or embezzlement. You can protect yourself by asking for approval from a supervisor to delete the output report, or by moving the report to an unassigned output queue. Moving the report to a different output queue will provide several advantages. First, the report will not show up on the user's output queue; second, the job will not inadvertently move up to the printing position in the job queue; and third, if the report is indeed necessary, the output can be moved back to an active queue for printing.

HINT

Before deleting printer output created by another user, consider whether your user profile contains *SPLCTL authority.

To display the contents of a spooled report,

Type   5   in the option column on the Work with Printer Output screen

Press   Enter

The ruled line marks the beginning of the actual data in the printer output, as shown in the example Figure 5.4. You can use the "Control" and "Find" fields at the top of the display to locate information within the spooled output. Two effective entries in the "Control" field are T for top and B for bottom. The "Find" field will locate any text typed in the variable area

Figure 5.4
Display Spooled
File Screen

```
                              Display Spooled File
            File . . . . . :   QPDSPJOB                      Page/Line   1/1
            Control . . . . .                                Columns    1 - 78
            Find . . . . . .
   *...+....1....+....2....+....3....+....4....+....5....+....6....+....7....+..
                               Work with Job

   Job . . . :   JCHARL1    User . . . :   JCHARLES    Number . . . . :    00

                            Job Status Attributes
            Status of job . . . . . . . . . . . . . . . :   ACTIVE
            Entered system:
            Date . . . . . . . . . . . . . . . . . . . :   10/09/96
            Time . . . . . . . . . . . . . . . . . . . :   08:20:37
            Started:
              Date . . . . . . . . . . . . . . . . . . :   10/09/96
              Time . . . . . . . . . . . . . . . . . . :   08:20:38
            Subsystem . . . . . . . . . . . . . . . . . :   QINTER
              Subsystem pool ID . . . . . . . . . . . . :   2
            Type of job . . . . . . . . . . . . . . . . :   INTER
            Special environment . . . . . . . . . . . . :   *NONE
            Program return code . . . . . . . . . . . . :   0
            Controlled end requested . . . . . . . . . :   NO
                                                                   More...
   F3=Exit    F12=Cancel    F19=Left    F20=Right    F24=More keys
```

with an exact match in the spooled file. For more information about either of these fields, place the cursor on the appropriate line and press the Help key.

Option 7, "Message," will display any messages relating to the spooled output. We will discuss printer messages in greater detail later in this chapter.

Use option 10, "Start printing," on the Work with Printer Output screen to assign spooled output to a printer. Type the name of the printer to be used in the "Printer" field, or press F4 to select from a list of all the printers on the system. If the printer is not started, the "Start Printing" message will be shown. The spooled output now appears under the name of the printer.

Option 11, "Restart printing," is used when a job has been stopped in the middle of printing — or more likely, when there has been a paper jam.

Commonly Used Function Keys

Occasionally, printed output is misplaced, or a spooled file may inadvertently be placed in a held output queue. One method that can help you locate the report is to verify that the spooled file was actually printed. To display the completed printer output screen,

Press   F6   from the Work with Printer Output screen

Because the completed output lists are generally lengthy, your may find it helpful to sort the information using the F10=Sort list function key. The "Sort list" option is useful for locating a specific report when numerous spooled output jobs are on a queue. (Note: F6 and F10 will be available on your AS/400 only if the system's job accounting function is active and is collecting printer completion information.)

To see another view of the same display,

Press   F11   for "Dates/pages/forms"

The Date/pages/forms view shows when the spooled output was created, the total number of pages, what types of forms are being used, and how many copies are to be printed. The date/time columns are helpful for you to calculate how long a job has been on the output queue and to predict approximately how long it will be before the job will begin printing.

Occasionally, you may make an error while you are typing in the printer name, or you might belatedly realize that a lengthy job has started printing. Fortunately, the F22 function key allows you to control the printers on your system. From the resulting "Work with Printers" display, you can start, stop, or restart a printer, or you can respond to messages that may indicate printer problems.

Working with Printer Output at the Intermediate Assistance Level

The AS/400 assistance level is designed to meet the changing needs of both users and computer center staff members. The WRKSPLF (Work with Spooled Files) command is an interesting example of this process, because the assistance level will display two different screens. You may find it helpful to set the assistance level to Intermediate when you are working with spooled files and print writers.

HINT

The F9 key is available to display a command line on screens that do not provide one automatically.

To work with spooled files at the Intermediate Assistance level,

Press	F9	to display a command line
Type	WRKSPLF ASTLVL(*INTERMED)	on any command line
Press	Enter	

Compare Figure 5.2, Work with Printer Output, with the system set at the Basic Assistance level, and Figure 5.5, Work with All Spooled Files, with the system set at the Intermediate Assistance level. Note that the Intermediate Assistance level displays a completely different screen of the same data. Typing the WRKSPLF command with the ASTLVL parameter *BASIC would display the Work with Printer Output screen.

The Work with All Spooled Files screen has three different displays, each providing you with slightly different information. The default view, or View 1, shown in Figure 5.5, lists the name of the job (under File), what user or program submitted the job, and the output queue where the spooled output is located. View 1 lists the spooled files in the order they are to be printed, assuming that all the spooled files have the same priority.

Figure 5.5
Work with All Spooled
Files Display, View 1
(Default)

```
                              Work with All Spooled Files

Type options below, press Enter.
  1=Send    2=Change    3=Hold    4=Delete    5=Display    6=Release    7=Message
  8=Attributes          9=Work with printing status

                        Device or                          Total    Cur
Opt     File            User        Queue     User Data  Sts  Pages  Page  Copy

___     QSYSPRT         QSYSOPR     PRTACT               WTR    1      1     1
___     QPJOBLOG        QSYSOPR     QSYSOPR              RDY    1            1
___     QPJOBLOG        QSYSOPR     QSYSOPR              RDY    1            1
___     QSYSPRT         QSYSOPR     QSYSOPR              RDY    1            1
___     QSYSPRT         QSYSOPR     QSYSOPR              RDY    1            1
___     QPDCDEVA        QSYSOPR     QSYSOPR              RDY    1            1
___     QSYSPRT         QSYSOPR     QSYSOPR              HLD    1            1




                                                              Bottom
Parameters for options 1, 2, 3 or command
===>
F3=Exit   F10=View 3   F11=View 2    F12=Cancel    F22=Printers    F24=More keys
```

The status column, Sts, reveals the condition of the job. Notice the first spooled file on the figure has a status of writer, WTR, while other spooled files are ready to print, RDY, or are held, HLD. For more information about status codes, see Figure 5.6.

Figure 5.6
Spooled File Status
Codes and Meanings

Status Code	Description
*CHG	Some change has been initiated on this spooled file. The *CHG will be displayed temporarily, until you press the F5=Refresh function key.
CLO	This printed report is finished (closed) but the entire job has not been completed.
DFR	Deferred is similar to held.
HLD *HLD	An operator has held the job. The *HLD status will be displayed temporarily until you press the F5=Refresh function key.
MSGW	The spooled output has a message waiting and will not print until the message is answered.
OPN	The job is unfinished or open.
PND	The spooled output status is pending, or in the process of waiting.
PRT	This job is currently being printed.
RDY	The job is ready to be turned over to the print writer when the job reaches the top of the queue.
RLS *RLS	An operator has released the job. The *RLS status will be displayed until you press the F5=Refresh function key.
SAV	The job has been printed with the save status. This means that all copies of the spooled output were printed, but the report file will be saved on the output queue until it is released or deleted.
SND	The spooled output has been sent to another system.
WTR	This job is being formatted by the print writer or is printing.

The "Spooled output schedule" (SCHEDULE) parameter controls whether a spooled file is available to print as soon as the individual report is closed, or whether the report must wait until the entire job that created it has finished. This parameter is particularly important for any spooled file that is created by an interactive job. Remember: An interactive job does not end until the user signs off. Any spooled file created with *JOBEND specified as the Spooled output schedule parameter (SCHEDULE) waits in an output queue with a status of CLO until the user signs off, possibly at the end of the day. If the operator notices a job that is on the output queue for an extended period of time, it may be appropriate to contact an administrator or programmer to request a change to *FILEEND, to print the job as soon as the spooled file is closed. This can be helpful if one program creates multiple reports. If the report must wait until the entire job has finished, use *JOBEND for this parameter.

Work with All Spooled Files, View 1

Many of the option and function keys perform the same function at both the Basic and the Intermediate Assistance levels. Therefore, this section will cover only the options or functions that are new or have a modified function at the different assistance levels.

Use option 1, "Send," on the Work with All Spooled Files screen, to send a spooled file to another system, or to another user's output queue on the same system. Type the user ID and network address for the user who will receive the file on the Send Network Spooled File (SNDNETSPLF) display. This option is helpful because most users do not have access to or authority to view or work with another user's output queue. If a user needs to view or work with a spooled file that is located in another user's output queue or system, it may be easier for you as the operator to copy the output to the current user's output queue. This function is *not* the same as changing the output queue for a printed report (Option 2). When you use Option 1, you are sending a *copy* of the printed output to another output queue, and the original will still remain in its original queue.

If the user receiving the spooled file is a user on another AS/400, the name of that system must be in the system directory. The system directory is a listing that identifies all users and systems allowed to communicate with your AS/400 and its users.

HINT

Use the DSPDIRE (Display Directory Entry) command to view the list of users and systems in your communications network.

HINT

To ensure that all the attributes of the spooled file are sent, press F4 and type *ALLDATA in the Data format field.

Use option 2, "Change," on the Work with All Spooled Files screen to assign a spooled output report to a printer, and to change other attributes of the printed output. Before the report is accepted for formatting by the print writer, you or the user must designate the printer to be used. Type the name of the printer to be used in the "Printer" field.

Option 7, "Message," will display any messages relating to the spooled output. In general, messages relate to a printer request. We will discuss printer messages in greater detail later in this chapter.

Option 8, "Attributes," displays the attributes that are listed when the program, the data, and the printer device files are combined. Certain attributes can be modified (using option 2), such as the number of copies to be printed. Other attributes, such as the number of lines on a page, cannot be altered.

Work with All Spooled Files, View 2

The second view of the Work with All Spooled Files screen, shown in Figure 5.7, has several new pieces of information that are of interest to the operator. The Form Type states what kind of paper is to be used for the printing process. To display an alternate view from the default screen,

Press   F11   for "View 2"

View 2 shows that all the spooled files are requesting standard forms. In the early days of computers, most documents for internal use were printed on green and white striped paper. Non-standard forms were typically preprinted documents, such as invoices or pay checks. Today the corporate standard is set partially by the printer hardware available and partially by individual preference. A chain printer with a wide carriage may still use the green and white striped paper, while a laser printer may be unable to use any paper wider than 8½ inches. Your computer center should have a list of the abbreviations and the forms that you are to use.

Figure 5.7
Work with All Spooled
Files Screen, View 2

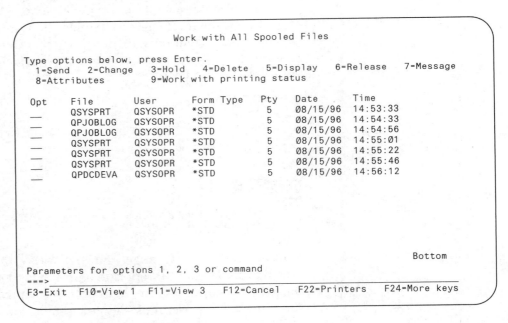

```
                        Work with All Spooled Files

 Type options below, press Enter.
   1=Send   2=Change    3=Hold    4=Delete    5=Display   6=Release    7=Message
   8=Attributes          9=Work with printing status

 Opt     File      User       Form Type   Pty   Date       Time
  __      QSYSPRT   QSYSOPR    *STD         5    08/15/96   14:53:33
  __      QPJOBLOG  QSYSOPR    *STD         5    08/15/96   14:54:33
  __      QPJOBLOG  QSYSOPR    *STD         5    08/15/96   14:54:56
  __      QSYSPRT   QSYSOPR    *STD         5    08/15/96   14:55:01
  __      QSYSPRT   QSYSOPR    *STD         5    08/15/96   14:55:22
  __      QSYSPRT   QSYSOPR    *STD         5    08/15/96   14:55:46
  __      QPDCDEVA  QSYSOPR    *STD         5    08/15/96   14:56:12




                                                                   Bottom
 Parameters for options 1, 2, 3 or command
 ===>
 F3=Exit   F10=View 1   F11=View 3   F12=Cancel   F22=Printers   F24=More keys
```

The priority of the spooled file is shown in View 2. Priorities may be assigned from a high of 1 to a low of 9. Notice in Figure 5.7 that all the jobs have the same priority; therefore, the spooled files will print in the order displayed.

Work with All Spooled Files, View 3

The third view of the Work with All Spooled Files screen, shown in Figure 5.8, lists the File name, the User name, and the Job number. You can combine these three pieces of information to construct the qualified job name. (We discussed the qualified job name and its importance in Chapter 4, "Working with Jobs and Message Handling.") To display the next view from View 2,

Press   F11   for "View 3"

Figure 5.8
Work with All Spooled
Files Screen, View 3

```
                         Work with All Spooled Files

Type options below, press Enter.
  1=Send    2=Change    3=Hold    4=Delete    5=Display    6=Release    7=Message
  8=Attributes          9=Work with printing status

                    File
Opt    File         Nbr    Job        User       Number    Queue       Library
  __   QSYSPRT       18     STAT1      QSYSOPR    075883    QSYSOPR     QSYSOPR
  __   QPJOBLOG      19     STAT1      QSYSOPR    075884    QEZJOBLOG   QUSRSYS
  __   QPJOBLOG      19     STAT1      QSYSOPR    075890    QEZJOBLOG   QUSRSYS
  __   QSYSPRT       20     STAT1      QSYSOPR    075892    QSYSOPR     QSYSOPR
  __   QSYSPRT       21     STAT1      QSYSOPR    075903    QSYSOPR     QSYSOPR
  __   QSYSPRT       22     STAT1      QSYSOPR    075908    QSYSOPR     QSYSOPR
  __   QPDCDEVA      23     STAT1      QSYSOPR    075014    QSYSOPR     QSYSOPR




                                                               Bottom
Parameters for options 1, 2, 3 or command
===>
F3=Exit  F10=View 2  F11=View 1   F12=Cancel   F22=Printers   F24=More keys
```

To return to View 1,

Press   F11

Print Writers

The print writer is an AS/400 system program that sends spooled output from an output queue to a physical printer. Any spooled file members on an output queue remain in the queue until a print writer has sent the report to a printer. For more information about print formatting, see Appendix A.

At the Intermediate Assistance level, use option 2, "Change," to assign output to a specific printer. Next, type the name of the printer to be used in the Printer field.

Changing Printer Output

During a work shift, you may send hundreds of jobs to the print writer and, therefore, to the printer. To send the output to be printed, you or the user must type in the name of the appropriate printer. Let's assume that 100 jobs are ready to be moved to the printer named PRTMFG. You would need to type a 2 in the Option column, press Enter, and type PRTMFG. This process would then need to be repeated 99 additional times. As you can see, this is a time-consuming process and surely some entries will be typed incorrectly. An easier and more error-free method would be to type the 2 in all the Option columns and then enter a single CL command parameter on the command line. The parameter, as shown in Figure 5.9, is OUTQ(printer name). When the system processes this change, all the jobs will be transferred to the print writer. Note that this technique requires the assistance level to be set to Intermediate for this user ID. To understand why this technique works, you need to first understand that Option 2 invokes the CHGSPLFA (Change Spooled File Attributes) command; OUTQ is a valid parameter for this command. When you type Option 2 in front of one or more reports, and include a value for the OUTQ parameter, the CHGSPLFA command executes for each report, using that parameter value.

Figure 5.9
Work with All Spooled Files Screen, with OUTQ CL Command

```
                          Work with All Spooled Files
Type options below, press Enter.
  1=Send   2=Change   3=Hold   4=Delete   5=Display   6=Release   7=Message
  8=Attributes           9=Work with printing status

                         Device or                      Total    Cur
 Opt    File             User      Queue    User Data  Sts Pages  Page  Copy

  2     QSYSPRT          QSYSOPR   PRTACT              WTR   1      1     1
  2     QPJOBLOG         QSYSOPR   QSYSOPR             RDY   1            1
  2     QPJOBLOG         QSYSOPR   QSYSOPR             RDY   1            1
  2     QSYSPRT          QSYSOPR   QSYSOPR             RDY   1            1
  2     QSYSPRT          QSYSOPR   QSYSOPR             HLD   1            1
  2     QSYSPRT          QSYSOPR   QSYSOPR             RDY   1            1
  2     QPDCDEVA         QSYSOPR   QSYSOPR             RDY   1            1

                                                               Bottom
Parameters for options 1, 2, 3 or command
===>OUTQ(PRTMFG)
F3=Exit  F10=View 3  F11=View 2   F12=Cancel   F22=Printers   F24=More keys
```

Working with Printer Messages

As system operator, you will find a myriad of messages associated with the printer. In this section, we will discuss the technique for answering messages in general, rather than discussing specific messages.

The AS/400 supports many types of messages. All messages provide a communications channel from the system to an operator or user. You should encourage users to view their message queue and delete their messages as soon as practical. This method will help ensure that messages are actually read and that disk space usage is kept to a minimum. However, as in Figure 5.10, it is recommended that you (as system operator) *not* use option 4, "Remove," and the F16 function key to remove messages not requiring a reply. These messages provide an audit trail for system activity (as does the job log). These messages provide copious information about system actions and they allow you to review actions taken earlier that may have caused the current problem.

Figure 5.10
Work with
Messages Screen

```
                              Work with Messages
User . . . . . . . . : JCHARLES                      System . . . . . . XXXXXXX
Type options below, then press Enter.
  4=Remove    5=Display detail and reply

Opt    Message
                                  Messages needing a reply
 __    Verify Alignment on Device PRTACT.  (I C G N R)

                               Messages not needing a reply

 __    Controller ETHLINET can not be varied on or off.
 __    SMTP job QTSMTPSRVR ended abnormally
 __    Device PCUSER1 no longer communicating.
 __    Device STAT05 no longer communicating.
 __    Verify alignment on printer PRTMFG. (I G N R E C)
 __       Reply . . :  I
 __    Device STAT09 no longer communicating.
 __    Device QPADEV0017 no longer communicating


F1=Help   F3=Exit   F5=Refresh   F6=Display system operator messages
F16=Remove messages not needing a reply       F17=Top    F24=More keys
```

As shown in Figure 5.10, the operator has a message relating to forms alignment. The forms alignment message provides you with five choices for the proper reply: I, C, G, N, and R. Because the AS/400 has many messages with multiple choices, as a novice operator you may wish to display the details before trying to answer the message. Typing a 5 in the option column for the message will display additional details about the message. Specific information about how to answer the message will be provided, as shown in Figures 5.11 and 5.12. You should type the appropriate response and press Enter.

Working with Printers

Most AS/400 installations have multiple printers connected to the system, and the status of each printer may be different. To look at printer status, and to work with printers at the Intermediate Assistance level (Figure 5.13),

Press   F22   "Printers" to display the Work with All Printers screen
Press   Enter

A print writer may have a status of END for many reasons: The printer may need repairs; a printer could be stopped after regular hours for security reasons; or if the paper jam occurred after hours, there would be no one available to correct the problem. To end a print writer, use option 4, "End," on the Work with All Printers screen. Press the Enter key on the Confirm End of Writer screen. After a printer is stopped, it must be restarted before any output can be generated. Use option 1, "Start," to begin the process to activate the printer. Press F5 to refresh the screen. When the printer's status is changed to start, STR, the system is in the process of activating the printer.

Figure 5.11
Additional Message
Information Screen

```
                          Additional Message Information

Message ID . . . . . : CPA4002              Severity . . . . : 99
Message type . . . . : INQUIRY
Job . . : XXXXX         User . . . XXXXXXX        Number . . . : 96584
Date sent . . . . . : 02/16/96                    Times sent . . . : 10:03:35
From Program . . . . : WRTYIP                      Instruction . . : 0000

Message . . . . . . : Verify Alignment on Device PRTACT.  (I C G N R)
Cause . . . . . . . : The forms may not be aligned correctly.  The first
  line for the file is 1.
Recovery . . . . . . : Do one of the following and try the request again.
Possible choices for replying to message . . . . . . . . . . . . . :
  I  -- To continue printing aligned forms starting with the next line of
        file, type an I.
  C  -- To cancel processing, type a C.
  G  -- To continue printing aligned forms skipping to the next form and
        printing the first line again, type a G.

                                                                   More...


Type reply, press Enter.
  Reply . . : _____
Press Enter to continue.
F3=Exit            F12=Cancel
```

Figure 5.12
Additional Message
Information Screen,
Continued

```
                          Additional Message Information

Message ID . . . . . : CPA4002              Severity . . . . : 99
Message type . . . . : INQUIRY
  N  -- To print the first line again on the next form and to verify the
        alignment,
        1. Press Stop only if Start and Stop are two keys, or press Reset.
        2. Advance the paper to the next form by pressing Form Feed/New Page
        3. Adjust the alignment with the forms adjust control
        4. Press Ready, Start, or Start/Stop.
        5. Type an N.
  R  -- To print the first line again on the current form and to verify the
        alignment if the forms are not aligned,
        1. Press Stop only if Start and Stop are two keys, or press Reset.
        2. Adjust the alignment with the forms adjust control.
        4. Press Read, Start or Start/Stop.
        5. Type an R.

                                                                 Bottom...


Type reply, press Enter.
  Reply . . : _____
Press Enter to continue.
F3=Exit            F12=Cancel
```

A forms-alignment message may appear when the printing restarts. If the status changes to "Message waiting," there may be a forms-alignment message that requires a response. Use option 7, "Display messages," to view the message and provide the appropriate response. Once the response has been accepted, the STR status will be shown.

Option 3, "Hold," allows you to hold the printer. All print jobs assigned to this printer are held. Printers that have been held have a status of *HLD or HLD.

Figure 5.13
Work with All
Printers Screen

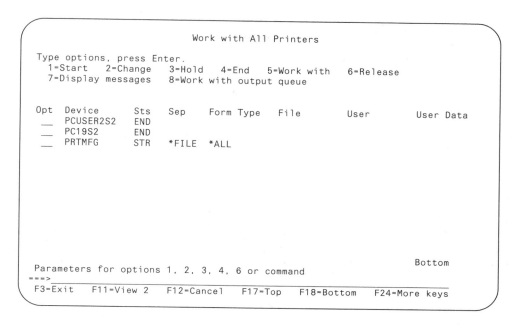

```
                         Work with All Printers
  Type options, press Enter.
   1=Start    2=Change    3=Hold    4=End    5=Work with    6=Release
   7=Display messages    8=Work with output queue


  Opt  Device      Sts    Sep   Form Type   File        User       User Data
  __   PCUSER2S2   END
  __   PC19S2      END
  __   PRTMFG      STR    *FILE  *ALL




                                                                   Bottom
  Parameters for options 1, 2, 3, 4, 6 or command
  ===>
  F3=Exit    F11=View 2    F12=Cancel    F17=Top    F18=Bottom    F24=More keys
```

To release the printers, use option 6, "Release," on the Work with All Printers screen. The status of the printer changes to RLS. Press F5=Refresh and the status changes to started, STR. If a printer is held, release it using option 6 on the Work with All Spooled Files display.

Option 8 allows you to change, hold, or release files on the output queue instead of having to work directly with the associated printer device.

Output Queues and Message Queues

Normally, an output queue exists for each printer on the system. Often, output queues have the same name as the printers on the system. These output queues are called default output queues. A system may have special output queues that do not have a printer name associated with them. For example, an output queue may be set aside for all printer output requiring special forms. As the operator, you would need to check this queue periodically to decide when to assign reports to a printer and what forms are needed. Another AS/400 system may have a separate output queue reserved for job logs.

To start a printer and assign it to a different output queue, enter the STRPRTWTR (Start Printer Writer) command and press F4 to prompt. In the printer parameter, specify the name of the printer to start. In the output queue parameter (OUTQ), specify the output queue name to use. If the output queue is not in the QGPL library or a library from your library list, type the name of the library and the output queue before the name of the output queue. For example, type lib/xxxxxxxx where *lib* is the name of the library and *xxxxxxxx* is the name of the output queue.

HINT

To change the characteristics of an output queue, use the CHGOUTQ (Change Output Queue) command.

Output queue descriptions can affect how output prints. The job separators parameter (JOBSEP), found in the output queue description, controls whether separator pages are printed between spooled files. Job separator pages provide identifying information about a spooled file. These pages are useful to help users locate their printed reports when many different people use a printer, or when a printer generates a large volume of output.

The order of the spooled output files on a queue controls the sequence in which output prints. The SEQ parameter controls the sequencing of the output. New spooled files are put after others on the queue (first in, first out), or they may be ordered by the time the job creating the output entered the system.

You may find the volume of messages in the QSYSOPR message queue is quite large. If so, it may be helpful to separate the messages for each printer to a different message queue, especially if the printers are in remote locations. To temporarily change the message queue, start the printer using the STRPRTWTR (Start Printer Writer) command, press F4, and change the parameter of the message queue name, MSGQ, to a valid message queue on the system.

HINT

To permanently change where print messages are located, use the WRKDEVD (Work with Device Description) command to specify the name of the printer whose message queue is to be changed, and the new message queue/library name, as appropriate.

Troubleshooting Report Problems

The Work with Spooled Files display is very helpful in determining why a report is not printing. Once you have located the spooled printer output on one of the displays, determine why that information is not printing. The "Status" column on the Work with Spooled Files screen will usually tell you. For more information, use option 9, "Work with printing status." The Work with Printing Status screen provides more detailed status descriptions than are available on other displays. The Work with Printing Status screen might also have more than one status message for the printer output. Use option 5, "Detailed description," on the Work with Printing Status screen for an explanation of the status and a list of alternative actions. This information can be helpful in solving any printer problems you might encounter.

A report may have already printed, but was distributed to the wrong person. In this case, you will want to display completed printer output. The system must be configured to save information about completed printer output. To display completed printer output on the Work with Printer Output screen, press F6=Completed printer output. On the Display Completed Printer Output screen, sort the information using function key F10=Sort list.

To further investigate why the spooled output isn't printing, gather information about the job and the output, such as the job name. If the output was created interactively, the job name is the name of the workstation the person was using. If the output was created by a batch job, the job name is assigned on the SBMJOB (Submit Job) command. Other questions to consider include the following: What user ID was used to create the output? On which printer does the output usually print? Does it print on special forms? How many pages is it? What is the output name? When was the job run? Based on the information you gather, where the report has been queued usually becomes obvious.

Key Terms

Assistance level	Print writer	Pending
Basic	Printer attributes	Printing
Intermediate	Qualified job name	Ready
Display a spooled file	Status of a spooled file	Released
Control field	Change	Saved
Find field	Deferred	Sent
Hold status	Held	User ID
Message queues	Message waiting	User profile
Output queues	Open	

Review Questions

1. How do you access the Operational Assistant at the Beginning Assistance level?

2. What criteria does the operating system use to select the next spooled output file for printing?

3. Why would you hold or release a spooled output file?

4. What is the difference between releasing a spooled output file and using option 10 to start printing?

5. If a user signs off from his or her terminal when (s)he goes to lunch, how would this affect the printing of the user's spooled output files?

6. What is a print writer? Why is it important?

7. In what situations would an operator need to change spooled output files to a different printer?

8. How do you stop a printer? Why would it be necessary to stop a printer?

9. Get two examples of common printer messages. Why do these messages occur?

10. What are the default message queue and default output queue? Why do they exist?

Exercises

1. Hold and release a print job.

2. Stop a printer.

3. Restart a printer.

Chapter 6

Device Configuration

Objectives

To recognize different types of network topologies

To understand

- ✓ the function of controllers
- ✓ the derivation of addresses
- ✓ what a device is
- ✓ what a common device status is
- ✓ the relationship among lines, controllers, and devices

To differentiate between device descriptions by address and by other attributes

To be able to

- ✓ display device descriptions for existing hardware
- ✓ copy a device description
- ✓ create device descriptions for new hardware
- ✓ perform basic problem resolution

Network Topologies

All devices on the AS/400, whether physical or logical, must connect in some orderly fashion to ensure that all data and requests are passed to the CPU and processed in sequence. The arrangement for how data is passed to the CPU and back to the user is referred to as the system's topology. After the topology scheme is defined, communications are passed down via lines, line controllers, and device addresses; finally, a connection to the device is established. Because communications and connectivity is a complex subject, we will discuss only the three most common network topologies in this chapter. We will then concentrate on connectivity tasks that the operator commonly performs, including setting up controllers, display devices, printers, tape drives, and diskette drives. We will first present an overview, and then walk you through the process of creating the device descriptions and of varying the devices on.

A computer network is a collection of computer nodes physically connected by a suitable communications medium. A computer node can be a personal computer, a computer workstation, a minicomputer (such as the AS/400), or a larger computer system (e.g., a mainframe). The arrangement and connection of these network nodes is referred to as the network topology.

The three common network topologies are bus, ring, and star (see Figure 6.1). The bus topology is the most commonly used. In a bus topology, one node of the network is connected to another by a single cable until the last node is reached; bus topology has two distinct ends. In a ring topology, the connections come full circle; in other words, the last node is connected to the first node to form a complete ring. In a star topology, a main server or computer handles or directs the communications, and all the nodes are attached to the main computer.

Figure 6.1
Common Network
Topologies

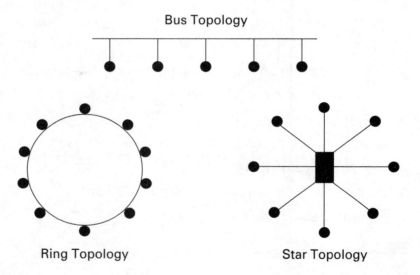

Once the particular topology has been selected, lines, controllers, and device addresses are required before a device can be connected and communications established with users.

The most common method for attaching display terminals to an AS/400 is a direct connection using twinaxial cable with a bus topology that is attached to a port. The port, in turn, attaches to a line extending out of the AS/400 (see Figure 6.2). Each display terminal is attached to an adapter that physically attaches to the twinaxial cable. The number of ports available depends on the AS/400 model and the hardware purchased.

Twinaxial data link control, *TDLC, is a direct link to an AS/400 using twinaxial cable. The *TDLC link is configured with a bus topology. Another type of connection, Ethernet, also employs a bus topology. Ethernet networks using the bus topology are frequently used in a PC LAN.

Figure 6.2
Relationship Between the
CPU, Ports, and Devices

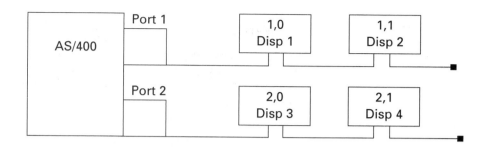

Other types of bus topology are available. Synchronous data link control, *SDLC, is generally used for communications between two remotely connected computers. The sending and receiving stations are commonly connected with each other, usually through telephone lines.

Token-Ring networks are generally the arrangement used in a PC LAN. Token-Ring networks send data in one direction throughout the ring by using the symbol of authority (a specialized transmission frame, consisting of starting, ending, and controlling bit sequences) called a token. The token controls the transmission, allowing any sending station in the network to send or receive data when the token arrives at the station. The flow of the token is a logical ring, regardless of how the network is physically cabled, so the token always ends up at the originating system. Think of the token as a person who delivers the mail to your house and returns to the post office when all the mail has been delivered. When the mail carrier comes to your mail box, you can send and/or receive mail. If you place a letter in your mail box after the mail carrier has passed your house, your letter must wait until the next day. This is the same concept Token-Ring topology uses; of course, Token-Ring is much faster.

In the star topology, each workstation connects directly to a port, providing exceptionally fast access. The AS/400 "listens" for the user to press the Enter key. When the AS/400 "hears" the request, it responds virtually immediately.

Lines, Controllers, Addresses, and Devices

Figure 6.3 displays the hierarchy of the relationship between lines, controllers (discussed in the next section), and devices (discussed on page 103).

Figure 6.3
Relationship Between
Lines, Controllers,
and Devices

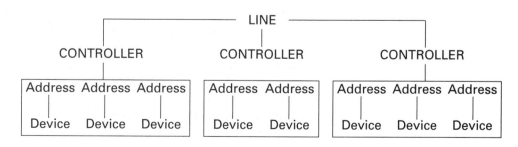

Lines

Most systems have multiple lines linking the AS/400 to its devices. Lines can be actual cables, phone lines, or other virtual types of lines; lines are the first level of connection from the AS/400. Because lines come in a variety of types, each line must have a line description, *LIND. A line description is an object that describes the attributes of a communications line for another system, controller, or network. More than one line description may exist for an individual line, but only one description can be varied on at a time. There are different categories of lines for different types of communications; for example, twinaxial data link control, *TDLC, is the category for a twinaxial connection.

Controllers

Controllers are a combination of a hardware card and software programs that are designed to handle a certain level of device transmission traffic. You might think of controllers as traffic cops. A police officer will allow a certain number of cars to pass though an intersection and will then stop the traffic, allowing the converging cars to have their turn crossing through the intersection. Controllers have a similar function of monitoring traffic to allow all the devices access to the CPU. Controllers exist to handle the hardware devices that are unique to a particular line, regardless of whether the devices are remote or local. Because controllers can support a variety of devices, a controller description is required. Controller descriptions define the type of physical devices that the controller will be handling.

Line and controller descriptions are created as part of your AS/400 installation and rely upon the type of communications topology installed. Operators are generally not responsible for maintaining and creating these descriptions. On the other hand, devices are added or removed frequently, such as for maintenance. And often it is the operator's job to maintain and control the changing of these devices.

Addresses

An AS/400 address is a means of uniquely identifying each device that is attached to the system. Refer to Figures 6.2 and 6.3, noting that each device has a unique address. An AS/400 computer address consists of two parts: a port and a switch setting. The port is the place where the line is physically attached to the AS/400. The switch setting uniquely identifies each device along the line. Two devices on the same line cannot have the same switch setting. The address is much like a street address, which includes a house number and a street name, such as 1000 College Drive. In computer terms, addresses are reversed, with the street name first (port number) and the house number last (switch setting), such as College Drive, 1000. Switch settings may range from 0 to 6. As long as a switch setting is not duplicated on a line, devices may be attached in any order. The address for the system console must always be 0,0.

Devices

A device description contains the attributes and characteristics of the device it describes. Because the AS/400 is capable of supporting many varieties of devices (i.e., workstations, printers, or tape drives), a device description is always required. The device description, *DEVD, provides a connection between a physical (or logical) device and the AS/400 with which it is communicating. A device description must exist for each device connected to a controller. The device description includes the type of device, the name of the controller to attach with, and the device's unique address.

Operational Assistant offers the system operator an easy menu-driven method to manage and view the various devices. Option 10 of the Operational Assistant menu includes many options, including "Display system status," "Run a backup," "Work with system operator messages," "Work with printer output," "Work with jobs," "Work with signed-on users," "Device status tasks," and "Customizing your system, users, and devices." To access these options (Figure 6.4),

Type	GO ASSIST	if you are not on the Operational Assistant menu
Press	Enter	
Type	10	for the "Manage your system, users, and devices" option
Press	Enter	

Figure 6.4
Mange Your System,
Users, and Devices Screen

```
 MANAGESYS              Manage Your System, Users, and Devices
                                                  System: XXXXXXX

 To select one of the following, type its number below and press Enter:

        1. Display system status
        2. Run a backup
        3. Work with system operator messages

       10. Work with printer output
       11. Work with jobs
       12. Work with signed-on users

       20. Device status tasks

       60. Customize your system, users, and devices




    Type a menu option below
       __

 F1=Help   F3=Exit   F9=Command line   F12=Cancel
```

Figure 6.5 describes options 1, 2, 3, 10, 11, 12, and 20 specified in Figure 6.4.

Figure 6.5	Option Number	Description
Operational Assistant Option 10 Choices and Meanings	1= Display system status	Allows the operator to look at the system status, displaying such things as disk space, users, and batch jobs.
	2= Run a backup	Allows the operator to run a daily, weekly, or monthly backup with other IBM backup options. We will discuss backup and restore in greater detail in Chapter 7.
	3= Work with system operator messages	Allows the operator to display and work with the system operator messages (discussed in Chapter 4).
	10= Work with printer output	Allows the operator to send, change, hold, delete, display, release, or modify attributes related to printing status with the spooled files (discussed in Chapter 5).
	11= Work with jobs	Allows the operator to hold, delete, release, display messages, and work with printer output on all jobs in the system (discussed in Chapter 4).
	12= Work with signed-on users	Allows the operator to send messages, sign off users, display details, and display messages of all users who are signed on at the present time (discussed in Chapter 4).
	20= Device status tasks	Allows the operator to work with the devices that are in the system, such as display devices, printer devices, tape devices, and diskette devices.

Device Status

The AS/400 supports a number of peripheral devices, including display devices, printer devices, and tape devices. Devices can be turned on or off, may be disconnected from the system while they are being repaired, or may be upgraded. Generally, the operator is responsible for controlling the various states of these hardware devices.

To access the Device Status Task menu from the Operational Assistant menu,

Type   20

Press   Enter

The Device Status Task menu subdivides hardware devices into display devices, printer devices, tape devices, and diskette devices, as shown in Figure 6.6.

HINT

To view the following screens with more specific information, you must be at the Intermediate Assistance level. While you are displaying one of the screens, you can change your assistance level by pressing F21 and choosing option 2.

Figure 6.6

Device Status Task Screen

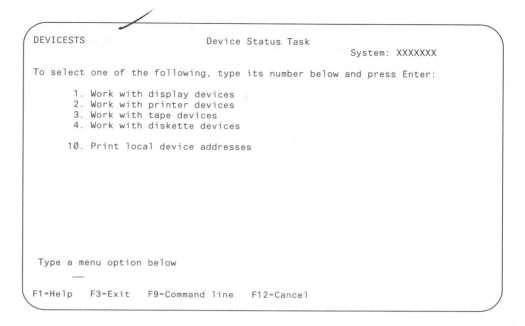

```
DEVICESTS                      Device Status Task
                                                   System: XXXXXXX

To select one of the following, type its number below and press Enter:

          1. Work with display devices
          2. Work with printer devices
          3. Work with tape devices
          4. Work with diskette devices

         10. Print local device addresses




   Type a menu option below
     __

 F1=Help    F3=Exit    F9=Command line    F12=Cancel
```

Device Status for Terminals and Display Devices
To access the Work with Display Devices screen (Basic Assistance level) or the Work with Configuration Status screen (Intermediate Assistance level),

> **Type**   1   from the Device Status Task screen
> **Press**   Enter

The Work with Configuration Status screen, as shown in Figure 6.7, contains the status of each display device on the system. You can make a device available, VARIED ON, or unavailable, VARIED OFF, by typing a 1 or a 2 in the Option column preceding the device type. You can use the "Varied on" and "Varied off" options to enhance security. For example, a device in a public place can be made unavailable during the evening and night hours. Any VARIED OFF device cannot be accessed after hours. You will need to vary the device on in the morning, making the device available before the first shift. The "Vary on" option and the "Vary off" option each takes some time to complete. Therefore, the system will display the VARY ON PENDING or VARY OFF PENDING message until the device status has changed.

Users should be encouraged to sign off their terminals whenever they will be gone for any length of time, such as to lunch or to a meeting. Again, this technique will enhance system security. When a user has signed off but has left the terminal powered on, the terminal status displayed will be SIGNON DISPLAY.

Refer to Figure 6.7 and note that the status of ACTIVE may be further defined to include ACTIVE/ALLOCATE, ACTIVE/DETACHED, ACTIVE/READER, ACTIVE/SOURCE, ACTIVE/TARGET, and ACTIVE/WRITER. The jobs that have ACTIVE further defined are generally

Figure 6.7
Work with Configuration
Status Screen (Displays)

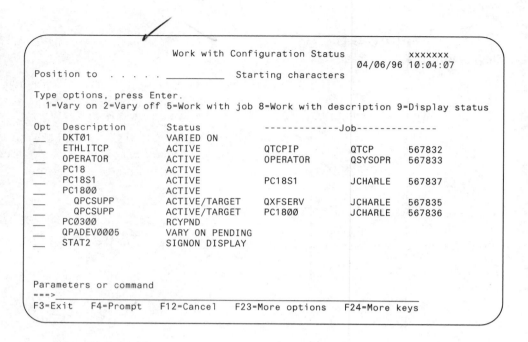

```
                          Work with Configuration Status        xxxxxxx
                                                                 04/06/96 10:04:07
   Position to  . . . . . _____   Starting characters

   Type options, press Enter.
     1=Vary on 2=Vary off 5=Work with job 8=Work with description 9=Display status

   Opt   Description        Status           ------------Job-------------
   ___   DKT01              VARIED ON
   ___   ETHLITCP           ACTIVE           QTCPIP        QTCP      567832
   ___   OPERATOR           ACTIVE           OPERATOR      QSYSOPR   567833
   ___   PC18               ACTIVE
   ___   PC18S1             ACTIVE           PC18S1        JCHARLE   567837
   ___   PC1800             ACTIVE
   ___     QPCSUPP          ACTIVE/TARGET    QXFSERV       JCHARLE   567835
   ___     QPCSUPP          ACTIVE/TARGET    PC1800        JCHARLE   567836
   ___   PC0300             RCYPND
   ___   QPADEV0005         VARY ON PENDING
   ___   STAT2              SIGNON DISPLAY



   Parameters or command
   ===> _____
   F3=Exit    F4=Prompt    F12=Cancel   F23=More options   F24=More keys
```

jobs that are called automatically and that are required for support or as a supplement to another job that is running.

The recovery pending (RCYPND) status indicator is generated when the system has noted an error and has automatically started an error-recovery task. Generally, these error-recovery tasks are for network interfaces, lines, and controllers. The system frequently will be able to correct the problem and the RCYPND status indicator will be replaced with VARY ON PENDING.

The three columns on the right in Figure 6.7 under the heading "Job" show three items of information. These three items are the same ones that make up the qualified job name. For interactive jobs, the first column contains the terminal or station number. For batch jobs, the job name will be the name of the batch job. The next column contains the user ID or user sign-on name. The last column contains a six-digit numeric number. These numbers are called job numbers and are assigned automatically by the system.

Device Descriptions for Terminals and Displays
Device descriptions fall into several broad categories: terminals, PCs with terminal emulation, remote devices, and the system console. An operator typically spends a large portion of time working with devices. Because devices provide the user with input and output capabilities to the system, the *IOSYSCFG special authority is required to work with devices.

To work with the description,

Type	8	on the option line for the device to be displayed, in this case, OPERATOR
Press	Enter	to go to the Work with Device Description screen

Type   5   to display the description

Press   Enter   to access the Display Device Description screen

The system console is shown in Figures 6.8 and 6.9. The name of the device is OPERATOR and the category of the device is a standard 3476 terminal, *DSP, which is directly cabled to the CPU as a local device, *LCL. The next several lines give the device type and model number. Note that IBM requires that the system console **must be** at port zero and switch zero to accommodate access during IPL and servicing.

Figure 6.8
Display Device
Description Screen,
Page 1

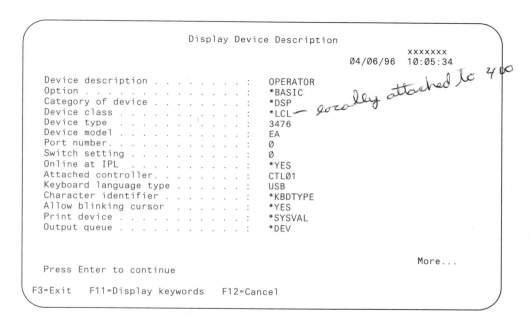

```
                              Display Device Description
                                                            xxxxxxx
                                                   04/06/96  10:05:34
        Device description . . . . . . . . :    OPERATOR
        Option . . . . . . . . . . . . . . :    *BASIC
        Category of device . . . . . . . . :    *DSP
        Device class . . . . . . . . . . . :    *LCL ← locally attached to 400
        Device type  . . . . . . . . . . . :    3476
        Device model . . . . . . . . . . . :    EA
        Port number. . . . . . . . . . . . :    0
        Switch setting . . . . . . . . . . :    0
        Online at IPL  . . . . . . . . . . :    *YES
        Attached controller. . . . . . . . :    CTL01
        Keyboard language type . . . . . . :    USB
        Character identifier . . . . . . . :    *KBDTYPE
        Allow blinking cursor  . . . . . . :    *YES
        Print device . . . . . . . . . . . :    *SYSVAL
        Output queue . . . . . . . . . . . :    *DEV


                                                               More...

        Press Enter to continue

      F3=Exit    F11=Display keywords    F12=Cancel
```

The second page of the Display Device Description screen (Figure 6.9) repeats the first three lines of the device name, option, and device category for clarification. The new data on this screen describes the default printer and any customizing performed on this device.

To view the device descriptions for a terminal, select the appropriate device and proceed as shown in the previous steps. An example is shown in Figure 6.10. Local terminal devices are those devices that have a port and switch address — in this example, port 5, switch 3. Local devices are generally connected to the AS/400 via a cable. These devices have a class of local, *LCL.

There are many types of display devices available on the AS/400, depending on how a device is connected. The previous discussion shows only a small sample of local display devices.

Figure 6.9
Display Device
Description Screen,
Page 2

```
                        Display Device Description
                                                        xxxxxxx
                                                04/06/96  10:05:34

    Device description . . . . . . . . . . :  OPERATOR
    Option . . . . . . . . . . . . . . . :  *BASIC
    Category of device . . . . . . . . . :  *DSP
    Printer file . . . . . . . . . . . . :  QSYSPRT
      Library . . . . . . . . . . . . . :     *LIBL
    Workstation customizing object . . . . :  *NONE
    Text . . . . . . . . . . . . . . . . :  CREATED BY AUTO-CONFIGURATION




                                                             Bottom
    Press Enter to continue

    F3=Exit    F11=Display keywords    F12=Cancel
```

Figure 6.10
Display Device
Description Screen,
Specific Device Selected

```
                        Display Device Description
                                                        xxxxxxx
                                                04/06/96  10:06:45
    Device description . . . . . . . . :  STAT14
    Option . . . . . . . . . . . . . . :  *BASIC
    Category of device. . . . . . . . :  *DSP
    Device class . . . . . . . . . . . :  *LCL
    Device type  . . . . . . . . . . . :  3476
    Device model . . . . . . . . . . . :  EA
    Port number . . . . . . . . . . . :  5
    Switch setting . . . . . . . . . . :  3
    Online at IPL . . . . . . . . . . :  *YES
    Attached controller . . . . . . . :  CTL02
    Keyboard language type . . . . . . :  USB
    Character identifier . . . . . . . :  *KBDTYPE
    Allow blinking cursor . . . . . . :  *YES
    Print device . . . . . . . . . . . :  *SYSVAL
    Output queue . . . . . . . . . . . :  *DEV


                                                             More...
    Press Enter to continue

    F3=Exit    F11=Display keywords    F12=Cancel
```

Device Status for Printers
To display the Device Status Tasks screen,

Press	F12	repeatedly until the Device Status Tasks menu is again displayed
Type	2	for the "Work with printer devices" option
Press	Enter	

Generally, the AS/400 has a variety of printers connected to the AS/400. Figure 6.11 shows the Work with Configuration Status screen with three printers attached. We recommend that printer names be descriptive to help differentiate between similar printers at different locations. In Figure 6.11, the printers are named by location, with one in the accounting department and the other on the manufacturing floor.

Figure 6.11
Work with Configuration
Status Screen (Printers)

```
                        Work with Configuration Status
                                                            xxxxxxx
                                                   04/06/96  10:07:16

 Position to  . . . . .  _____    Starting characters

 Type options, press Enter.
   1=Vary on   2=Vary off   5=Work with job   8=Work with description
   9=Display mode status ...

 Opt  Description        Status            -------------Job-------------
  __   LASER             VARIED OFF
  __   PRTACT            ACTIVE/WRITER      PRTACT     QSPLJOB     049041
  __   PRTMFG            VARY ON PENDING



                                                               Bottom
 Parameters or command
 ===>_____
 F3=Exit   F4=Prompt   F12=Cancel   F23=More options   F24=More keys
```

Device Description for Printers
A printer, like every other device attached to the AS/400, must have a description to identify its attributes to the AS/400. To work with the description, from the Work with Configuration Status screen,

Type	8	on the option line for the device
Press	Enter	to go to the Work with Device Description screen
Type	5	to display the description
Press	Enter	to go to the Display Device Description screen for PRTACT

The printer (*PRT) in Figure 6.12 represents a locally attached (*LCL) printer (*PRT) that communicates through the CTL01 controller. The display devices in the earlier examples were attached to the CTL02 controller.

Note the "Port number" and "Switch setting" parameters. Unlike tape units and diskette drives, printers attached locally must have an address, like a display station. If auto configuration was the method used to generate the device description, the "Text" parameter will be "Created by auto-configuration," as shown in Figure 6.13.

Figure 6.12
Display Device
Description Screen for
Specified Printer

```
                        Display Device Description
                                                              XXXXXXX
                                                   04/06/96  10:07:43
      Device description . . . . . . . . :    PRTACT
      Option . . . . . . . . . . . . . :    *BASIC
      Category of device. . . . . . . . :    *PRT
      Device class . . . . . . . . . . :    *LCL
      Device type . . . . . . . . . . . :    *IPDS
      Device model. . . . . . . . . . . :    0
      Advanced function printing. . . . . :    *NO
      Port number . . . . . . . . . . . :    1
      Switch setting . . . . . . . . . . :    0
      Online at IPL . . . . . . . . . . :    *YES
      Attached controller. . . . . . . . :    CTL01
      Font:
         Identifier . . . . . . . . . . :    011
         Point size. . . . . . . . . . . :    *NONE
      Form feed . . . . . . . . . . . . :    *CONT


                                                              More...

      Press Enter to continue

      F3=Exit    F11=Display keywords    F12=Cancel
```

Figure 6.13
Display Device
Description Screen
Showing Auto-
Configuration

```
                        Display Device Description
                                                              XXXXXXX
                                                   04/06/96  10:07:43
      Device description . . . . . . . . :    PRTACT
      Option . . . . . . . . . . . . . :    *BASIC
      Category of device . . . . . . . . :    *PRT
      Separator drawer . . . . . . . . . :    *FILE
      Printer error message. . . . . . . :    *INQ
      Message queue . . . . . . . . . . :    QSYSOPR
         Library . . . . . . . . . . . . :      *LIBL
      Text . . . . . . . . . . . . . . :    CREATED BY AUTO-CONFIGURATION






                                                              Bottom

      Press Enter to continue

      F3=Exit    F11=Display keywords    F12=Cancel
```

Device Status for Tape Drives
With most standalone PCs, backup consists of copying files to a floppy drive. While this approach to backup may be inconvenient for the PC user, it is manageable. However, with the AS/400's single-level approach to memory storage and the large volume of objects stored on the CPU, tape backup becomes mandatory. The following material explains how to display a tape drive's status and device description.

To return to the Device Status Tasks screen,

Press	F12	repeatedly from the Display Device Description screen until you return to the Device Status Tasks screen; then
Choose	option 3	from the Device Status Tasks screen to "Work with tape devices"
Type	8	on the option line of the Work with Tape Devices screen for the device to be displayed; in this case, TAP01
Press	Enter	to go to the Work with Device Description screen
Type	5	to display the description on the Work with Configuration Status screen
Press	Enter	

Figures 6.14 and 6.15, presented in the order in which you will access them on the system, show the status of the tape drive.

Figure 6.14
Work with Configuration
Status Screen
(Tape Devices)

```
                    Work with Configuration Status
                                                    XXXXXXX
                                        04/06/96  10:08:15
Position to  . . . . . _____   Starting characters

Type options, press Enter.
  1=Vary on   2=Vary off   5=Work with job   8=Work with description
  9=Display mode status ...

Opt  Description      Status              ------------Job-------------
 __   TAP01           VARIED ON



                                                        Bottom
Parameters or command
===>_____
F3=Exit    F4=Prompt    F12=Cancel    F23=More options   F24=More keys
```

Tape devices must be VARIED ON and therefore made available for use like other devices on the AS/400. You can modify the status of the device from the Work with Configuration Status screen.

Figure 6.15
Display Device
Description Screen
(Tape Device)

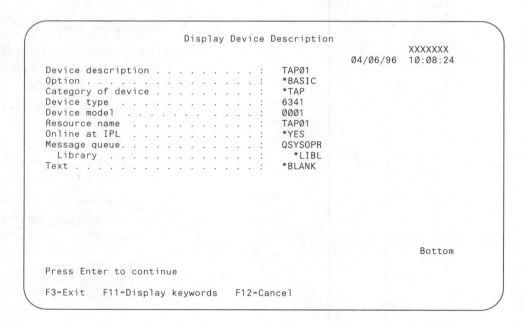

```
                         Display Device Description
                                                           XXXXXXX
                                                    04/06/96  10:08:24
Device description . . . . . . . . . :    TAP01
Option . . . . . . . . . . . . . . . :    *BASIC
Category of device . . . . . . . . . :    *TAP
Device type  . . . . . . . . . . . . :    6341
Device model  . . . . . . . . . . .  :    0001
Resource name  . . . . . . . . . . . :    TAP01
Online at IPL  . . . . . . . . . . . :    *YES
Message queue. . . . . . . . . . . . :    QSYSOPR
  Library  . . . . . . . . . . . . . :      *LIBL
Text . . . . . . . . . . . . . . . . :    *BLANK



                                                            Bottom

Press Enter to continue

F3=Exit    F11=Display keywords    F12=Cancel
```

The tape device description, TAP01, represents a 6341 tape device, online at IPL. Note that the "Text" parameter is blank. Unlike the printer device description referred to earlier, this tape drive was not generated by automatic configuration. However, text could have been entered when the tape drive device description was created. The tape drive device description does not display or require a local address, because tape drives are directly connected via a controller card, through a special address called a *resource name.*

Device Status for Diskette Drives
Return to the Device Status Tasks screen and

Press	F12	repeatedly to return to the Device Status Tasks screen
Choose	Option 4	from the Device Status Tasks screen to "Work with devices"
Type	8	on the option line of the Work with Devices screen to "Work with description" for the device; in this case, DKT01
Press	Enter	to go to the Work with Device Description screen
Type	5	to display the description on the Work with Device Description screen
Press	Enter	

Figures 6.16 and 6.17 show the status of the diskette drive. The diskette drive device description does not display a local address because diskette drives connect directly to a controller card, through a resource name.

Figure 6.16
Work with Configuration
Status Screen (Diskettes)

```
                        Work with Configuration Status
                                                        XXXXXXX
                                                04/06/96  10:08:34

 Position to  . . . . .  _____    Starting characters

 Type options, press Enter.
   1=Vary on 2=Vary off 5=Work with job 8=Work with description 9=Display status

 Opt   Description      Status          -------------Job-------------
 __    DKT01            VARIED ON




                                                            Bottom
 Parameters or command
 ===>_____
 F3=Exit    F4=Prompt    F12=Cancel    F23=More options    F24=More keys
```

Figure 6.17
Display Device
Description Screen
(Diskettes)

```
                          Display Device Description
                                                        XXXXXXX
                                                04/06/96  10:08:44

 Device description . . . . . . . . :   DKT01
 Option . . . . . . . . . . . . . . :   *BASIC
 Category of device. . . . . . . . :   *DKT
 Device type . . . . . . . . . . . :   6133
 Device model . . . . . . . . . . . :   0000
 Resource name . . . . . . . . . . :   DKT01
 Online at IP . . . . . . . . . . . :   *YES
 Text. . . . . . . . . . . . . . . :   CREATED BY AUTO-CONFIGURATION




                                                            Bottom
 Press Enter to continue

 F3=Exit    F11=Display keywords    F12=Cancel
```

Creating Device Descriptions

Before you add new devices to the AS/400, you should first document your
system hardware. Draw a layout of the physical location of your local twinaxial
devices (a simplified layout is shown in Figure 6.2). Be sure to include the
device addresses in this document. The *AS/400 Device Configuration Guide*
contains Form C1, a Local Work Station Diagram (Twinaxial Cabling) to document your addresses and other information needed to configure displays,

printers, and other devices. Use Form E1 for Tape and Tape Controllers. Use Form E2 for Diskette and Diskette Controllers. Make as many copies of these forms as you need for the number of ports or controllers on your system. Refer to the literature with each display station, printer, and other devices to complete Form C1. The Local Work Station Diagram will bring together in an organized manner most of the information you need to create your display and printer device descriptions. You can use various forms located in your *AS/400 Device Configuration Guide* (you will find copies of these forms in Appendix B of this text) to document your hardware information. You will find these forms to be exceptionally helpful, but you need to be sure to keep them up-to-date. And if devices are moved or replaced, update all related forms.

Now that you as the operator are comfortable with the concept of device descriptions and how to access existing descriptions, the next question is, "How are descriptions created?" There are several methods available to configure devices. The AS/400 can configure devices automatically. For automatic configuration, the system value Automatic Configuration, QAUTOCFG, must be set to 1 (on). As the operator, you will plug in a new device and ensure the device is turned on; the AS/400 will then configure the device and vary it on during the next IPL.

Automatic configuration has several disadvantages. If the QAUTOCFG system value is allowed to remain on, each IPL sequence may create extraneous device descriptions for devices that are powered on. This understandably creates confusion for operators and system staff. The authors recommend that auto-configuration is turned off immediately after a device description has been created. To turn automatic configuration off, change the QAUTOCFG system value to 0.

Another disadvantage of automatic configuration is that the system staff has no control over the name assigned to the device. The system will assign a name that probably will mean nothing to the operator. The staff usually will find it more convenient to have names that are easy to identify for later problem resolution. The AS/400 lets you change object names with the RNMOBJ (Rename Object) command, but this is an extra step.

Copying Device Descriptions for Display Stations
Configuring other devices manually is frequently faster than auto-configuration, and manual configuration also provides meaningful names for the new devices. If you need to configure a display station that is the same type as one that already exists, copy the description of the existing display station and change the old address to the appropriate address for the new device.

To display the Work with Device Descriptions screen (shown in Figure 6.18),

Type   WRKDEVD   on the command line

Figure 6.18
Work with Device
Descriptions Screen

```
                        Work with Device Descriptions
                                                  System: XXXXXXX
 Position to  . . . . .  _____   Starting characters _____

 Type options, press Enter.
   2=Change  3=Copy  4=Delete  5=Display  6=Print  7=Rename
   8=Work with status              9=Retrieve source

 Opt   Device      Type    Text
  _    DKT01       6133    CREATED BY AUTO-CONFIGURATION
  _    ETHLITCP    *NET    CREATED BY AUTO-CONFIGURATION
  _    OPERATOR    3476    CREATED BY AUTO-CONFIGURATION
  _    TEST        3476    Created for exercise
  _    OVERHEAD    5150    Overhead projector PC support config
  _    OVERHEADS1  3197    Device created for OVERHEAD
  _    OVERHEAD00  *APPC   AUTOMATICALLY CREATED BY QLUS
  _    OVERHEAD01  *APPC   AUTOMATICALLY CREATED BY QLUS
  _    PCUSER1     5150
  _    PCUSER1S1   3197

                                                           More...
 Parameters or command
 ===>_____
 F3=Exit F4=Prompt F5=Refresh F6=Create F9=Retrieve F12=Cancel F14=Work status
```

In large AS/400 shops, the Work with Device Descriptions screen may be many pages in length. Prompting the WRKDEVD command lets you choose the specific types of device descriptions to work with, filtering out the others. This gives you a more user-friendly working environment.

To select a specific device type, use the following sequence:

Press F3   to cancel the previous display

Type WRKDEVD   on the command line

Press F4   to prompt the Work with Device Descriptions command

Press F4   to prompt the Device description parameter

As Figure 6.19 shows, many different types of devices can be attached to the AS/400. As you might expect, the device descriptions are either three- or six-character words. To specify a device description for a display station,

Type *DSP   as the device description

Press Enter

To copy a device description, position the cursor on the option column for the 3476 display device named TEST, as shown in Figure 6.18.

Type 3   in the option column of the device description TEST

Press Enter

When you copy the device description, you must provide a new name and new address for the new device, as shown in Figure 6.20.

Figure 6.19
Specify Value for
Parameter Device
Description (DEVD)
Screen

```
                     Specify Value for Parameter DEVD

Type choice, press Enter.

Type . . . . . . . . . . . . . :   GENERIC NAME
Device description . . . . . . . >  *DSP

    *ALL                                *SNPT
    *CMN
    *DKT
    *DSP
    *LCLDSP
    *RMTDSP
    *VRTDSP
    *LOC
    *PRT
    *LCLPRT
    *RMTPRT
    *VRTPRT
    *TAP




F3=Exit  F5=Refresh  F12=Cancel  F13=How to use this display  F24=More key
```

Figure 6.20
Create Device Desc
(Display) (CRTDEVDSP)
Screen

```
                  Create Device Desc (Display) (CRTDEVDSP)


Type choices, press Enter.

Device description . . . . . . .    _____      Name
Device class . . . . . . . . . >  *LCL          *LCL, *RMT, *VRT, *SNPT
Device type . . . . . . . . . >  3476          3101, 3151, 3161, 3162...
Device model . . . . . . . . . >  EA            0, 1, 2, 4, 11, 12, 23...
Port number . . . . . . . . . >  5             0-17
Switch setting . . . . . . . . >  0             0, 1, 2, 3, 4, 5, 6
Online at IPL . . . . . . . . >  *YES          *YES, *NO
Attached controller . . . . . >  CTL02         Name
Keyboard language type . . . . >  USB           *SYSVAL, AGB, AGI, BLI...
Allow blinking cursor . . . . >  *YES          *YES, *NO
Text 'description' . . . . . . >   *BLANK



                                                              More...

F3=Exit   F4=Prompt   F5=Refresh   F10=Additional parameters   F12=Cancel
F13=How to use this display     F24=More keys
```

The operator must name the device and change the "Port number" and "Switch setting" to the correct address of the new device. Device addresses must be unique. To replace a device that requires maintenance, see Appendix A. To name the device and change the port number and switch setting,

Type	TEST2	in the parameter for the "Device description" name
Type	5	for the "Port number" parameter
Type	6	for the "Switch setting" parameter
Press	Enter	

Creating a Device Description for a Display Station

If you choose to, or need to, create a display station description because one does not exist to copy, type CRTDEVDSP (Create Device Description Display) on the command line and press Enter. A screen similar to Figure 6.21 will be shown. After you have completed entering the parameters, press Enter.

Figure 6.21
Create Device Desc
(Display) (CRTDEVDSP)
Screen

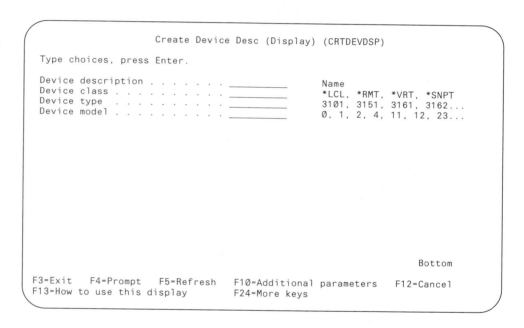

```
                          Create Device Desc (Display) (CRTDEVDSP)
 Type choices, press Enter.

 Device description . . . . . . . .  _____    Name
 Device class . . . . . . . . . . .  _____    *LCL, *RMT, *VRT, *SNPT
 Device type  . . . . . . . . . . .  _____    3101, 3151, 3161, 3162...
 Device model . . . . . . . . . . .  _____    0, 1, 2, 4, 11, 12, 23...




                                                                       Bottom
 F3=Exit    F4=Prompt    F5=Refresh    F10=Additional parameters    F12=Cancel
 F13=How to use this display           F24=More keys
```

Now that the AS/400 operating system is prepared for a new display station, the display station itself must be programmed. Locate the documentation that accompanied the hardware to find out how to access the address screen. Some of the newer IBM models require that you hold the space bar down while the device is powering on. Other older IBM or System/36 stations require you to adjust actual physical switches on the device. When the address screen is available, enter the same port and switch setting that you defined on the Create Device Description screen.

HINT

Add to Form C1 how to access the address screen for each display station.

Type   8   on the Work With Device Descriptions screen
    or   next to the device you wish to work on
Type   WRKCFGSTS   on the command line if you are not on the
                         Work With Device Descriptions display

Press   Enter

After the display station has been configured and addressed, turn the power off and then on again. Go to an operator's console and vary the new device on. Use the Work with Device Description display to verify that the new device has VARIED ON.

Troubleshooting
If the newly installed display station will not vary on, ensure that the following steps have been successfully completed:

1. Create the device description, including selecting a unique port and switch address.
2. Assign the same port and switch address to the display station address screen.
3. Vary the device on.

If the display station will not vary on, it is possible that the controller is not active. The controller for the port must be active for the devices attached to it to function. The CTL02 in Figure 6.22 is the description for the controller that handles the device description TEST2. Use option 1, "Vary on," next to the controller name. When the controller is shown as ACTIVE, vary the display device on. The new display station should now be ready for use.

Figure 6.22
Work with Configuration
Status Screen

```
                        Work with Configuration Status          XXXXXXX
                                                                 03/06/96
        Position to  . . . . . _____   Starting characters _____

        Type options, press Enter.
          1=Vary on   2=Vary off   5=Work with job   8=Work with description
          9=Display mode status ...

        Opt  Description       Status            -------------Job-------------
             CTL02             ACTIVE
               TEST2           VARY OFF PENDING




                                                                   Bottom
        Parameters or command
        ===>_____
        F3=Exit   F4=Prompt   F12=Cancel   F23=More options   F24=More keys
```

To cancel the Work with Configuration Status screen,
Press   F12

Creating Device Descriptions for Tape and Diskette Drives
You can create tape and diskette descriptions the same way you create display device descriptions — by copying one that already exists. You should update Form E1 for every new tape or tape controller device. You should use Form E2 for a diskette or diskette controller unit connected to your system.

If you wish to create a new tape drive description manually instead of copying an existing one, use the CRTDEVTAP (Create Device Tape) command, as shown in Figure 6.23. When you are creating a tape device description, use the information on the E1 form.

Figure 6.23
Create Device Desc (Tape)
(CRTDEVTAP) Screen

```
                          Create Device Desc (Tape) (CRTDEVTAP)

 Type choices, press Enter.

 Device description . . . . . . . > TEST          Name
 Device type  . . . . . . . . . .  _____     2440, 3422, 3430, 3480...
 Device model . . . . . . . . . .  ___            1, 2, A01, A12, B01, ....
 Resource name  . . . . . . . . .  _____     Name
 Switch setting . . . . . . . . .  _              0-F
 Online at IPL  . . . . . . . . .  *YES           *YES, *NO
 Attached controller  . . . . . .  _____     Name
 Message queue  . . . . . . . . .  QSYSOPR        Name, QSYSOPR
   Library  . . . . . . . . . . .  *LIBL          Name, *LIBL, *CURLIB
 Text 'description' . . . . . . .  *BLANK

                              Additional Parameters

 Authority  . . . . . . . . . . .  *LIBCRTAUT     Name,*LIBCRTAUT,*CHANGE...



                                                                  Bottom
 F3=Exit   F4=Prompt   F5=Refresh   F12=Cancel  F13=How to use this display
 F24=More keys
```

To create a new diskette unit description instead of copying an existing one, use the CRTDEVDKT (Create Device Diskette) command, as shown in Figure 6.24. When you are creating a diskette device description, use the parameters with the information from the E2 form.

Figure 6.24
Create Device Desc
(Diskette) (CRTDEVDKT)
Screen

```
                    Create Device Desc (Diskette) (CRTDEVDKT)

 Type choices, press Enter.

 Device description . . . . . . .  _____    Name
 Device type . . . . . . . . . . .              6131, 6132, 6133, 9331
 Device model. . . . . . . . . . .  _            0, 1, 2
 Resource name . . . . . . . . . .  _____   Name
 Online at IPL . . . . . . . . .    *YES         *NO, *YES
 Text 'description' . . . . . . .   *BLANK


                         Additional Parameters

 Authority . . . . . . . . . .      *LIBCRTAUT   Name,*LIBCRTAUT,*CHANGE.




                                                              Bottom
 F3=Exit   F4=Prompt   F5=Refresh   F12=Cancel   F13=How to use this display
 F24=More keys
```

Figure 6.25
Create Device Desc
(Printer) (CRTDEVPRT)
Screen

```
                    Create Device Desc (Printer) (CRTDEVPRT)

 Type choices, press Enter.

 Device description . . . . . . . . > TEST       Name
 Device class . . . . . . . . . . .  _____       *LCL, *RMT, *VRT, *SNPT
 Device type . . . . . . . . . . .   _____       3287, 3812, 4019, 4201...
 Device model . . . . . . . . . . .  _           0, 1, 2, 3, 4, 10, 13
 Emulated twinaxial device. . . . .              3812, 5219, 5224, 5256
 Advanced function printing . . . .  *NO         *NO, *YES




                                                              Bottom
 F3=Exit   F4=Prompt   F5=Refresh   F12=Cancel   F13=How to use this display
 F24=More keys
```

Creating Device Descriptions for Printers
If you wish to create a new printer device description manually, use the CRTDEVPRT (Create Device Printer) command, as shown in Figure 6.25.

The screen in Figure 6.25 is the first screen that will appear after you type the CRTDEVPRT (Create Device Printer) command. After you supply the parameters with the correct information from your printer documentation, a screen similar to Figure 6.26 will be displayed.

Figure 6.26
Create Device Desc
(Printer) (CRTDEVPRT)
Screen

```
                          Create Device Desc (Printer) (CRTDEVPRT)
            Type choices, press Enter.

            Device description . . . . . . . > TEST          Name
            Device class . . . . . . . . . . > *LCL          *LCL, *RMT, *VRT
            Device type  . . . . . . . . . . > 3287          3287, 3812, 4019
            Device model . . . . . . . . . . > 1             0, 1, 2, 3, 4, 10, 13,
            Emulated twinaxial device. . . . > 5219          3812, 5219, 5224, 5256
            Port number  . . . . . . . . . .   __            0-17
            Switch setting . . . . . . . . .                 0, 1, 2, 3, 4, 5, 6
            Online at IPL  . . . . . . . . .   *YES          *YES, *NO
            Attached controller  . . . . . .                 Name
            Font:
              Identifier . . . . . . . . . .   __            3, 5, 11, 12, 13, 18,
            Point size . . . . . . . . . . .   *NONE         000.1-999.9, *NONE
            Form feed  . . . . . . . . . . .   *CONT         *CONT, *CUT, *AUTOCUT
            Separator drawer . . . . . . . .   *FILE         *FILE, 1, 2, 3


                                                                          Bottom

            F3=Exit    F4=Prompt   F5=Refresh   F12=Cancel   F13=How to use this display
            F24=More keys
```

You can find the parameter information (other than the device description) for creating a printer description on the C1 form. Maintaining the system layout and C1, E2, and E3 forms are important operator tasks to provide smooth transitions while you are adding new devices or dealing with devices that require maintenance. Meaningful device names and mapping locations of devices are also helpful for troubleshooting purposes. This level of organization is invaluable when hardware device problems arise and users are in immediate need of a replacement device.

Key Terms

Addresses	Device status	Topology
Configuration status	Display stations	bus
Controllers	Lines	ring
Devices	Port	star
Device descriptions	Terminals	

Review Questions

1. How do the bus, Token-Ring, and star topologies differ?

2. The physical address of a device consists of two parts. What are they?

3. How do you determine whether the automatic configuration for devices is turned on?

4. What status is required for a controller to allow a device attached to it to function?

5. Are physical addresses required for printers attached to the AS/400 using a twinaxial connection?

Exercises

1. Fill out form C1 to describe a workstation and a local twinaxial printer. Copy the form from Appendix B as required.

Chapter 7

Backup, Restore, and PTFs

Objectives

To understand

- ✓ the concept behind save/restore commands
- ✓ the importance of quarterly, monthly, weekly, and daily backup procedures
- ✓ tape concepts and the need for initialization
- ✓ diskette concepts and the need for initialization
- ✓ what function "Clean Up" performs
- ✓ how to set up a backup procedure
- ✓ the concepts of how to restore different object types
- ✓ the concept of a Program Temporary Fix (PTF)
- ✓ how to order PTFs
- ✓ how to load PTFs
- ✓ how to load a cumulative PTF
- ✓ how to verify a PTF installation

To be able to

- ✓ do backup and recovery planning
- ✓ run a backup
- ✓ restore an object

Creating a Backup Plan

Backing up your system is a time-consuming, but necessary, task. If your system crashes and the information it contained was not backed up, the loss to your company, both in time spent trying to re-create the data lost and in the dollars lost for data that cannot be replaced, can be critical. Many scenarios would require backed-up information to be restored. For example, someone accidentally or intentionally deletes an object, a disk drive is damaged, or a virus enters your system. Whatever the scenario, the need to back up your system regularly is critical, and your backup plan should always be documented.

In all backup plans, it is necessary to balance the time required to back up an object with the time constraints for restoring the object. Because restoring data generally represents an emergency situation, most backup plans emphasize the time required to restore an object. The backup guidelines used in this text represent a balance between the recovery time of a potential disaster and the time required to back up all data as required for a potential disaster recovery. So a primary question becomes "When and how often should a given object be backed up?" One good rule of thumb is to back up objects whenever there is a significant change to the data. For example, a payroll system may need to be backed up weekly, while a customer order-entry system probably requires daily backups.

Save Commands

To prevent data loss, a dependable backup plan must ensure that every object and every category of object is saved regularly. The AS/400 operating system offers seven separate save commands to back up different classes of objects. The following material discusses the various save commands and then ties these commands into a comprehensive quarterly, weekly, and daily procedure.

The simplest save method uses the SAVSTG (Save Storage) command. SAVSTG saves every object on the system. The disadvantage of this command is that it saves a sector-by-sector copy of the total contents of DASD storage. With SAVSTG, you cannot restore individual libraries or objects. A SAVSTG is a disk-image save and is not very flexible. But a SAVSTG backup is the quickest way to restore an exact copy of all data to the same hardware configuration when a complete restore is required. Because SAVSTG is not very flexible for restoring objects to a system, most installations opt for an organized strategy of full system backup, using other backup commands.

The SAVSYS (Save System) command saves the AS/400 Licensed Internal Code (LIC), the operating system, and all security data. This save command requires the system to be in a restricted state, which means users cannot be signed on to the system during the SAVSYS procedure.

HINT

Before the release of the AS/400 64-bit PowerPC boxes, many AS/400 hardware systems required Model Unique Licensed Internal Code (MULIC) or Feature Unique Licensed Internal Code (FULIC), installed from tapes supplied in the AS/400's service kit. These tapes contained licensed internal code specific to your model. These tapes are very important, and management should decide where they should be kept. If the MULIC/ FULIC tape is damaged and is not immediately available for restoration, the system may not function. If your tape is damaged or lost, you can request a new one from IBM and receive it within 48 hours.

The SAVLIB (Save Library) command saves libraries that contain IBM licensed programs, such as RPG/400, COBOL/400, OfficeVision/400, and so on. SAVLIB also saves IBM-defined libraries such as QGPL, QUSRSYS, QRCL, and most other libraries that begin with Q but that are not related to a specific licensed program. More importantly, SAVLIB saves user libraries. User libraries usually contain the corporate data and represent the largest volume of variable information that requires backup.

The SAVSECDTA (Save Security Data) command saves all security data including user profiles and authorization lists that allow access to your system. This information is also saved by the SAVSYS command, mentioned earlier.

The SAVCFG (Save Configuration) command saves configuration objects such as lines, controllers, devices, and other communications objects defined to support AS/400. These objects are also saved by the SAVSYS command, mentioned earlier.

The SAVDLO (Save Documents Library Object) command saves documents stored in folders for OfficeVision objects.

The SAVCHGOBJ (Save Changed Objects) command saves objects only if they have been changed since the last backup. IBM-supplied libraries such as QGPL, QUSRSYS, QRCL, and all other Q* libraries may not have changes. The SAVCHGOBJ backup command will conserve time and is commonly used in the daily backup cycle.

The SAV (Save) command can save the entire system. We recommend, however, that you continue to use existing backup commands, as discussed above, and that you use the SAV command for the Integrated File System (IFS) objects.

Sample Backup Plan

Now that we have briefly discussed some of the save commands, what is a reasonable way to implement a backup plan? Figure 7.1 shows a suggested schedule for backing up all objects on the system. The various save commands presented combine to save all the system objects at a minimum of every three months. This comprehensive backup plan incorporates the various save commands to isolate data in relatively small blocks. The small size of the objects balances the varying needs of changing objects and keeps restore time to a minimum. Note that different save commands require different restore commands, as presented in Figure 7.1.

Notice the "Accept path" (ACCPTH (*YES)) parameter in the SAVLIB and SAVCHGOBJ commands in Figure 7.1. This parameter specifies that the access paths are to be included in the save. Saving the access paths does increase backup time and requires more storage on backup media, but doing so greatly reduces restore time when you are restoring during a full system recovery. However, each organization should evaluate the savings balanced with the additional time required to save these access paths. Saving access paths can take at least 20 percent to 50 percent longer for production data libraries. Those same libraries may see as little as a 10 percent reduction in restore time. Also, more tapes are required if access paths are saved. Finally, with all of this in mind, how often has your MIS department had to do a full recovery? Some businesses will not see an advantage in saving access paths.

Figure 7.1

An Example of Backup Procedures and Related Restore Commands

Quarterly Backup Procedure	Quarterly Restore Commands
SAVSYS *Save System*	RSTUSRPRF, RSTCFG, RSTAUT
SAVSECDTA *Save Security Data*	RSTUSRPRF, RSTAUT *Restore User Profile Restore Config Restore Authori*
SAVDLO DLO(*ALL) FLR(*ANY)	RSTDLO *Restore Documents Library*
SAVLIB LIB(*IBM) ACCPTH(*YES) *IBM Library access Path*	RSTLIB
SAVLIB LIB(*ALLUSR) ACCPTH(*YES)	RSTLIB

SAVDEV('QSYS.LIB/TAP01.DEVD')   *Save device*
     OBJ(('/*') ('QSYS.LIB' *OMIT)
     ('/QDLS' *OMIT)) UPDHST(*YES)
	RST

Weekly (or Monthly) Backup Procedure	Weekly (or Monthly) Restore Commands
SAVDLO DLO(*ALL) FLR(*ANY)	RSTDLO
SAVLIB LIB(*ALLUSR) ACCPTH(*YES)	RSTLIB

SAVDEV('QSYS.LIB/TAP01.DEVD')
     OBJ(('/*') ('QSYS.LIB' *OMIT)
     ('QDLS' *OMIT)) UPDHST(*YES)
	RST

Daily Save Procedure	Daily Restore Commands
SAVSECDTA	RSTUSRPRF, RSTAUT
SAVCFG	RSTCFG
SAVDLO DLO(*CHG)	RSTDLO

SAVDEV('QSYS.LIB/TAP01.DEVD')
     OBJ(('/*') ('QSY.LIB' *OMIT)
     ('QDLS' *OMIT))
     CHGPERIOD(*LASTSAVE)
     UPDHST(*NO)
	RST

SAVCHGOBJ OBJ(*ALL) LIB(*ALLUSR) OBJJRN(*YES) ACCPTH(*YES)	RSTOBJ

DSPOBJD OBJ(QSYS/QSAV*)
     OBJTYPE(*DTAARA)
     DETAIL(*FULL)
     OUTPUT(*PRINT)	

You should implement the quarterly save procedure every three months *and* after PTFs have been applied.

You should follow the monthly save procedure every month on the same relative day; for example, the last day of the month, whether it is February 28th, August 30th, or September 31st. A general monthly backup should be performed after month-end processing.

You should also perform the weekly save procedure the same day every week, after any required weekly processing is complete.

You should conduct the daily save procedure each day at the end of the day (e.g., 5:00 p.m.), after the day's processing has been completed.

HINT

You can run the procedures in Figure 7.1 from your command line or they can be set up by your Security Officer in Operational Assistant, which allows customized menus to execute your saves.

Tape Considerations

The most common media for backing up your system is tape. The AS/400 supports numerous types of backup tape devices, including ½-inch reels, ½-inch cartridges, ¼-inch cartridges, and 8mm cartridges. You can use diskettes to back up smaller objects (because of their smaller storage capacity) or to transfer files between computer systems. Whatever the media, the basic backup procedures are the same.

To access the Tape menu shown in Figure 7.2,

Type   GO TAPE   on any command line
Press   Enter

As you can see, the Tape menu provides nearly all the commands you will need for tape functions or to resolve a tape problem.

Figure 7.2
Tape Menu

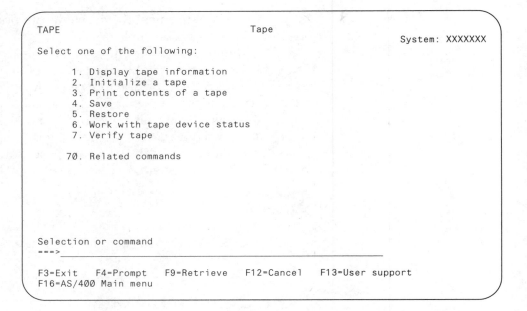

```
TAPE                                    Tape
                                                        System: XXXXXXX
Select one of the following:

        1. Display tape information
        2. Initialize a tape
        3. Print contents of a tape
        4. Save
        5. Restore
        6. Work with tape device status
        7. Verify tape

       70. Related commands




Selection or command
===>_____

F3=Exit   F4=Prompt   F9=Retrieve   F12=Cancel   F13=User support
F16=AS/400 Main menu
```

The stored header information (option 1, "Display tape information") provides you with a summary of data concerning the tape currently in the drive. To access this information from the Tape menu,

Type   1   to display the tape information
Press   Enter

The Display Tape (DSPTAP) screen shown in Figure 7.3 will be presented. As this figure shows, the parameter "Tape device" defines a valid tape drive. This name will be required in later processing. The "Output" parameter allows either *PRINT (printer spooled file to be generated) or * (information to display on the screen). If the AS/400 system has multiple tape drives, you may wish to print the Display Tape screen if you're a novice operator, to help you remember the correct spelling of the tape device name. The "Data type" parameter gives you the option to display the labels or to display the save/restore information that is stored on the tape.

Initializing Tapes

Initializing a tape is similar to formatting a diskette on a DOS system, and the initialization must be completed before information can be stored on a tape. Additionally, the initialization process will set up the tape label and other required parameters, as shown in Figure 7.4. You can also use the INZTAP (Initialize Tape) command to erase data from a tape before you reuse the tape.

Figure 7.3
Display Tape
(DSPTAP) Screen

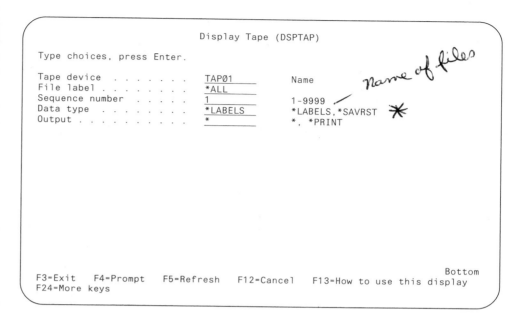

```
                          Display Tape (DSPTAP)

Type choices, press Enter.

Tape device  . . . . . . .     TAP01        Name
File label . . . . . . . .     *ALL
Sequence number  . . . . .     1            1-9999
Data type  . . . . . . . .     *LABELS      *LABELS,*SAVRST
Output . . . . . . . . . .     *            *, *PRINT
```

(handwritten: name of files)

```




                                                              Bottom
 F3=Exit    F4=Prompt    F5=Refresh    F12=Cancel    F13=How to use this display
 F24=More keys
```

To return to the Tape menu from the Display Tape (DSPTAP) Screen,

Press	F3	to return to the TAPE menu
Type	2	to initialize a tape
Press	Enter	

You will now see the Initialize Tape (INZTAP) screen shown in Figure 7.4.

Figure 7.4
Initialize Tape
(INZTAP) Screen

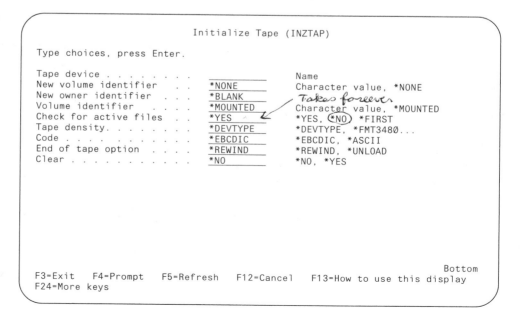

```
                         Initialize Tape (INZTAP)

Type choices, press Enter.

Tape device  . . . . . . . .                  Name
New volume identifier   . .    *NONE          Character value, *NONE
New owner identifier  . . .    *BLANK
Volume identifier  . . . .     *MOUNTED       Character value, *MOUNTED
Check for active files  . .    *YES           *YES, *NO *FIRST
Tape density . . . . . . .     *DEVTYPE       *DEVTYPE, *FMT3480...
Code . . . . . . . . . .       *EBCDIC        *EBCDIC, *ASCII
End of tape option . . . .     *REWIND        *REWIND, *UNLOAD
Clear  . . . . . . . . . .     *NO            *NO, *YES
```

(handwritten: Takes forever)

```




                                                              Bottom
 F3=Exit    F4=Prompt    F5=Refresh    F12=Cancel    F13=How to use this display
 F24=More keys
```

To begin the initialization process, you must enter the "Tape device" parameter. This is the name of your tape drive defined on the Display Tape screen. A maximum of 10 characters is allowed.

The "New volume identifier" parameter, NEWVOL, attaches an internal volume ID name to the tape. Volume IDs help to keep multiple tapes from the same application separate and confirm when a tape is approved for reuse. Volume IDs can have a maximum of six characters.

The "New owner identifier" parameter, NEWOWNID, writes an owner's name to the tape. An application name is commonly used here and is more effective than the owner's name. A maximum of 14 characters is allowed.

The "Volume identifier" parameter, VOL, is the volume name that was attached to this tape the last time it was initialized. To change the volume ID, enter a maximum of six characters. Each tape should have a unique volume ID to avoid unintentionally overwriting data. This parameter value can also be *MOUNTED. If the value is entered as *MOUNTED, the initialization will continue for any tape regardless of the previous name.

The "Check for active files" parameter, CHECK, specifies whether the AS/400 operating system checks for active files on the tape before initialization. If *YES is specified and the system finds data on the tape, the system will not initialize the tape.

The "Tape density" parameter, DENSITY, should always be specified as *DEVTYPE so that the tape is initialized to the density supported by the tape drive.

The collating sequence of the backup refers to the CODE parameter. For continued use on the AS/400, this parameter value should be *EBCDIC. Use the value *ASCII to restore this tape to an ASCII computer system.

The "End of tape" option, ENDOPT, indicates whether the tape should only be rewound, or rewound and unloaded (ejected) after initialization is complete. Generally, *UNLOAD is preferred only for unattended backups.

The "Clear" parameter, CLEAR, defines whether the tape's data is to be deleted before initialization. Clearing the data takes more time and the initialization process will duplicate this step. Therefore, this parameter value is generally *NO.

Diskette Considerations

Diskettes are another magnetic medium you can use for system backup. The AS/400 supports two sizes of diskettes: 8-inch and 5.25-inch. Both diskette types are considered "local" devices on the AS/400. Many AS/400s connect with PCs, which have either 5.25-inch or 3.5-inch diskettes as part of the hardware. We will not discuss these PC diskettes here as a backup medium because they use ASCII as their base language, and they are considered either remote or virtual devices by the AS/400 operating system.

Let's go to the Diskette menu now so you can become familiar with the options there. From the Initialize Tape (INZTAP) screen,

Press   F3   to "Exit"

Type   GO DISKETTE   on the command line

Press   Enter

The Diskette menu shown in Figure 7.5 provides the functions you will need to work with a diskette drive or to resolve a diskette problem.

Figure 7.5
Diskette Menu

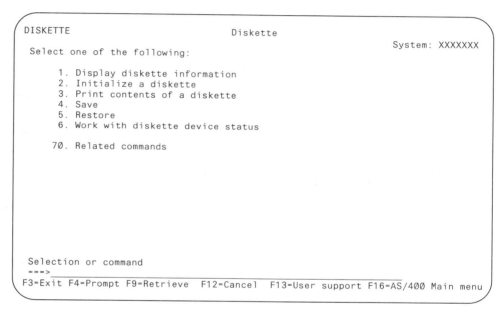

```
DISKETTE                          Diskette
                                                        System: XXXXXXX
   Select one of the following:

        1. Display diskette information
        2. Initialize a diskette
        3. Print contents of a diskette
        4. Save
        5. Restore
        6. Work with diskette device status

       70. Related commands




   Selection or command
   ===>_____
   F3=Exit F4=Prompt F9=Retrieve  F12=Cancel  F13=User support F16=AS/400 Main menu
```

Taking option 1 on the Diskette menu will display the diskette's volume identification and the data file names stored on the diskette. This list is similar to a DOS directory listing and is called a file list. The stored directory information provides you with a summary of data concerning the diskette drive. To access the Display Diskette (DSPDKT) screen shown in Figure 7.6,

Type   1

Press   Enter

As Figure 7.6 shows, the "Diskette device" parameter defines a valid diskette drive. The diskette device name will be required in later processing. The "Output" parameter allows either a spooled file to be generated (*PRINT), or the information to display on the screen (*). If the AS/400 system has multiple diskette drives, you may wish to print the Display Diskette screen to help you remember the correct spelling of the diskette device name. The "Data type" parameter gives you the option to display the label or to display the save/restore information that is stored on the diskette.

Figure 7.6
Display Diskette
(DSPDKT) Screen

```
                              Display Diskette (DSPDKT)

 Type choices, press Enter.

 Diskette device  . . . . . .    DSK01         Name
 Diskette label . . . . . . .    *ALL
 Data type  . . . . . . . . .    *LABELS       *LABELS, *SAVRST
 Output   . . . . . . . . . .    *             *, *PRINT




















                                                                        Bottom
 F3=Exit    F4=Prompt    F5=Refresh    F12=Cancel    F13=How to use this display
 F24=More keys
```

You must initialize a diskette before its first use; you can also use the initialization procedure to remove all data files on a diskette before it is reused. Initializing a diskette serves the same purpose as formatting a DOS diskette.

To access the Initialize Diskette (INZDKT) screen from the Diskette menu,

Press	F3	to cancel the Display Diskette menu
Type	2	to select "Initialize a diskette"
Press	Enter	

As Figure 7.7 shows, you must enter the "Diskette device" parameter (DEV). This is the name of the diskette drive that is holding the diskette that is to be initialized. A maximum of 10 characters is allowed for the device name. You can find this device name in the Display Diskette (DSPDKT) screen (Figure 7.6). The "Data type" parameter on this screen gives you the option to display the labels or to display the save/restore information that is on the diskette. The "Output" parameter allows you to have the information moved to a spooled print file (*PRINT) or allows the information to be displayed on the screen (*).

The "New volume identifier" parameter (NEWVOL) attaches a volume ID name to the diskette. Volume IDs can have a maximum of six characters.

The "New owner identifier" parameter (NEWOWNID) attaches an owner's name for this diskette. Frequently, the owner identifier is an application name.

You use the "Diskette format" parameter (FMT) either for save/restore (*SAVRST) operations or to save other formats for exchange between other systems and the AS/400.

Figure 7.7
Initialize Diskette
(INZDKT) Screen

```
                        Initialize Diskette (INZDKT)

Type choices, press Enter.

Diskette device  . . . . . . . .                        Name
New volume identifier  . . . . .     *NONE              Character value, *NONE
New owner identifier . . . . . .     *BLANK
Diskette format. . . . . . . . .     *DATA              *DATA, 1, 2, 2D, *DATA2...
Sector size. . . . . . . . . . .     *STD               *STD, 128, 256, 512, 1024
Check for active files . . . . .     *YES               *YES, *NO
Code . . . . . . . . . . . . . .     *EBCDIC            *EBCDIC, *ASCII




F3=Exit    F4=Prompt    F5=Refresh    F12=Cancel    F13=How to use this display
F24=More keys
```

The "Sector size" parameter (SCTSIZ) specifies the sector size for the format indicated in the FMT parameter. Sector size is comparable to the tape density parameter. The default standard value *STD is commonly used to ensure that the sector size is supported by the diskette drive.

The "Check for active files" parameter (CHECK) specifies whether the system checks for active files on the diskette. If *YES is specified and the system finds data on the diskette, an error message will halt the initialization. Leave this value at *YES if you would like to be notified if the diskette contains data. If you wish to overwrite all the data files on the diskette, enter *NO.

The "Code" parameter (CODE) is the collating sequence of the backup. For the AS/400, this value should always be *EBCDIC. You can use the value *ASCII if you are going to restore this diskette of information to an ASCII computer system.

To exit the Initialize Diskette screen,

Press   F3

HINT

Another way to erase diskette data is to use the CL command CLRDKT DEV(device name) VOL(*MOUNTED) CHECK(*NO)

HINT

Initialize all tapes and/or diskettes before you begin a backup procedure. Wise operators usually have extra tapes and diskettes prepared, because file sizes generally grow rather than shrink.

HINT

All archived media should have an associated inventory list. This list should include the volume ID and the purpose of the data. The off-site media should be physically inventoried annually.

Reclaiming Storage

Periodically reclaiming storage is important to the maintenance of single-level storage on the AS/400. Remember that single-level storage allows main memory and DASD to be treated as a single accessible unit. As a result of power or equipment failures, an object may be lost or damaged (an object that cannot be found in a library or that has no ownership connection is considered to be lost). A damaged item is not usable. The RCLSTG (Reclaim Storage) command may correct damaged or lost data. The RCLSTG command searches for all objects that are not in a library, all objects without an owner, and all damaged or destroyed objects. When the Reclaim Storage process finds objects that meet these requirements, the system creates a library named QRCL. The RCLSTG command copies these reclaimed objects to the QRCL library and then deletes them from the inappropriate locations. You must run the RCLSTG command interactively from the system console; it cannot be submitted to batch. You must first be sure all subsystems are ended. Finally, it's important to know that reclaiming storage may be a lengthy process, so you should schedule it accordingly.

Cleaning Tasks

After the diskettes and tapes are prepared and storage has been reclaimed, it is important to clean up old files and objects that no longer are useful and should not be saved via backup. Each time a program is compiled, a backup object is created in library QRPLOBJ. The system gives the backup object a name that starts with a Q and ends with a number. In companies that employ programmers, the QRPLOBJ library typically becomes very full. You should routinely clear out these objects with the CLRLIB (Clear Library) command. Using positional notation, you can enter this command as

```
CLRLIB QRPLOBJ
```

and press Enter.

The OS/400 keeps journals, journal receivers, and logs for tracking system activity. These objects accumulate information daily and use DASD storage. Cleaning up old journals and journal receivers helps keep your system running smoothly. You can automatically clean up objects that are no longer needed by scheduling clean-up activities using the Operational Assistant's Cleanup Tasks menu. To access the Cleanup Tasks menu,

Type   GO CLEANUP   on any command line
Press   Enter

The Cleanup Tasks menu will be displayed as shown in Figure 7.8.

Figure 7.8
Cleanup Tasks Menu

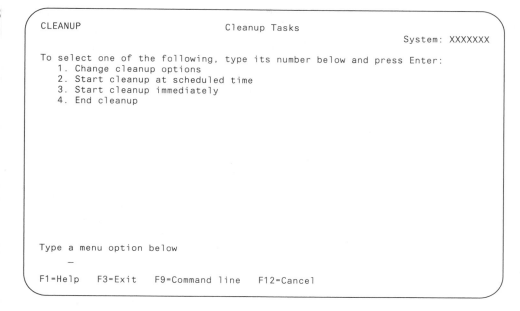

```
CLEANUP                        Cleanup Tasks
                                                      System: XXXXXXX

To select one of the following, type its number below and press Enter:
    1. Change cleanup options
    2. Start cleanup at scheduled time
    3. Start cleanup immediately
    4. End cleanup






Type a menu option below
    _

F1=Help    F3=Exit    F9=Command line    F12=Cancel
```

The Cleanup Tasks menu option 1 allows customization of the cleanup activities. You can also use the CHGCLNUP (Change Cleanup) command to modify the options. The cleanup options include when to automatically start cleanup, what objects to delete, and after how many days. To use the Cleanup command or menu option, you must be signed on as security officer or have been given authority to use this command. Objects located in the QRCL library (created by a Reclaim Storage activity) should be moved to proper locations or deleted if they are unusable.

Option 2 will schedule the cleanup activities to be run automatically. These cleanup tasks are frequently scheduled daily on second or third shift. The CL command to start cleanup at the scheduled time is STRCLNUP OPTION(*SCHED). The cleanup will start automatically at the time specified in option 1.

HINT

You can also access the Cleanup Tasks menu via the Operational Assistant menu. To do so, type GO ASSIST on any command line, then choose "Customize your system, users, and devices" (option 11). Next, select "Cleanup tasks" (option 2).

Option 4 allows you to end the cleanup tasks immediately. "End cleanup" will terminate the cleanup job if it is waiting on the job queue, or you can use the ENDCLNUP command to terminate cleanup activities.

"Start cleanup immediately" starts the cleanup job immediately. This allows the cleanup job to run on demand instead of waiting for its scheduled time. You can also use the CL command STRCLNUP OPTION(*IMMED).

For practice, let's "Start cleanup at the scheduled time." From the Cleanup Tasks menu,

Type   2   on the Cleanup Tasks menu option line
Press   Enter

When the cleanup tasks are completed, you can start the actual system backup.

Running a Backup

Now that the backup plan has been completed, ensuring that all objects will be saved, the diskettes or tapes have been initialized, storage has been reclaimed, and the cleanup tasks are finished, you can start the system backup. As with all AS/400 commands, there are multiple ways to complete a given task. In this text, we will use the Operational Assistant's customization feature.

To access the AS/400 Operational Assistant menu,

Type   GO ASSIST   on the command line
Press   Enter

The AS/400 Operational Assistant menu will be displayed as shown in Figure 7.9.

Figure 7.9
AS/400 Operational
Assistant Menu

```
ASSIST                    AS/400 Operational Assistant Menu
                                                              System: XXXXXXX
 To select one of the following, type its number below and press Enter:

       1. Work with printer output
       2. Work with jobs
       3. Work with messages
       4. Send messages
       5. Change your password

      10. Manage your system, users, and devices
      11. Customize your system, users, and devices

      75. Information and problem handling

      80. Temporary sign-off




 Type a menu option below
   __

 F1=Help    F3=Exit    F9=Command line    F12=Cancel
```

From this menu, select option 11, "Customize your system, users, and devices."

Type   11   as your menu option choice

Press   Enter

The customization menu, as shown in Figure 7.10, provides access to the backup procedures.

HINT

You can access the customization menu directly by typing GO SETUP on any command line.

Figure 7.10
Customize Your System, Users, and Devices Menu

```
 SETUP                 Customize Your System, Users, and Devices
                                                          System: XXXXXXX
 To select an option, type its number below and press Enter:

       1. Change system options
       2. Cleanup tasks
       3. Power on and off tasks
       4. Disk space tasks
       5. Backup tasks

      11. Change passwords for IBM-supplied users

      20. Communications configuration tasks




 Type a menu option below
       __

 F1=Help   F3=Exit   F9=Command line   F12=Cancel
```

To begin the backup tasks from the Customize your System, Users, and Devices menu,

Type   5   as your menu choice

Press   Enter

The Backup Tasks menu will be displayed, as shown in Figure 7.11.

Figure 7.11
Backup Tasks Menu

```
 BACKUP                        Backup Tasks
                                                           System: XXXXXXX
 To select one of the following, type its number below and press Enter:

     1. Run backup
     2. Display backup status

    10. Set up backup

    20. Initialize a tape
    21. Initialize a tape set




 Type a menu option below
   __
   F1=Help    F3=Exit    F9=Command line    F12=Cancel
```

If your Security Officer has created a backup procedure for your system, choose option number 1 in Figure 7.11. Otherwise, you can only use the "Set up backup" option if you are signed on with either Security Officer authority or have been granted authority to use this menu. For practice purposes, assume you have this authority and choose the "Set up backup" option:

Type   10   for "Set up backup"

Press   Enter

The Set Up Backup menu will be displayed as shown in Figure 7.12. This menu allows for changes to the daily, weekly, or monthly backup procedures. Additionally, you can change the library backup list, the folders backup list, or the backup schedule from this menu.

After you have defined the backup procedures as appropriate, press F3 to return to the Backup Tasks menu (shown in Figure 7.11).

The backup procedures should be run under a user profile with *SAVSYS (Save System) authority. SAVSYS authority speeds up the backup because the system does not have to perform authority checking on each object.

Restricting access to the system when you are performing saves is a good practice. Many save commands do not require restricted access, but that is the only way to ensure the save contains the most current object a user may be using. If any user has an update or exclusive lock on a file while you run your backups, the object cannot be saved.

Before you do a restricted backup, send all users a message telling them to sign off the system. Use the SNDMSG (Send Message) command or the SNDBRKMSG (Send Break Message) command. For either command, always

Figure 7.12
Set Up Backup Menu

```
 SETUPBCKUP                        Set Up Backup
                                                         System: XXXXXXX
 To select one of the following, type its number below and press Enter:

        1. Change daily backup options
        2. Change weekly backup options
        3. Change monthly backup options

       10. Change library backup list
       11. Change folder backup list

       20. Change backup schedule




 Type a menu option below
    __

  F1=Help    F3=Exit    F9=Command line    F12=Cancel
```

specify the time the system will be taken down and when the users can expect the system to be available.

You must end all subsystems except the controlling subsystem QCTL for a complete system save. Use the ENDSBS (End Subsystem) command for each subsystem. As an alternative to using separate ENDSBS commands, you can use the ENDSYS (End System) command, which ends all subsystems and brings the system to a restricted state.

Now you are ready to do the system backup. Choose option 1, "Run backup," to begin copying data to the tapes. Follow the displayed instructions until the backup is complete.

Using Save Files

If your backup strategy requires that you occasionally do an unattended backup, when you might not have an operator available to change tapes, you can consider the option of saving objects to a "save file." A save file is an object you as the operator must create to hold a compressed version of backed-up objects. All the objects you have requested for backup will be compressed and placed into this save file. The save file can be transferred to a tape at a later date.

HINT

You cannot do a save operation on a file that is being updated or that is allocated exclusively to another job, with the exception of a journal receiver.

It is important to use caution in this process, because saving to a save file requires a great deal of DASD. Make sure that, when the amount of memory required by the files you are saving is added to existing DASD storage, you will not be creating a total DASD usage in excess of 80 percent. DASD usage in excess of 90 percent will seriously degrade system performance. And if an error is made and DASD is over-committed (more than 100 percent), then it will be necessary to do a total reload of the system.

To create a save file, use the following CL command:

Press F9 to display a command line

Type CRTSAVF on any command line

Press F4 to prompt

The Create Save File screen will be displayed as shown in Figure 7.13.

Figure 7.13
Create Save File
(CRTSAVF) Screen

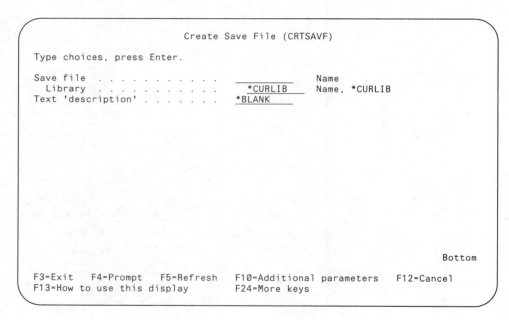

```
                          Create Save File (CRTSAVF)
 Type choices, press Enter.

 Save file . . . . . . . . . . .  _____   Name
   Library . . . . . . . . . .   *CURLIB     Name, *CURLIB
 Text 'description' . . . . . . .  *BLANK



                                                                       Bottom
 F3=Exit   F4=Prompt   F5=Refresh   F10=Additional parameters   F12=Cancel
 F13=How to use this display        F24=More keys
```

To practice creating a save file, on the Create Save File (CRTSAVF) screen,

Type Your name for a practice "save file" name. (A descriptive name usually is preferred.)

Type Practice as the text description of the file

Press Enter

After you have created a save file to store information, save your library to the save file using the SAVLIB command.

Type SAVLIB on the command line

Press F4 to prompt

At this point, the Save Library screen will be displayed, as shown in Figure 7.14.

Figure 7.14
Save Library
(SAVLIB) Screen

```
                           Save Library (SAVLIB)

Type choices, press Enter.

Library  . . . . . . . . . . . .   _____   Name, *NONSYS, *ALLUSR, *IBM
                 + for more values  _____
Device . . . . . . . . . . . . .   _____   Name, *SAVF
                 + for more values
Volume identifier  . . . . . . .   *MOUNTED     Character value, *MOUNTED
                 + for more values
Sequence number  . . . . . . . .   *END         1-9999, *END
Label  . . . . . . . . . . . . .   *LIB
File expiration date . . . . . .   *PERM        Date, *PERM
End of tape option . . . . . . .   *REWIND      *REWIND, *LEAVE, *UNLOAD




F3=Exit    F4=Prompt    F5=Refresh    F10=Additional parameters    F12=Cancel
F13=How to use this display          F24=More keys
```

To execute the SAVLIB command, enter the following value:

Type   Your name   for library name

Type   *SAVF   for device

Press   Enter

This command saves your entire library to a save file on disk. After a save file exists on disk, you can copy it to tape with the SAVSAVFDTA command (see Figure 7.15).

Restoring Objects

Hopefully, the ultimate disaster will not strike your system, but it is important to be organized and prepared if the worst should happen. You must use the restore commands, with the corresponding save commands, to replace damaged or deleted objects. At first glance, our sample backup plan may appear to be overkill. However, you can only restore objects in a certain way. In other words, how the objects were saved determines how the restore can be executed. The sample backup plan furnished in the text provides flexibility for restoring quickly.

Before any backup plan is complete, you must be sure that full system backups are done on the Alternate Load IPL Device. An initial program load (IPL) requires that the tape device be specified as the Alternate Load IPL device. Check with your system administrator to see which device is your Alternate Load IPL Device.

Figure 7.15
Save Save File Data
(SAVSAVFDTA) Screen

```
                    Save Save File Data (SAVSAVFDTA)

Type choices, press Enter.

Save file . . . . . . . . . . .                      Name
  Library  . . . . . . . . . .    *LIBL             Name, *LIBL, *CURLIB
Device . . . . . . . . . . . .                       Name
            + for more values
Volume identifier  . . . . . .    *MOUNTED           Character value, *MOUNTED
            + for more values
Sequence number . . . . . . . .   *END               1-9999, *END
End of Tape option . . . . . .    *REWIND            *REWIND, *LEAVE, *UNLOAD
Clear . . . . . . . . . . . .     *NONE              *NONE, *ALL, *AFTER

                       Additional Parameters

File expiration date . . . . .    *PERM              Date, *PERM
Data compaction . . . . . . . .   *DEV               *DEV, *NO
Output . . . . . . . . . . . .    *NONE              *NONE, *PRINT, *OUTFILE


                                                              More...
F3=Exit   F4=Prompt   F5=Refresh   F12=Cancel   F13=How to use this display
F24=More keys
```

To completely restore your system, you should take the following steps:

1. Restore licensed Internal Code (LIC) and Model Unique Licensed Internal Code (MULIC). IBM's *Backup: Recovery — Basic Guide*, explains how to restore the LIC and MULIC. Restore the LIC from your most recent SAVSYS tapes.

   If your system displays system reference code A6xx6051 (where *xx* is a MULIC tape number), restore the MULIC from your service kit tapes. Then restore the operating system from your SAVSYS tapes.

   Your sign-on must be as the Security Officer, QSECOFR. If the Security Officer's password has changed since the last system save, you must use the old password to ensure a password match.

2. Type GO RESTORE and press Enter to go to the Restore menu.

3. Take Option 21, "System and user data." This will restore all the IBM Licensed Program Products, user libraries, document library objects, and IFS objects, all with full prompting.

4. At the End Subsystem command prompt, press Enter.

5. Press Enter to respond to informational messages.

6. At the User Profile command prompt screen,
   - Press F10 for additional parameters.
   - Change "Allow object differences" to *ALL.
   - Change "Output member options replace or add records" to *ADD.
   - Press Enter.

7. At the Configuration command prompt screen,
   - Change "System resource management" to *NONE.
   - Press F10 for additional parameters.
   - Change "Allow object differences" to *ALL.
   - Change "Output member options replace or add records" to *ADD.
   - Press Enter.

8. At the Restore Library command prompt,
   - Press F10 for additional parameters.
   - Change "Database member option" to *ALL.
   - Change "Allow object differences" to *ALL.
   - Change "Output member options replace or add records" to *ADD.
   - Press Enter.

9. At the Restore Document Library Objects command,
   - Press F10 for additional parameters.
   - Change "Allow object differences" to *ALL.
   - Change "Output member options replace or add records" to *ADD.
   - Press Enter.

10. At the Restore Authority command, press Enter.

11. At the Start Subsystems command, press F3 to exit.

12. Type SIGNOFF *LIST to send the JOBLOG to an output queue and press Enter.

13. Sign on.

14. Turn the keylock to normal.

15. Type PWRDWNSYS *IMMED and press Enter.

16. When the IPL is complete, use DSPTAP to inventory the latest SAVCHGOBJ tapes so you know which libraries and objects are represented.

17. Using the DSPTAP lists, use the RSTOBJ command to restore changed objects.

When a complete system restore is not required, you may find it more convenient to use the following menu options:

Type   GO RESTORE   on the command line
Press   Enter

Figure 7.16 displays the restore commands explained earlier in the text. Use the prompt screen for additional options.

Figure 7.16
Restore Menu

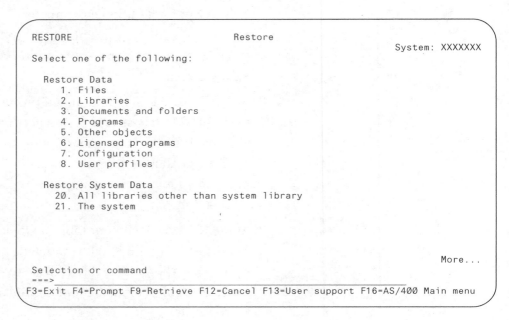

As we've said, the need to restore an object or to recover from a disaster will, hopefully, never occur; but good planning and documentation will provide an organized process to correct any unforeseen problems. Regular system backups are a necessary prerequisite for peace of mind.

Program Temporary Fixes (PTFs)

When IBM becomes aware of a problem in its software (problems are either discovered by IBM staff or reported to IBM by AS/400 users), IBM first generates an authorized program analysis report (APAR) to study the problem. If necessary, IBM creates a program temporary fix (PTF) to correct the problem. A PTF is labeled temporary because IBM documents the problem and incorporates the correction into the next release or modification of the software. When a PTF is generated, it usually corrects one problem and is called an individual PTF. However, IBM also puts together cumulative (CUM) PTF packages, which are aggregates of the individual PTFs. A convenient way for you to manage PTFs is through the cumulative PTF packages.

Individual PTFs include a cover letter that explains what device or software required the correction, as well as other pertinent information. Always read the cover letter, because you may find important information there about how the PTF will correct a problem your system may be experiencing. Follow the instructions exactly.

You can order PTFs through IBM's Electronic Customer Support (ECS) system. When you use ECS, the cover letter is stored in a file named

QAPZCOVER in the QGPL library. Version 2 users will note that the QAPZCOVER file will contain a member name starting with a P followed by the PTF number. Version 3 users will note that the member name now starts with a Q. To display the cover letter, use the DSPPFM (Display Physical File Member) command or print the cover letter with the CPYF (Copy File) command, specifying QSYSPRT for the "To file" parameter.

High-impact and pervasive (HIPER) PTFs are critical PTFs, because they fix problems that can crash the computer or severely degrade performance, or they correct a multitude of machine problems. HIPER PTFs are usually in a separate classification from other PTFs and should receive top priority to be loaded onto the system.

To order individual PTFs, you will need the PTF number. IBM has created some reserved PTF numbers that you can use to order particular types of PTFs. In the list that follows in Figure 7.17, **v** is the OS/400 version number, **r** is the release number, and **m** is the modification level. Therefore, for V3R1M0, **vrm** would be replaced by 310. Note that some of the PTFs are informational reports, not program objects.

Figure 7.17
PTF Numbers and Related Descriptions

Number	Description
MF98vrm	Preventive service planning information report for licensed internal code.
SF97vrm	PTF summary listing.
SF98vrm	Preventive service planning information report for licensed programs. Includes the date of the latest CUM PTF package.
SF99vrm	CUM PTF package.
SHnnnnn	Individual PTF for MAPICS or CMAS. Each *n* represents a numeral of a five-digit sequence number.

To order PTFs through ECS, use the SNDPTFORD (Send Program Temporary Fix Order) command. In Figure 7.18, the parameter "PTF Parts" offers a choice of receiving the cover letter and the PTF code, *ALL, or just the cover letter, *CVRLTR. Because your particular AS/400 may not have the hardware or the software associated with the PTF, it may be helpful to initially download only the cover letters.

The "Delivery method" parameter with the *ANY value indicates that if the PTF is small enough, it should be transmitted electronically through the ECS modem line. Most PTF listings and reports are delivered electronically. The delivery method parameter of *ANY is replaced with the *LINKONLY value and the PTF is sent through the ECS line. The ECS program will download the PTF save file to DASD. If the PTF exceeds the *LINKONLY size, such as with a CUM PTF, IBM will mail a tape within 48 hours of when you placed the order.

The "Order parameter" with the *REQUIRED value performs additional PTF verification. If the needed PTF has a prerequisite, both PTFs will be sent. You can request the *PTFID value, which lists the prerequisite PFT IDs. This may be helpful to determine whether the earlier PTF has previously been installed.

The "Reorder parameter" value can be either *YES or *NO. Specifying *NO will cause the system to check whether the PTF is already loaded and/or applied on your system. If the PTF is loaded, the SNDPTFORD command ends with an error. The system is attempting to avoid a duplicate order.

To reorder the cover letter only, specify *CVRLTR for the value of the "PTF parts" parameter and change the "Reorder" parameter to *YES.

Figure 7.18
Send PTF Order
(SNDPTFORD) Screen

```
                        Send PTF Order (SNDPTFORD)

 Type choices, press Enter.

 PTF description:
   PTF identifier . . . . .   SF99250      Character value
   Product  . . . . . . . .   *ONLYPRD     F4 for list
   Release  . . . . . . . .   *ONLYRLS     *ONLYRLS, VxRxMx
           + for more values
 PTF parts  . . . . . . . .   *ALL         *ALL, *CVRLTR
 Remote control point . . .   *IBMSRV      Name, *IBMSRV, *SELECT
 Remote network identifier    *NETATR      Name, *NETATR

                        Additional Parameters

 Delivery method  . . . . .   *ANY         *ANY, *LINKONLY
 Order  . . . . . . . . . .   *REQUIRED    *REQUIRED, *PTFID
 Reorder  . . . . . . . . .   *NO          *NO, *YES

                                                              Bottom
 F3=Exit  F4=Prompt  F5=Refresh  F12=Cancel  F13=How to use this display
 F24=More keys
```

Figure 7.18 shows a sample of an order for an individual PTF. To order a cumulative PTF package, type the following command: SNDPTFORD SF99vrm. The vrm is the version, release, and modification level of your system. For example, to order a CUM tape for Version 3 Release 1 Modification level 0, type SNDPTFORD SF99310.

Loading Individual PTFs

From time to time, you may need to apply individual PTFs. You can order them in small groups of up to 20 at a time via the ECS modem. If the ECS modem is a 2400 bps modem, or if the quantity of PTFs is more than just a few, then you can change the DELIVERY method to *ANY, so you can receive the PTFs on tape. Custom Preventive Service Packages are usually mailed within 48 hours after order placement..

PTFs are of two general types: Microcode Fixes, or PTFs that begin with MF; and System Fixes, for all other PTFs that begin with SF. All PTFs can be applied Permanent, applied Temporary, and some may be applied

Immediate. Most fixes are best applied Temporary, but occasionally they must be applied Permanent right away. Consult the cover letter that comes with the PTF. Look for special instructions, and follow them. You can usually remove temporarily applied PTFs if they cause a problem. You cannot remove permanently applied PTFs.

PTFs usually require an IPL before they are applied. There are PTFs that you can apply "Immediate." Even PTFs that are "Immediate" usually carry special instructions to become active, and they may be more conveniently applied with the next unattended IPL.

Any and all PTFs can be Loaded and Applied during regular hours and marked for "Apply at the next IPL." Because you can normally do an IPL after a weekly unattended full-system save, the PTFs will be applied without any additional effort. You should be aware that applying PTFs during an IPL can greatly increase how long it will take to perform the IPL.

Microcode Fixes (MFs) carry special importance because they affect basic machine functions, or those basic services that are below the machine interface (MI). Because of their importance, there are actually two copies of these fixes: One group contains all the Permanently applied MFs and is called the A side; the other group contains all of the MFs, including the latest Temporary applied MF PTFs. Because of the importance of the Microcode to the entire computing environment, if a new Temporary applied MF PTF causes a problem, the system can be IPLed to the A side and, in essence, be restored immediately.

The front panel of the AS/400 can show an A or a B, but that is not the best place to look to see on which "side" of the Microcode the system is running. Often, during the automatic install process of a CUM tape, the front panel can show A but the system is actually running on the B side. The system is just looking ahead. To make sure, type DSPPTF and press Enter. The first group of PTFs displayed will be the MFs, and the top of the screen is the last IPL source. Most systems in a normal production environment should run on the B side. Most temporary PTFs are running on the B side. When the PTFs are made permanent, they are, essentially, copied to the A side; the machine will then IPL from side A.

Figure 7.19 displays the Program Temporary Fix menu. All the options needed to manage PTFs are located on this menu. Temporary fixes that are not transferred electronically from ECS are mailed either on tape or diskette media, and they need to be loaded onto the system.

To access the Program Temporary Fix (PTF) menu,

Type   GO PTF on any command line

Press   Enter

Option 1 on the above menu loads individual PTFs from tape, diskette, or a save file (*SAVF). (Remember, a save file is a compressed and unreadable file.) To load a PTF,

Figure 7.19
Program Temporary
Fix (PTF) Menu

```
 PTF                        Program Temporary Fix (PTF)
                                                              System: XXXXXXX
 Select one of the following:

       1. Load a program temporary fix
       2. Apply a program temporary fix
       3. Copy a program temporary fix
       4. Remove a program temporary fix
       5. Display a program temporary fix
       6. Order a program temporary fix
       7. Install a program temporary fix from a list
       8. Install program temporary fix package

      70. Related commands




 Selection or command
 ===> _____

 F3=Exit F4=Prompt  F9=Retrieve   F12=Cancel   F13=User support
```

Type	1	"Load a program temporary fix" option
Press		Enter

This will take you to the Load Program Temporary Fix (LODPTF) screen, shown in Figure 7.20. The "PTF numbers to select" and the "PTF numbers to omit" options shown in this figure are referring to the PTF numbers that identify the PTFs. All PTFs are identified by a unique number, to connect the PTF with the hardware device or application software problem that necessitates the correction.

Now let's return to the Program Temporary Fix (PTF) menu:

Press	F3	to "Exit"

Loading Cumulative PTFs

CUM tapes should be installed using the instructions sent with the tape. Usually, those instructions will lead you through many preparatory steps that are necessary to ensure the successful installation on the CUM PTFs. The CUM tape can be installed during normal business hours. Just remember to change the option "Automatic IPL after install?", as shown in Figure 7.21, to *NO. Additional PTFs may also be applied and marked for IPL action. Then let the next unattended IPL, after the dedicated system save, apply all the above.

Now you're ready to load the cumulative PTFs. From the Program Temporary Fix (PTF) menu,

Type	8	to "Install program temporary fix package"
Press	Enter	

Figure 7.20
Load Program Temporary
Fix (LODPTF) Screen

```
                        Load Program Temporary Fix (LODPTF)

 Type choices, press Enter.

 Product  . . . . . . . .   _____      F4 for list
 Device . . . . . . . . .   *SERVICE      Name, *SERVICE, *SAVF
 PTF numbers to select  .   *ALL          Character value, *ALL
     + for more values
 PTF numbers to omit. . .   _____      Character value
     + for more values
 Superseded PTFs  . . . .   *APYPERM      *APYPERM, *NOAPY
 Release  . . . . . . . .   *ONLY         *ONLY, VxRxMx




                                                                  Bottom
 F3=Exit   F4=Prompt   F5=Refresh   F12=Cancel  F13=How to use this display
 F24=More keys
```

Figure 7.21
Install Options for
Program Temporary
Fixes Screen

```
                Install Options for Program Temporary Fixes
                                                      System: XXXXXXX
 Type choices, press Enter.

    Device . . . . . . .  _____      Name, *SERVICE

    Automatic IPL  . . .     Y          Y=Yes
      N=No

    PTF type . . . . . .     1          1=All PTFs
                                        2=HIPER PTFs and HIPER LIC fixes only
                                        3=HIPER LIC fixes only




 F3=Exit   F12=Cancel
```

Verifying PTF Installation

Use the Manage Licensed Programs menu to verify that the PTFs were successfully installed. To access this menu,

Type   GO LICPGM   to display the Manage Licensed Programs menu
Press   Enter

Type	50	to review PTF installations
Press	Enter	
Press	Enter	again, to view PTF installation messages

The system presents a series of messages that inform you whether the PTF was installed successfully. Look for the word "failed" anywhere in the messages, such as "Loading of PTFs failed" or "Marking of PTFs delayed, application failed" or even "Applying PTFs failed." Occasionally, IBM issues PTFs that do more damage than good; these PTFs are reported in the HIPER PTF packages as "PTFs in error." Anytime before a PTF is applied permanently, you can remove it with the "Remove a program temporary fix," option 4, on your Program Temporary Fix menu. Ensure that the PTFs are, in fact, working properly before you apply them permanently.

To return to the PTF menu,

Press	F3	to "Exit"

Anytime after you load and/or apply PTFs, and before you apply PTFs permanently, you should display them. The DSPPTF (Display PTF) command, in its simplest form, provides a list of all PTFs currently on the system and their status. The status can be applied temporarily, permanently, loaded, or superseded. To display the PTF status, go to the PTF menu, then

Type	5	on the PTF menu option line
Press	Enter	

This will take you to the Display Program Temporary Fix (DSPPTF) screen, shown in Figure 7.22.

Figure 7.22
Display Program
Temporary Fix
(DSPPTF) Screen

```
                      Display Program Temporary Fix (DSPPTF)

 Type choices, press Enter.

 Product  . . . . . . . . . . .      *ALL      F4 for list
 PTF numbers to select  . . . . .    *ALL      Character value, *ALL...
 Release  . . . . . . . . . . .      *ALL      *ALL, VxRxMx
 Cover letter only  . . . . . . .    *NO       *NO, *YES
 Output . . . . . . . . . . . .      *         *, *PRINT, *OUTFILE












                                                                       Bottom
 F3=Exit   F4=Prompt   F5=Refresh   F12=Cancel   F13=How to use this display
 F24=More keys
```

This additional information is brief (and sometimes confusing), but it can be helpful. The DSPPTF (Display Program Temporary Fix) command accepts several parameters to help you narrow the list of PTFs. For example, prompt the "Product" parameter to select just the PTFs for a particular application package. Request that the list be sent to *PRINT to generate a spooled output file, then place the report with other system documentation.

To return to the PTF menu,

Press   F3   to "Exit"

PTFs are a necessary part of AS/400 maintenance. We recommend that you load and apply a CUM PTF package every three or four months. If your system has problems that you can't seem to pinpoint, the solution may already be waiting in a PTF. To further avoid problems, you should keep a printed list of all PTFs near the CPU. If your computer is experiencing problems and cannot IPL, this list can be very beneficial to the IBM support group as they help you resolve the problems.

Key Terms

Backup
PTF
   cumulative
   temporary

Review Questions

1. Why should you have an AS/400 system backup plan?

2. Why does the system require several different save commands?

3. Why does the system require several different restore commands?

4. Why does the AS/400 accumulate files that need to be deleted by the operator or the automatic clean-up process?

5. Why is it necessary to initialized tapes and diskettes? What other purpose will initialization serve?

6. The "Delivery method" parameter with the SNDPTFORD command defines what? What is the difference between the value choices? Why choose either one?

7. PTFs should be loaded and installed on what area displayed on the CPU panel?

Exercises

1. Create a sample backup plan.

2. Print a program temporary fix list for the OS/400.

3. Create a "save file" of your library.

Chapter 8

Subsystems and Performance

Subsystems

As we mentioned in Chapter 1, all work on the AS/400 is carried out in subsystems. Subsystems are started when the AS/400 powers up and loads the operating system and other necessary objects into main memory. When the AS/400 is first installed, practically all work, including interactive and batch jobs, is performed by subsystem QBASE. This simple arrangement is convenient for installation but doesn't take advantage of the system's capabilities. Separating the work load into additional subsystems improves performance; in fact, some individual software applications available on the AS/400 are designed to run in their own subsystems. Many administrators have found maximum AS/400 efficiency by placing each specific type of job into its own subsystem. For example, establishing separate subsystems for batch, interactive, and communications jobs provides much more control over creating system performance consistency.

The AS/400 comes preloaded with the basic subsystems to be used in a multiple subsystem configuration: QCTL, QINTER, QSPL, QCMN, and QBATCH. QCTL is the controlling subsystem in a multiple subsystem configuration. QINTER is the subsystem that supports interactive jobs. The QSPL subsystem handles spooled file jobs, including placing files or jobs into disk storage for later processing or printing. The QCMN subsystem supports communications jobs. Finally, QBATCH is the subsystem that supports batch jobs. Although the AS/400 allows for virtually any combination of jobs within subsystems, you should not override the defaults because doing so will reduce the system's efficiency.

The system console is attached to the QCTL subsystem. This configuration is important for many reasons, but the most important concerns IPL. When the AS/400 performs an IPL, the system console is the only display station capable of carrying out functions until the IPL is complete. Specifically, QCTL begins an auto-start job at IPL. The auto-start job then starts the four system-supplied subsystems: QINTER, QSPL, QCMN, and QBATCH.

Each time a subsystem is created, a subsystem description is required. A subsystem description is another type of object. Changing from a single subsystem to multiple subsystems is a very simple procedure. The system value QCTLSBSD (Controlling Subsystem Description) holds the name of the initial subsystem. If you change the name of the controlling subsystem to QCTL, the AS/400 understands to start using multiple subsystems.

HINT

To change the controlling subsystem requires Security Officer authority. If you have the appropriate authority, you would use the CHGSYSVAL (Change System Value) command to change your controlling subsystem.

To check whether the controlling subsystem on your AS/400 is QCTL, use the DSPSYSVAL (Display System Value) command, as shown below.

Type	DSPSYSVAL	on any command line
Press	F4	to prompt for DSPSYSVAL command parameters
Type	QCTLSBSD	for the "System value" parameter
Press	Enter	

You will be shown the Display System Value screen, represented in Figure 8.1, which displays the value for the controlling subsystem. In this example, QCTL is the controlling subsystem and it is located in library QSYS.

To work with a subsystem on the AS/400, use the WRKSBS (Work with Subsystem) command. To designate a particular subsystem, type WRKSBS [subsystem name] using positional notation. The default for the name of the

Figure 8.1
Display System
Value Screen

```
                              Display System Value


    System value . . . . . :   QCTLSBSD
    Description  . . . . . :    Controlling subsystem


    Controlling subsystem  . . . :    QCTL
      Library  . . . . . . . . . :      QSYS












    Press Enter to continue.

    F3=Exit    F12=Cancel
```

subsystem parameter is *ALL. To access the Work with Subsystems screen
(shown in Figure 8.2),

Press	Enter	to exit the DSPSYSVAL screen
Type	WRKSBS	on the command line
Press	Enter	

Figure 8.2
Work with
Subsystems Screen

```
                              Work with Subsystems
                                                         System: XXXXXXX

    Type options, press Enter.
      4=End subsystem   5=Display subsystem description
      8=Work with subsystem jobs


                         Total     ------Subsystem Pools------------
    Opt  Subsystem    Storage (K)  1  2  3  4  5  6  7  8  9 10  _
    __   QBATCH            0        2
    __   QCMN              0        2
    __   QCTL              0        2
    __   QINTER            0        2  4
    __   QSPL              0        2  3
    __   QSYSWRK           0        2
    __   QTCP              0        2
    __   QXFPCS            0        2



                                                          Bottom
    Parameters or command
    ==>_____
    F3=Exit   F5=Refresh   F11=Display system data    F12=Cancel
    F14=Work with system status
```

The Work with Subsystems screen shows all the subsystems that are currently active. If a subsystem is not active, it will not be displayed.

HINT

To start a subsystem, use the STRSBS (Start Subsystem) command on any command line.

The WRKSBS display lets you as the system operator "Work with subsystem jobs" by typing 8 in the option column next to the appropriate name of the subsystem. This is a convenient way to verify if, and how many, jobs are running in a subsystem.

System Pools

As we have discussed, subsystems are generally created to improve system performance for different departments, or for different users' needs. Each subsystem is defined to run in a system pool based on how many resources the job is likely to require. A system pool, also called a storage pool, is a logical division of main memory reserved for processing a job or group of jobs. AS/400 subsystems are preassigned to main memory pools by the operating system.

We can compare system pools to multiple swimming pools. A reasonable approach to sharing the swimming pools would be to dedicate each swimming pool to a particular type of swimmer. One pool might be dedicated to lap swimming, one to diving practice, and one to children for splashing and playing. System pools work in the same way, with work divided into types of jobs.

Each storage pool has a predefined size and activity level. Activity levels are the maximum number of jobs that can be run simultaneously in the particular storage pool. We can also relate activity levels to the swimming pools example. The lap pool might only have eight lanes, while the diving pool may be able to efficiently handle a dozen divers, and the children's pool may have a maximum limit of 75 children.

By limiting the number of jobs sharing the storage pool, each job secures just enough resources to run efficiently. Having a large number specified for the activity level will allow many more jobs to enter main storage. These jobs will compete for system resources, ultimately slowing the completion of all the jobs.

When the AS/400 is shipped, all of main storage resides in two system pools: the machine pool (*MACHINE) and the base pool (*BASE). The machine pool must be defined to support your system hardware; the amount of main storage allocated to the machine pool is hardware-dependent and varies with each AS/400.

The base pool is the main storage that remains after the machine pool is reserved. *BASE can be designated as a shared pool for all subsystems to use to process work, or *BASE can be divided into smaller pools of shared and private main storage. Other shared storage pools you can define include *INTERACT (for interactive jobs), *SPOOL (for printers), and *SHRPOOL 1 to *SHRPOOL 10 (for pools that you can define for your own purposes).

Shared pool sizes are controlled via the CHGSHRPOOL (Change Shared Storage Pool) or WRKSHRPOOL (Work with Shared Storage Pools) commands. Figure 8.3 shows a WRKSHRPOOL screen, on which the pool size or activity level can be modified simply by changing the entries.

Figure 8.3
Work with Shared Pools Screen

```
                        Work with Shared Pools
                                                    System:    xxxxxxx
  Main storage size (K)  . :        8192

  Type changes (if allowed), press Enter.

              Defined    Max    Allocated   Pool   -Paging Option--
  Pool        Size (K)  Active  Size (K)     ID    Defined  Current
  *MACHINE      5480     +++       5480       1     *FIXED   *FIXED
  *BASE         1478       4       1478       2     *CALC    *CALC
  *INTERACT     1202       4       1202       3     *CALC    *CALC
  *SPOOL          32       1         32       4     *CALC    *CALC
  *SHRPOOL1        0       0                        *FIXED
  *SHRPOOL2        0       0                        *FIXED
  *SHRPOOL3        0       0                        *FIXED
  *SHRPOOL4        0       0                        *FIXED
  *SHRPOOL5        0       0                        *FIXED
  *SHRPOOL6        0       0                        *FIXED


                                                          More...
  Command
  ===>
  F3=Exit    F4=Prompt    F5=Refresh    F9=Retrieve    F11=Display text
  F12=Cancel
```

The AS/400's default controlling subsystem (QBASE) and the default spooling subsystem (QSPL) are configured to take advantage of shared pools. QBASE uses the *BASE pool and the *INTERACT pool, while QSPL uses *BASE and *SPOOL.

To see what pools a subsystem is using, use the DSPSBSD (Display Subsystem Description) command; for instance, when you execute the command in keyword notation:

```
DSPSBSD QBASE OUTPUT(*PRINT)
```

the following pool definitions for QBASE will be listed (if the defaults have not been changed):

```
QBASE   ((1 *BASE) (2 INTERACT))
```

The parentheses group together two definitions, each containing two distinct parts (the subsystem pool number and size. In this example of the QBASE pool definitions, the (1 *BASE) represents the subsystem pool number of 1 and the special value of *BASE to indicate the pool size, meaning that the system will use all of the *BASE as a shared pool. A third part of the pool definition doesn't appear on this screen: the activity level. The system value QBASACTLVL contains this value. The second pool definition for QBASE is (2 *INTERACT). Because pools can be modified by other commands (such as

CHGSHRPOOL or WRKSHRPOOL), the activity level is not listed for this subsystem description.

Be careful not to confuse *subsystem* pool numbering with *system* pool numbering. The AS/400's two predefined system pools, *MACHINE and *BASE, are defined as system pool number 1 and system pool number 2, respectively. (The *MACHINE storage pool is reserved for hardware needs. The *BASE storage pool is shared and drawn from as needed for batch jobs or other jobs not able to acquire enough memory from other pools. The *SPOOL storage pool is used for spooling output jobs, and the *INTERACT pool is used for interactive jobs. The values for pools will vary depending on your system hardware resources.)

Pool numbering within a subsystem is unique to that subsystem, and only the routing entries in that subsystem use it to determine which pool jobs will use, based on the routing data associated with each job. As subsystems define new storage pools (shared or private) in addition to the two predefined system pools, the system simply assigns the next available system pool number to use as a reference on the WRKSYSSTS display.

For example, with the above pools for QBASE and the following pools for QSPL,

```
QSPL    ((1 *BASE) (2 *SPOOL))
```

the system pool numbering might correspond to the subsystem pool numbering shown in Figure 8.4.

Figure 8.4
System and Subsystem
Pool Numbering

	Subsystem Pool Number	
System Pool Number	**QBASE**	**QSPL**
1 Machine Pool		
2 *BASE Pool	1	1
3 *INTERACT Shared Pool	2	
4 *SPOOL Shared Pool		2

A private pool is a specific allocation of main storage reserved for one subsystem. It's common to use a private pool when the system uses the controlling subsystem QCTL instead of QBASE. Although using QBASE as the controlling subsystem lets you divide main storage into separate pools, using QCTL is inherently easier to manage and administer in terms of controlling the number of jobs and performance tuning.

Now let's look again at Figure 8.2 (page 155). In this example, the Subsystem Pools area (numbered 1-10) identifies which system storage pools are used by each subsystem storage identifier. The numbers below the Subsystem Pools heading, which correspond to the subsystem name, are the identifiers for the system pools. To attach a name to the system pool number in use, you will need to access the WRKSYSSTS (Work with System Status) display, shown in Figure 8.5. To do so,

Type   WRKSYSSTS   on the command line

Press   Enter

The System Pool column in Figure 8.5 displays the number that corresponds to the system pool numbers displayed vertically in Figure 8.2 on the Work with Subsystems display.

Figure 8.5

Work with System Status Screen

```
                              Work with System Status               xxxxxxx
                                                      04/09/96  15:27:23
  % CPU used . . . . . :        7.1    Auxiliary storage:
  Elapsed time . . . . :    00:07:54     System ASP    . . . . . :      1442 M
  Jobs in system . . . :        112      % system ASP used   . :    60.8611
  % addresses used:                      Total . . . . . . . . :      1442 M
    Permanent   . . . :      1.617       Current unprotect used :       359 M
    Temporary   . . . :      1.012       Maximum unprotect  . . :       367 M

  Type changes (if allowed), press Enter.

  System    Pool     Reserved    Max
  Pool    Size (K)   Size (K)   Active    Pool        Subsystem   Library
    1       4229       2717       +++     *MACHINE
    2      13117          0         7     *BASE
    3        146          0         2     *SPOOL
    4       2988          0        15     *INTERACT


                                                                  Bottom
  Parameters or command
  ===> _____
  F3=Exit    F4=Prompt        F5=Refresh    F9=Retrieve    F10=Restart
  F11=Display paging option   F12=Cancel    F24=More keys
```

Ending Subsystems

You can use the ENDSBS (End Subsystem) command to end any subsystem. For example, you might want to end a remote subsystem at the end of the day so there is no access at night. But remember to be careful not to end subsystems while users are running valid jobs within them.

When you need to end a subsystem with the ENDSBS command (the End Subsystem command screen is displayed in Figure 8.6), the system will prompt you for the name of the subsystem you wish to end; the prompt is for either a controlled end, *CNTRLD, or an immediate end, *IMMED.

A controlled end allows all active jobs to continue for as long as the "Delay time" parameter specifies. You can change the value of the "Delay time" parameter for a given number of seconds, or you can specify no maximum, *NOLIMIT, so that all active jobs continue indefinitely.

Immediate end forces the system to take drastic measures to end the jobs; if users are updating files (especially keyed files), the AS/400 operating system may have to repair the files the next time you IPL, which could cause the IPL to take much longer.

Figure 8.6
End Subsystem (ENDSBS)
Command Screen

```
                              End Subsystem (ENDSBS)

 Type choices, press Enter.

 Subsystem  . . . . . . . . . .                    Name, *ALL
 How to end . . . . . . . . . .  *CNTRLD           *CNTRLD, *IMMED
 Delay time, if *CNTRLD . . . .  *NOLIMIT          Seconds, *NOLIMIT







                                                                    Bottom
 F3=Exit        F4=Prompt      F5=Refresh          F12=Cancel
 F13=How to use this display   F24=More keys
```

System Performance

Everyone who has worked on an AS/400 has experienced days when the system seems especially slow. Interactive processing needs usually are high between 8:00 a.m. and 5:00 p.m.; at midnight of the same day, processing needs are generally quite different. Disk storage (DASD), main memory (storage pools), central processing Unit (CPU) time slices, run priorities, and job states combine to execute the system duties and user tasks with various degrees of efficiency.

The AS/400 automatically adjusts pool sizes and activity levels with the QPFRADJ (Automatic Performance Adjustment) system value. The QPFRADJ value indicates whether the system should not adjust resources, should adjust resources at IPL or at regular intervals, or should do both. Activity level and pool sizes will be calculated by the system and changed during IPL if the value 1 is specified. The system will calculate and change pool sizes and activity levels at regular intervals and at IPL if the value 2 is indicated. A value of 3 for the QPFRADJ system value indicates that the system will calculate and change resources at regular intervals but not at IPL.

However, many systems can benefit from additional minor tuning changes to improve their performance. The AS/400 MIS staff can monitor system performance and tune the AS/400 for maximum efficiency. Security Officers are generally the only people who can actually modify the system. However, system operators often monitor AS/400 performance; it is the job of the system operator to inform the Security Officer that changes may be needed. The following discussion will demonstrate how to observe and calculate the best performance balance for your system, and how to prevent bottlenecks from occurring.

The computer department should first define the organization's preference for system performance goals. One possible definition might be that programmers should have system priority for compiles and testing. Another definition might be that the customer-support department have the highest system priority. By pinpointing the areas within the organization where performance is most important, the computer department can more easily balance DASD, main memory, and the CPU. Any one of these areas can become a bottleneck. Main memory and DASD are finite resources, having room for only a certain number of jobs. The OS/400 operating system effectively manages the efficient use of the AS/400's disk drives. But it is necessary to monitor disk usage to ensure that total disk usage does not exceed 80 percent of the available disk space. If disk usage exceeds 80 percent, performance may become very poor and the possibility of a system crash is significant. If disk usage does exceed 80 percent, removing seldom-used applications or purchasing more DASD may be necessary.

CPU Issues and Considerations

CPU considerations are varied and are considerably different from those related to main memory and DASD. The CPU uses time slices, run priorities, and job states to effectively manage the jobs that are submitted for processing.

Time Slices and Run Priorities

A time slice is the amount of processor time a job has available before the CPU moves to other jobs of equal or higher priority. The run priority indicates the importance of the job. Within a single storage pool, the job that has been given higher priority will acquire system resources first. On the AS/400, the run priority number is a ranking from 1 to 99, with 1 being the highest priority. Do not confuse the run priority (which determines the priority of the job while it is executing) with the job priority (which determines the relative order of a job waiting on the job queue).

As an example of how the system prioritizes jobs, AS/400 print writers have higher priority than interactive jobs, because printers use so little processor time that they don't significantly delay other jobs. Giving print writers high priority makes better use of the printer and speeds system throughput. Additionally, the system values usually give higher priority to interactive work than to batch jobs, just as you would give higher priority to people who are waiting on the phone than to requests you have received in the mail. Batch jobs generally have the lowest priority and access system resources only when jobs with higher priority are inactive.

Job States

Another concept related to jobs is the job state. Jobs running on the AS/400 are in one of three states: active, waiting, or ineligible. A job is considered active when it is occupying storage, using the processor, and has not exceeded the activity level of the storage pool. We can relate the "active" status to a swimmer actually swimming in the lap pool and using one of the lanes.

A waiting job is generally inactive until the next user request is initiated. For example, the interactive user may be discussing a problem with a customer and not currently entering any data into the computer. This job takes one of the activity level slots because the user may press a function key or the Enter key at any time.

An ineligible job cannot occupy storage or use the processor because the activity level has reached its maximum limit.

Jobs shift between job states automatically, depending on the system's work load. For example, when a user presses the Enter key at the workstation and there is room within the activity level range, the user's interactive job passes from the "wait" to the "active" mode. If, however, the activity level limit has been reached for that storage pool, the job changes from "wait" to "ineligible" and remains ineligible until some other job leaves the active state. The ineligible job will then make the job transition from "ineligible" to "active." If an active job request reaches the end of the time slice without conclusion, the system checks to determine whether some other job of equal or higher priority in the same storage pool is in the ineligible state. If a job is ineligible, the active job transfers from an "active" to an "ineligible" state to allow the other jobs to run. This means, then, that if another job of equal or higher priority in the same storage pool is ineligible, the current job becomes ineligible when it reaches the end of its time slice. This lets other jobs move into the active or wait states to be executed or wait their turn. When a job is completed or an interactive user signs off, the job is removed from the system.

Now that you have the information you need to understand the basic concepts underlying system performance, let's look at how you can specifically measure that performance.

Measuring System Performance

You can identify system performance values by observing the Work with System Status (WRKSYSSTS), the Work with Active Jobs (WRKACTJOB), and the Work with Disk Status (WRKDSKSTS) screens and then completing some minimal calculations. For a one-week period, run these three commands several times a day, trying to do so at approximately the same time each day. Take your measurements during a busy time. Take five "snapshots" of each screen about one minute apart to record average response times for interactive jobs. An easy way to do this is to use the Print Screen key and the F5 (Refresh) key.

Working with the System Status

To access the Work with System Status screen,

Type   WRKSYSSTS   on any command line
Press Enter

Figure 8.7

Portion of Work with
System Status
(WRKSYSSTS) Screen

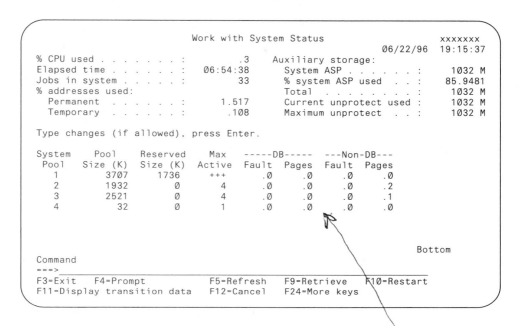

```
                         Work with System Status              xxxxxxx
                                                     06/22/96  19:15:37
% CPU used . . . . . . . :          .3   Auxiliary storage:
Elapsed time . . . . . . :    06:54:38     System ASP . . . . . . :      1032 M
Jobs in system . . . . . :          33     % system ASP used  . . :   85.9481
% addresses used:                          Total  . . . . . . . . :      1032 M
  Permanent  . . . . . . :       1.517     Current unprotect used :      1032 M
  Temporary  . . . . . . :        .108     Maximum unprotect  . . :      1032 M

Type changes (if allowed), press Enter.

System    Pool     Reserved    Max    -----DB-----   ---Non-DB---
 Pool    Size (K)  Size (K)  Active  Fault   Pages   Fault   Pages
   1       3707      1736      +++     .0      .0      .0      .0
   2       1932         0        4     .0      .0      .0      .2
   3       2521         0        4     .0      .0      .0      .1
   4         32         0        1     .0      .0      .0      .0


                                                             Bottom
Command
===>
F3=Exit    F4=Prompt           F5=Refresh   F9=Retrieve    F10=Restart
F11=Display transition data    F12=Cancel   F24=More keys
```

The machine shown in Figure 8.7 has four system pools. The pool size is the amount of main memory storage available, expressed in pages. Pages are blocks of information set aside to hold information required for the jobs that are running. If a pool is not large enough to hold all the information needed for the job, then the information must be retrieved from DASD. This retrieval time will slow job completion and may cause other jobs to be placed in an "ineligible" job state.

The machine pool's reserved size shows the amount of memory that is reserved for each pool. The system calculates the reserved size using storage pool sizes and activity levels. You cannot directly change it.

The maximum number of jobs that can be in main storage simultaneously is shown in the next column. This number is not the same as the maximum number of jobs that are currently active.

Database Faults is the value that indicates the number of times per second that database information was requested but was not available in main storage. This data must then be retrieved from disk and placed into main storage, ultimately slowing down the system. Database Pages is the rate per second that database pages (512 byte blocks of information) are being retrieved from disk into main storage. The Non-Database Faults and Pages columns indicate the same information for data that doesn't fall into the database category, such as program code.

The machine pool (system pool 1), which contains low-level system code and OS/400 licensed programs, plays a significant role in affecting system performance. The size of the machine pool is held in system value QMCHPOOL. You will not usually change this system value, because setting the storage pool too small will adversely affect performance. You can monitor general system performance by observing the machine pool faulting and paging rates on the WRKSYSSTS display. The chart in Figure 8.8a illustrates typical faulting ranges, and how they usually affect performance.

Figure 8.8a
Sample from Work with System Status (WRKSYSSTS) Screen

System Pool	Pool Size (K)	Reserved Size (K)	Max Active	DB Faults	DB Pages	Non-DB Faults	Non-DB Pages
1	12064	7446	+++	.0	.0	.0	.0

MAIN STORAGE CONFIGURED	GOOD	ACCEPTABLE	POOR
12 MB OR LESS	2	2-4	>4
MORE THAN 12 MB	1	1-2.5	>2.5

If monitoring reveals that the machine pool performance is poor, you should make your Security Officer aware of the actual values.

Other Pools

The guidelines for system pools 2, 3, and 4 are not as simple as those for the machine pool (see Figure 8.8b). You must consider each of these pools individually. The purge attribute of jobs in the pool and the AS/400 model affect the evaluation of system performance. The purge attribute is a work management tuning parameter. The PURGE parameter value is either *YES or *NO. The recommended value for most environments is *YES. The *YES purge attribute is the capability of a job to be removed from memory (or to be paged out) at the end of its time slice. If there are long waiting times, or if a job requires great quantities of memory, the *YES frees memory for other jobs to use. The purge value of *NO tends to create higher default rates. When jobs are small or memory is plentiful, however, *NO lets a job stay in main storage until the job can become active again.

For each pool, add the database faults and the non-database faults to create a result. Find the figure from Table 8.1 that applies to your system's hardware model type. You can use the appropriate figure, purge attribute, and the result calculated above to evaluate your system's performance.

If monitoring reveals that a pool performance is poor, you should inform your Security Officer of the actual values.

In summary, find the system memory pools that have the highest page-faulting rates, and look for any unusual causes for faulting. For example, these might include compiles in the wrong pool, large queries running simultaneously, and/or interactive save/restore operations. Determine whether the causes for high faulting are likely to occur regularly; if so, scheduling changes

Figure 8.8b

Sample from Work with System Status (WRKSYSSTS) Screen

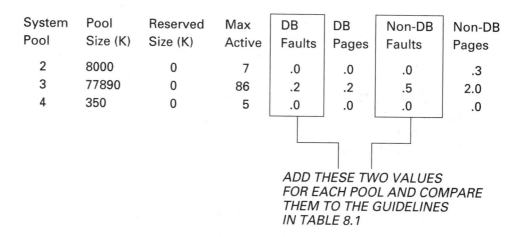

System Pool	Pool Size (K)	Reserved Size (K)	Max Active	DB Faults	DB Pages	Non-DB Faults	Non-DB Pages
2	8000	0	7	.0	.0	.0	.3
3	77890	0	86	.2	.2	.5	2.0
4	350	0	5	.0	.0	.0	.0

ADD THESE TWO VALUES FOR EACH POOL AND COMPARE THEM TO THE GUIDELINES IN TABLE 8.1

Table 8.1

Model Performance Guidelines

MODEL	PURGE ATTRIBUTE	GOOD	ACCEPTABLE	POOR
B10 AND B20; C04-C20; D04-D10 E02 and E04	*YES	<10	10-15	>15
	*NO	<15	15-20	>20
B30 AND B40-45; C25; D20; D35 E06 and E10	*YES	<15	15-20	>20
	*NO	<20	20-25	>25
B50, B60, AND B70; D25-D60; E20-E60	*YES	<20	20-30	>30
	*NO	<25	25-35	>35
D70 AND D80 E70-E80	*YES	<25	25-35	>30
	*NO	<30	30-40	>40
E90 and E95	*YES	<25	25-35	>35
	*NO	<35	35-45	>45

may be in order. If your system needs a more permanent solution, purchasing additional memory or disk drives may be necessary.

Working with Active Jobs

Possible signs of bottlenecks would involve variations in job priority within the same storage pool, unusually high CPU usage, and slow response time. Jobs in the same memory pool with different priority may cause problems, because jobs with low priorities cannot compete with jobs of higher priority. Because programmers tend to have higher system priority and use more resources when they are compiling or testing applications, other users could become locked out. One possible suggestion to prevent this from happening might be to separate programming jobs from other interactive users by giving programmers a separate subsystem.

To monitor the CPU usage of individual jobs, access the Work with Active Jobs screen by typing WRKACTJOB on a command line and pressing Enter. Using the same measuring techniques as you did for the WRKSYSSTS screens, collect the new data (an example is shown in Figure 8.9). From the initial display, press the F11 key to generate the Elapsed Time display, then print the screen. You rarely use the WRKACTJOB screen, because displaying the information for each job requires considerable system overhead. In this text, we specifically do not have all the students perform the WRKACTJOB command during the class period, because when everyone in a large class requests this screen, the system response time will degrade dramatically.

Figure 8.9

Sample from Work with Active Jobs (WRKACTJOB) Screen

| | | | | | ----------Elapsed---------- | | | | |
Opt	Subsystem/job	Type	Pool	Pty	CPU	Int	Rsp	AuxIO	CPU%
	QBASE	SBS	2	0	98.5			10	.2
	DSP02	INT	3	20	5.4	0	.0	0	.0
	DSP07	INT	3	20	.3	0	.0	11	.9
	DSP08	INT	3	20	8.5	1	.5	0	.0

If CPU usage is high since a particular job has begun, it might be wise to submit this job as a batch job instead of an interactive job. For example, query jobs use great quantities of CPU time, effectively locking out other interactive users; such jobs are generally better if they are submitted as batch jobs.

Another area that can point out problems in performance is the "Rsp" column of the Work with Active Jobs, Elapsed Time screen, as shown in Figure 8.9. This column represents the average interactive response time for a job, expressed in seconds. Response is generally expressed numerically. However, if the response is noted as a series of pluses (+++), then this particular job or workstation is not getting its share of time slices. Many factors could contribute to this situation. It is possible that the job is not getting its time slice because it is sharing a pool with jobs that have a higher priority. Another reason might be that all the system resources are being used on a large job that might better be submitted at night. Another reason might be that a large number of interactive users are active, requesting the same resource at the same time. Sometimes, the +++ will appear for only a few seconds until the system processes the requests — the +++ should not occur for long periods. If the situation persists, notify your Security Officer.

Working with Disk Status

One disk unit will always be used more because this unit contains the system programs. This is also the disk unit from which the operating system will load. All other non-system unit usage should be relatively balanced. As we previously mentioned, the total disk storage used should not exceed 80 percent of the total available space. If any of the non-system disk units becomes exceedingly full, poor performance and possible disk crash may result.

To obtain disk storage information,

Type   WRKDSKSTS   on any command line
Press   Enter

This will display the Work with Disk Status screen (Figure 8.10). Again, please note that the following figure is only a portion of this screen.

Figure 8.10
Portion of Work with Disk Status (WRKDSKSTS) Screen

```
              Size   %     I/O   Request  Read Write Read Write  %
Unit  Type    (M)   Used   Rqs   Size (k) Rqs  Rqs  (K)  (K)   Busy
 1    9332    200   99.9    .0     .0      .0   .0   .0    .0    0
 2    9332    200   76.8    .0     .0      .0   .0   .0    .0    0
 3    9332    200   77.0    .0     .0      .0   .0   .0    .0    0
```

The unit column in Figure 8.9 refers to the number assigned to each individual disk drive. The % Busy value should not exceed 40 percent. When the busy percentage is high, the AS/400 will have long queues of waiting jobs and all the time slices will be used as the system attempts to access the data required for the jobs in the queues. Users will note system degradation and longer turnaround times. Scheduling jobs at non-peak periods may be one way to relieve the daytime load on the system. If rescheduling jobs does not correct the problem, your organization may have to purchase additional DASD for the system.

If system performance has degraded because of excessive disk usage, you should delete unnecessary files from the disk. Occasionally, you may be able to back up seldom-used application packages and programs and remove them from the system. You can place these programs back in DASD when they are needed. One such example might be a budget package that is only used during one or two months of the year.

An AS/400 Performance Tools program is also available from IBM. The Performance Tools program supplies tools to measure performance and interprets the results and makes recommendations from the results. Often, the Performance Tools program recommends running batch jobs when the system is not so busy.

Powering Down the AS/400

Powering down a computer system as sophisticated as the AS/400 is not like turning the power switch off on a personal computer. Often, the system will be running jobs that you might not even be aware of, and you must be careful to not interrupt those jobs by powering down the system. For example, the AS/400 may be running batch jobs that communicate with remote systems or that are printing reports.

You can check system activity with the WRKACTJOB (Work with Active Jobs) command. The Work with Active Jobs screen, shown in Figure 8.11, shows what jobs are currently active — that is, what jobs are actually running. Some jobs are system jobs that you'll see all the time, even when you're the only user on the system. To access the Work with Active Jobs screen,

Type   WRKACTJOB   on the command line
Press Enter

Remember that you should use the WRKACTJOB command infrequently because the system requires considerable overhead to display information about each job.

If you don't need to see all active jobs during your normal daily work, you should consider using the WRKUSRJOB (Work with User Jobs) command, which displays jobs by user profile name, or the WRKSBSJOB (Work with Subsystem Jobs) command, which displays jobs by subsystem name (Note that the easiest way to confirm that no new jobs start on the system is to end all the subsystems.)

Figure 8.11
Work with Active
Jobs Screen

```
                        Work with Active Jobs                       xxxxxxxx
                                        04/10/96  19:52:04
    CPU %:      .0    Elapsed time:   00:00:00    Active jobs:   30
 Type options, press Enter.
   2=Change 3=Hold  4=End  5=Work with  6=Release  7=Display message
   8=Work with spooled files    13=Disconnect ...

 Opt  Subsystem/Job   User      Type  CPU %  Function        Status
 __   QBATCH          QSYS      SBS    .0                     DEQW
 __   QCMN            QSYS      SBS    .0                     DEQW
 __   QCTL            QSYS      SBS    .0                     DEQW
 __     QSYSSCD       QPGMR     BCH    .0    PGM-QEZSCNEP     EVTW
 __   QINTER          QSYS      SBS    .0                     DEQW
 __     QPADEV0011    QSYSOPR   INT    .0    CMD-WRKACTJOB    RUN
 __   QSPL            QSYS      SBS    .0                     DEQW
 __     PRT01         QSPLJOB   WTR    .0                     PRTW
 __   QSYSWRK         QSYS      SBS    .0                     DEQW

                                                            More...
 Parameters or command
 ===>
 F3=Exit F5=Refresh F10=Restart statistics 11=Display elapsed data F12=Cancel
 F23=More options   F24=More keys
```

You should send a message to all your users before you power down. This message should be friendly yet authoritative. Allow users plenty of time to end the tasks they're performing. The best way to announce an anticipated power down is to send everyone a break message using the SNDBRKMSG (Send

Break Message) command. This command sends a message that is immediately displayed at the user's screen, interrupting whatever the user is doing. The user will probably read the message and be forced to press the Enter key to return to whatever (s)he was doing. The Send Break Message (SNDBRKMSG) command screen is displayed in Figure 8.12.

Figure 8.12
Send Break Message
(SNDBRKMSG) Command
Screen

```
                    Send Break Message (SNDBRKMSG)

 Type choices, press Enter.

 Message text . . . . . . . Shutting down the system in 30 minutes.
 Please sign off as quickly as possible. 04/13/96




 To work station message queue  .  *ALLWS        Name, *ALLWS
    Library . . . . . . . . . . .  *LIBL         Name, *LIBL
                  + for more values

 Message type . . . . . . . . . .  *INFO         *INFO, *INQ
 Message queue to get reply . . .  QSYSOPR       Name
    Library . . . . . . . . . . .    *LIBL       Name, *LIBL




                                                            Bottom
 F3=Exit      F4=Prompt     F5=Refresh      F12=Cancel
 F13=How to use this display              F24=More keys
```

In the example shown in Figure 8.12, the same message is sent to *all* display stations. Unfortunately, this means that, for any display stations that are not active at the time the message is sent, the message will be displayed to the next user who signs on at that station, possibly the next day.

The PWRDWNSYS command actually turns off the system. As shown in Figure 8.13, the screen is similar to that displayed with the ENDSBS command, in the respect that this screen also has a "How to end" parameter that accepts either *CNTRLD or *IMMED. This parameter is of value only if you haven't ended the subsystems beforehand. If all subsystems are ended, the value you select in this parameter is irrelevant. Shutting down the system with the PWRDWNSYS command doesn't cut electrical power from peripheral devices such as display stations and printers; these devices must be shut off individually.

The "Restart after power down" parameter of this command is very important. Specifying *NO for this parameter causes the system to actually shut itself down, removing electrical power from all CPU components. If you choose *YES for the "Restart after power down" parameter, the system goes through the motions of powering down; but before the power is shut off, it starts again. This is how you can perform an IPL without shutting down the system entirely.

Figure 8.13
Power Down System
(PWRDWNSYS)
Command Screen

```
                           Power Down System (PWRDWNSYS)

 Type choices, press Enter.

 How to end . . . . . . . . . . .   *CNTRLD    *CNTRLD, *IMMED
 Delay time, if *CNTRLD . . . . .   3600       Seconds, *NOLIMIT
 Restart after power down . . . .   *NO        *NO, *YES
 IPL source . . . . . . . . . .    *B         *PANEL, A, B, D








                                                                    Bottom
 F3=Exit      F4=Prompt     F5=Refresh      F12=Cancel
 F13=How to use this display              F24=More keys
```

Key Terms

Database faults
Job states
Machine pool
Non-database faults

Page
QCTL
QBASE
Shared pools

Subsystems
Time slices

Review Questions

1. When you are running the AS/400 in multiple-subsystem configuration, what are the four basic subsystems? What is the controlling subsystem?

2. Subsystems are created for what purpose?

3. When you are ending a subsystem, define the difference between a controlled end and an immediate end.

4. What is the disadvantage of using the WRKACTJOB command during your normal daily activities?

5. Looking at the screen below, what is the +++? Why is this happening?

```
Opt    Subsystem/job  User      Type    CPU%      Function      Status
       QBASE          QSYS      SBS      .0                      DEQW
         DSP02        TMPROKOP  INT      .0      *-CMDENT        DSPW
         DSP07        MHUFFAR   INT      .0      *-CMDENT        DSPW
         DSP08        BDSNYDER  INT      .0      *-CMDENT        DSPW


                                        ------Elapsed--------
Opt    Subsystem/job  Type  Pool   Pty   CPU  Int  Rsp  AuxIO   CPU%
       QBASE          SBS   2      0    98.5              10     .2
         DSP02        INT   3      20    5.4   0  +++      0     .0
         DSP07        INT   3      5      .3   0   .0     11     .9
         DSP08        INT   3      5   308.5   1   .5      0     .0
```

Review Questions Continued

Review Questions continued

6. Looking at the screen print below, is this acceptable performance for an AS/400 Model C25 system with more than 12 MB of memory? Is the Purge Attribute *YES acceptable for the model C25?

```
                      Work with System Status           xxxxxxxx
                                                 03/10/96  08:54:06
 % CPU used . . . . . . . :       22.6    Auxiliary storage:
 Elapsed time . . . . . . :    00:04:56     System ASP . . . . . . :   1442 M
 Jobs in system . . . . . :        105      % system ASP used  . . :   61.6977
 % addresses used:                          Total  . . . . . . . . :   1442 M
   Permanent  . . . . . . :      2.116      Current unprotect used :    364 M
   Temporary  . . . . . . :      4.311      Maximum unprotect  . . :    374 M

 Type changes (if allowed), press Enter.

 System    Pool    Reserved   Max   -----DB-----  ---Non-DB---
  Pool   Size (K)  Size (K)  Active  Fault  Pages  Fault  Pages
    1      4223      2725     +++     .0     .0    3.0    1.2
    2     11616        0       6     3.9     .6    3.3    8.3
    3        92         0       2     1.8     .0    4.7     .0
    4      4549         0      15     3.1     .0    2.9    5.3


                                                              Bottom
 Command
 ===>
 F3=Exit   F4=Prompt          F5=Refresh   F9=Retrieve   F10=Restart
 F11=Display transition data  F12=Cancel   F24=More keys
```

Exercise

1. Using the WRKSBS display, print the subsystem description for the QINTER subsystem.

Chapter 9

PC Support/400 and Client Access for OS/400

Objectives

To understand

✓ what PC Support/400 and Client Access for OS/400 are

✓ Client/Server terminology as it relates to PC Support/400 and Client Access for OS/400

✓ the different versions of PC Support/400 and Client Access for OS/400

✓ the installation process

✓ how to start PC Support/400 and Client Access for OS/400

✓ the features of PC Support/400 and Client Access for OS/400

PC Support/400 and Client Access for OS/400 Defined

PC Support/400 and Client Access for OS/400 are IBM licensed software products that provide AS/400-to-Personal Computer (PC) connectivity and communications. These products provide such features as terminal and printer emulation, data transfer, and shared folders, among others. We will discuss the details of these and other PC Support and Client Access features in later sections of this chapter. Before Version 3 of OS/400, IBM's AS/400-to-PC connectivity and communications product was called PC Support/400. With Version 3 of OS/400, PC Support/400 was replaced with Client Access for OS/400. Because many AS/400 shops have not upgraded to OS/400 Version 3, as a system operator you are likely to encounter both PC Support/400 and Client Access for OS/400 (referred to as PC Support and Client Access from here on). The two products share many of the same capabilities, but their features may be presented differently depending on whether the DOS or Microsoft Windows version is used.

PC Support and Client Access are implementations of client/server technology. The client application resides on the PC and the server application resides on the AS/400. The philosophy behind client/server technology is that certain tasks can be performed better on one computer platform than on another. Tasks are distributed to the appropriate platform to achieve optimal performance, reliability, and usability. For example, the

AS/400 is an excellent database server, while the PC uses a Graphical User Interface (GUI) to enhance the appeal and usability of applications. The AS/400 provides the data while the PC is responsible for formatting and displaying the data. Client/server technology has become very important in the world of computers as more users' terminals have been replaced by PCs on their desks. Users depend on PC applications as well as on AS/400 applications to do their jobs.

As you become familiar with PC Support or Client Access, you'll find different variations on how to install and use the software. The following sections describe the different versions, present an installation overview, and discuss how the features of each product are commonly used.

Client Versions

Like many software applications, PC Support and Client Access have different options that can be installed. Each install option has different hardware and software requirements.

The *DOS* option provides the basic connectivity and communications features using a terminate-and-stay-resident (TSR) program under the MS-DOS conventional memory structure. Under this conventional memory structure, only 640K of the computer's memory is used to run programs. The DOS option has the fewest hardware requirements and runs on most PCs. The DOS option, however, does not take advantage of any extended memory that most of today's PCs have — nor does it offer a graphical user interface.

With the *Extended DOS* option, part of the application is loaded in extended memory, saving valuable conventional PC memory for other applications. Extended memory uses memory in the PC over the 640K boundary. With PC Support, the Extended DOS option provides features to run PC Support under Microsoft Windows.

Client Access provides a *DOS* and an *Extended DOS* option as well, but Client Access also has a *Client Access/400 for Windows* option that allows it to be installed and operate within the Windows environment. The Client Access implementation is enhanced to provide better Windows operability than PC Support's implementation with Windows.

At the time of this writing, IBM recently released *Client Access for Windows 95*. The Client Access/400 for Windows version mentioned above does not work with Windows 95. And though we do not discuss it in this text, IBM provides a version for OS/2 as well.

Install Overview

Because PC Support and Client Access are client/server applications, there is an install process for the AS/400 and for each PC. Before the software is installed, the PC must be able to communicate with the AS/400 through some type of physical connection. The PC can be connected to the AS/400 directly with a twinaxial emulation card wired to the AS/400's workstation controller. The PC also can be connected to the AS/400 via a local area network (LAN), where the PC has a network card and network access, and the LAN provides the access to the AS/400. For remote communications, the software can be configured to work over modems.

On the AS/400, the server portion is usually loaded when you initially install the operating system or when you upgrade from a previous version. If the AS/400 operating system is upgraded to Version 3, Client Access replaces PC Support during the upgrade process. To view the version currently on the AS/400, follow these steps:

Type   GO LICPGM   on any command line

Select   Option 10   to "Display installed licensed programs"

As shown in Figure 9.1, the Display Installed Licensed Programs screen displays the licensed program number, the description, and the current version. Use this information to verify that the version of the client application being installed on the PC is compatible with the version of the server application on the AS/400.

Figure 9.1
Display Installed
Licensed Programs

```
                      Display Installed Licensed Programs
                                            System:    S1019033
   Licensed                                            Installed
   Program      Description                            Release

   5763RG1      ILE RPG/400 - RPG/400                     V3R1M0
   5763XA1      Client Access/400 Family - Base           V3R1M0
   5763XA1      Client Access/400 - PC Tools Folder       V3R1M0
   5763XB1      Client Access/400 for DOS with Ext Memory V3R1M0
   5763XB1      Client Access/400 - Ext DOS SBCS          V3R1M0
   5763XB1      Client Access/400 - Ext DOS DBCS          V3R1M0
   5763XC1      Client Access/400 for Windows 3.1         V3R1M1
   5763XC1      Client Access/400 - Windows 3.1 SBCS      V3R1M1
   5763XL1      Client Access/400 for DOS                 V3R1M0
   5763XL1      Client Access/400 - DOS SBCS              V3R1M0
   5763XL1      Client Access/400 - DOS DBCS              V3R1M0




                                                        More...
   Press Enter to continue.

   F3=Exit    F12=Cancel
```

If PC Support or Client Access needs to be installed on the AS/400, select option 11, "Install Licensed Programs," from the Work with Licensed Programs menu.

Once the licensed program is installed on the AS/400, you can perform many tasks from the PC Support Task menu and Client Access Task menu, including enrolling users in PC Support and Client Access. You must have Security Officer authority to enroll users. To display the task menu,

TYPE   GO PCSTSK   on a command line

Install Overview for PC Support
and Client Access on the PC

Before installing the client software, you should be familiar with the DOS operating system and Microsoft Windows if you are installing any of the Windows options. You also should have read through the install guide that is available with PC Support and Client Access. Both products offer several install options that affect how the products work and appear to the user. The additional reference section at the end of this chapter lists the IBM books on CD that explain each option and the related requirements for installation.

The install process for PC Support and Client Access require that the PC has enough random-access memory (RAM) and hard disk space to accommodate the options you select. As a general guide, the DOS version requires a PC with 640K of RAM and a single diskette drive. The Extended DOS version requires a PC with 1 MB of RAM, a hard drive, and a single diskette drive. The Windows version requires a PC using Windows 3.x, 1 MB of RAM, a hard drive, and a single diskette drive. With Windows, the more memory and hard drive space you have the better an application will run.

PC Support and Client Access provide install programs that guide you through the process. Depending on the type of connection to the AS/400, you may need to know the name of the AS/400, a workstation address, the connection type, or a TCP/IP address. Be aware that the install process may modify your AUTOEXEC.BAT and CONFIG.SYS files, so it is important that you create a backup of these files before you begin the install.

PC Support can be installed from diskettes; Client Access can be installed from diskettes or compact disk (CD). To begin the installation process using DOS, load the first diskette and, from a PC prompt,

Type   <drive>:INSTALL

Using Windows, follow these steps to begin the install process:

Select	File	from Program Manager
Select	Run	to start an application
Type	<drive>:INSTALL	in the Command Line entry
Press	Enter	to start the process

During the install process, you will indicate where the software is installed, the type of connection to the AS/400, and start-up options. For most installs, the application is copied to a directory named PCS or CAWIN on the hard drive of the PC. A start-up batch file named STARTPCS.BAT is created that contains start-up commands and start-up options that were selected during the install process. A configuration file named CONFIG.PCS is also created that contains configuration and connection information. If you install either PC Support with the Microsoft Windows feature or Client Access for Windows, group windows are created with icons by which you can access the various programs.

Starting PC Support

You usually run the batch file STARTPCS.BAT to start PC Support. You can place STARTPCS.BAT in the AUTOEXEC.BAT file, so that STARTPCS.BAT starts when the PC is powered on. STARTPCS.BAT contains calls to other PC Support programs. Most importantly, STARTPCS.BAT calls the programs that load the adapter handler and the router. The adapter-handler program communicates with the PC hardware device that handles the communications with the AS/400. Each adapter handler program works with the specific hardware device. The adapter-handler program for a twinaxial card is different from the adapter-handler program used for connecting through a LAN. The router handles the receipt and transfer of the requests and data between the PC and the AS/400. It is the router's job to play traffic cop and make sure requests and data are routed to the AS/400 or to other PC Support programs.

After the adapter handler and router are loaded, other options in STARTPCS.BAT are loaded. These other options may include starting a terminal emulation session, starting a shared folder, or establishing a virtual printer where the PC can print to an AS/400 printer. The options that load are initially set during the installation process, but you can change them at any time by modifying the STARTPCS.BAT file or by running the CFGPCS program.

Starting Client Access

Similarly to PC Support, the DOS versions of Client Access can be started with STARTPCS.BAT. With Client Access for Windows, however, this is not necessary because the application runs through Windows. With the icons provided within the Client Access group, you can "click" with a mouse on an icon and start Client Access. The two icons that start Client Access are shown in Figure 9.2.

Figure 9.2
Icons to Start
Client Access

Client Access   AS/400
Startup   Connection

The Client Access Startup icon establishes the connection with the AS/400, and it can start other Client Access options such as terminal emulation, shared folders, and virtual printers. The AS/400 Connection icon only establishes the connection with the AS/400. If you use the AS/400 Connection icon, you must start other features separately by selecting their icons.

Using PC Support and Client Access Features

Once PC Support or Client Access is connected to the AS/400, either through the adapter handler and router under DOS or through the session connection icons under Windows, you can use other features of the products. The DOS versions of Client Access appear similar to the DOS versions of PC Support. When we explain features in the following sections, we show the sample screens as DOS or Windows screens. Though the screens look different depending on whether you are using the DOS or Windows version, the functionality of the features is the same.

We cover shared folders in detail in a later section, but it is important to note here that depending on how PC Support and Client Access was installed, the program names mentioned may be located in the PCS subdirectory on the PC's hard drive, or the programs may reside on the AS/400 in a shared folder. The advantage of using a shared folder on the AS/400 is that it minimizes the amount of hard-drive space that the products require on the PC. The disadvantage to shared folders is that accessing the AS/400 is slower than accessing the PC's local hard drive, so you must consider the performance impact when you use shared folders.

Using DOS, you can configure and perform many PC Support and Client Access features using the PCSMENU program. As shown in Figure 9.3, the PCSMENU program provides easy access to many of the application's features from a menu. You can also access the features by typing in the program's name at a DOS prompt. For example, to transfer data from the AS/400 to the PC, you can either select "Transfer data" from the menu or type in the command RTOPC at the DOS prompt.

Figure 9.3
PCSMENU Main Menu

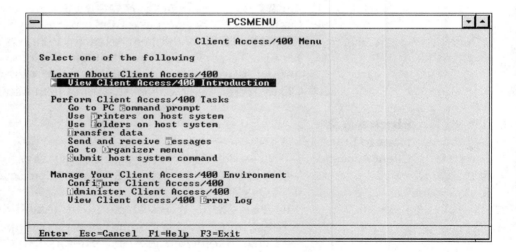

With Windows, you access the features by clicking on icons in the group window. Figure 9.4 displays the group window for Client Access.

Terminal and Printer Emulation

Terminal emulation allows the PC to act as, or *emulate*, a terminal. The AS/400 communicates with terminals using a data packet format called the 5250 Data Stream. The terminal emulation program translates the data stream between the AS/400 and the PC.

Figure 9.4
Client Access/400 for
Windows Group Window

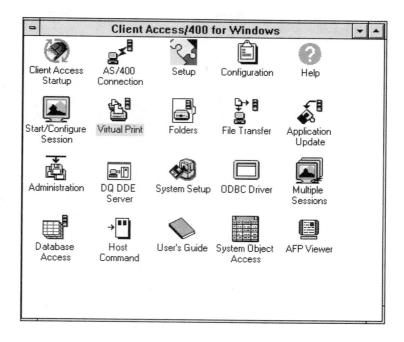

Printer emulation allows a printer attached to the PC to emulate an AS/400 printer, which can provide an inexpensive and convenient method for users to print reports close to their work area.

Under DOS, terminal and printer emulation are handled by the Work Station Function programs. The Work Station Function programs create and save session information. A session can be a terminal emulation session or a printer emulation session. The CFGPCS program is used to configure sessions. The WSF program is used to start the sessions.

Under Windows, Client Access provides two emulation packages that can be installed: Personal Communications/400 from IBM, and RUMBA/400 from Wall Data, Inc. Both solutions provide quick and easy ways to define a terminal or printer session. The Personal Communications/400 package appears as the Start/Configure Session icon in the Client Access/400 for Windows group window. RUMBA/400 has its own group window with icons to define sessions. Figure 9.5 shows the AS/400 sign-on screen using Personal Communications/400. Emulation software usually provides features such as custom screen and keyboard layout, macro maintenance, and copy/paste features for use with other Windows programs. (Macros are files that contain key strokes than can be played back at a later time. Using macros can simplify repetitive keystroke tasks and reduce the risk of keying errors.) The toolbar that displays below the menu options lets users access key features of the software simply by clicking on an icon in the toolbar.

You can create a printer session by using the Communication-Configure option and selecting Printer as the session type. Advanced features let you customize the type of printer and the printer characteristics such as font, the

Figure 9.5

Personal
Communications/400
Display Session

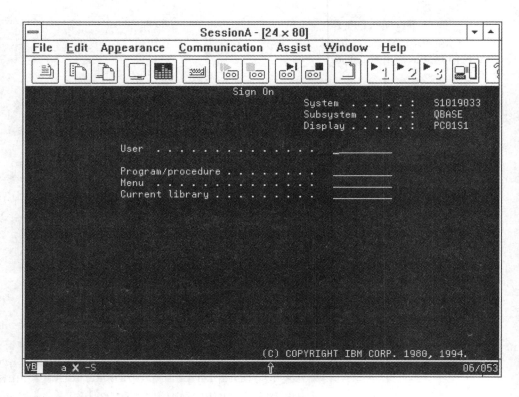

drawer of a laser printer to pull the paper from, and message queue. When the printer session is activated, the output queue and writer device are created on the AS/400. The session then displays a window indicating the current status of the emulated printer, as shown in Figure 9.6. The figure shows that the emulated printer is PC01P2, and that PC01P2 is on-line and ready to print. Anybody on the AS/400 can send spooled files to PC01P2 and the spooled files will print on the printer attached to the PC.

Figure 9.6

Personal
Communications/400
Printer Session

S1019033 / PC01P2

Status

Ready

Job in Process

On-Line

START   STOP   Cancel

Shared Folders

Shared folders are AS/400 folders that are assigned as a PC directory so the PC can use the AS/400's DASD just as the PC would use a hard drive. If you are using shared folders, files that need to be accessed by multiple individuals can be maintained and shared on the AS/400. For example, an accounting department can store its Microsoft Excel budget spreadsheets in an AS/400 folder named BUDGET. Individuals in the accounting department can view, edit, and save the spreadsheets to the BUDGET folder from their PCs. This process saves the tedious and error-prone task of sharing PC files by copying the files to a floppy diskette and reloading the files on another computer.

Another use for shared folders is to archive PC files. PC files can be copied to a shared folder and then saved using AS/400 backup hardware as part of a centralized backup plan. Continuing with our accounting department example, if the department contained 20 PCs, backing up all the necessary files on 20 individual PCs would be a labor-intensive job. Using shared folders, important documents can be copied to the AS/400 folder from each PC; and as part of the nightly AS/400 backup, the folder is saved with other important AS/400 objects.

From the AS/400, you maintain folders with the WRKFLR (Work with Folders) command. Figure 9.7 shows the Work with Folders screen. Documents are stored in folders. The documents can be AS/400 documents or PC files. The WRKFLR command allows you to create, remove, and work with the documents within the folders. You can also create folders within other folders. Using our accounting department again as an example, additional folders could be created within the BUDGET folder to keep the budget files separated by fiscal year.

Figure 9.7
Work with Folders Screen

```
                                  Work with Folders
      Folder  . . . /
      Position to . . . . . .               Starting characters

      Type options (and Folder), press Enter.
        1=Create           3=Next level      4=Delete        5=Work with documents
        7=Rename           8=Details        14=Authority

      Opt  Folder          Opt  Folder

           BUDGET               QIWSFLRD
           CONVERT              QIWSFL2
           DQTECH               QIWSFL2D
           IMAGES               QIWSTOOL
           QBKBOOKS             QOTTMFLR
           QDIADOCS             QPWXCSO
           QFOSDIA              QPWXCWN
           QIWSADM              SOURCE
           QIWSFLR

                                                              Bottom
      F3=Exit                    F5=Refresh      F6=Print list    F9=Work with
      F11=Display descriptions   F12=Cancel      F13=Previous level
```

Before a PC can use an AS/400 folder as a shared folder, the folder must be *assigned* or *connected* to the PC. As shown in Figure 9.8, multiple folders can be assigned to different drive letters, allowing the PC to access several folders at once. Figure 9.8 shows that three drives letters — I, J, and K — have been assigned to three AS/400 folders. From the same program, connected drives can be disconnected when access to the folder is no longer needed.

Figure 9.8
Folder Connections

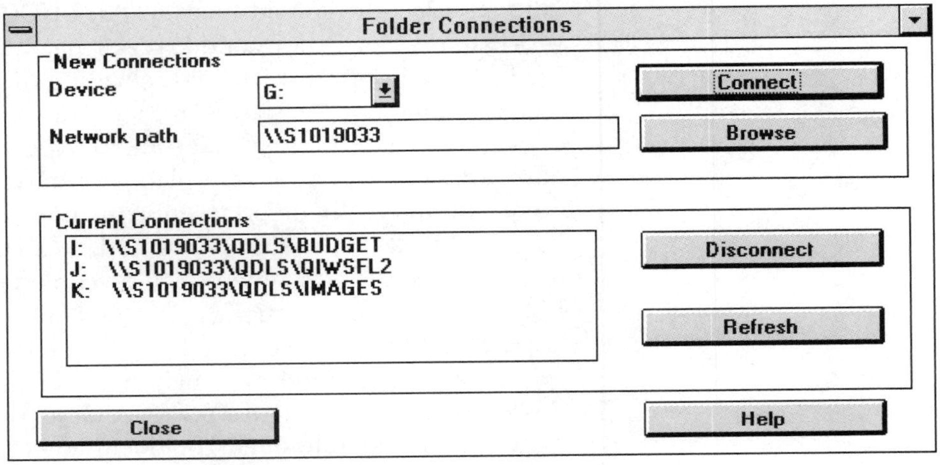

Wherever a shared folder can be assigned, the program offers the option of browsing the AS/400 to view the folders. The browse feature helps you find folders on the AS/400. The browse feature allows you to select folders, view folders within folders, or view folders on a different AS/400. Figure 9.9 displays the Browse Folder window when you are connecting shared folders from Client Access for Windows.

After the shared folder has been assigned or connected, PC applications are aware that the folders are available to use. Figure 9.10 shows the Windows File Manager program. The drive icons indicate that drives I, J, and K are available. The file listing displays the documents stored in the AS/400 folder named IMAGE, which the PC is using as the K drive.

For DOS versions, folders are assigned and configured the same way as they are with the Windows version. You use the STARTFLR command to start shared folders. You use the FSPC command to assign and release the shared folders. In the following DOS batch file example, the commands start the shared folders function, assign the folder IMAGES to the K drive, and copy files from the PC's hard drive to the shared folder:

```
REM Start shared folders, then assign K drive
STARTFLR
FSPC ASSIGN K: IMAGES
XCOPY C:\IMAGES\*.* K: /S
```

Figure 9.9
Browse Folders

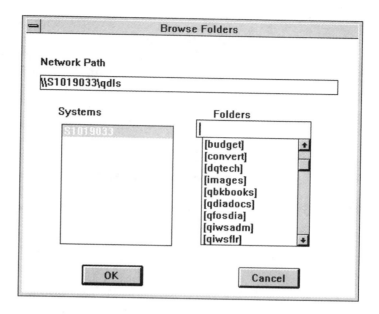

Figure 9.10
Windows File Manager
with Connected Drives

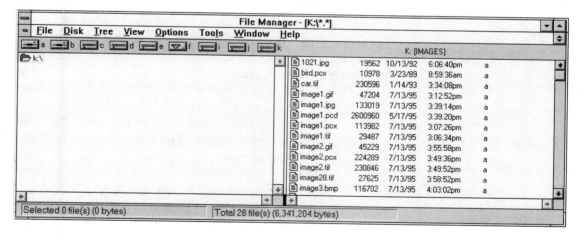

In summary, shared folders offer a simple and convenient way for PCs to use AS/400 DASD as a hard drive. Shared folders facilitate users sharing files and provide a method for archiving PC files with an automated and centralized process.

Data Transfer/File Transfer

Data transfer, or *file transfer*, involves transferring files from the AS/400 to the PC, known as *downloading*, or transferring files from the PC to the AS/400, known as *uploading*. To transfer files, a transfer request is created that indicates where the file is coming from (the source), where the file is going (the target), which records to transfer, and the source-file and target-file formats. Transfer requests can be saved so they can be recalled to use again or to modify. The source-file format is how the data is currently stored on the source computer. The target-file format is how the data will be stored once it is transferred to the target platform. When the transfer takes place, the data is automatically converted from EBCDIC to ASCII and vice versa, unless the transfer request specifically indicates not to convert to the target computer's character code set.

On the AS/400, file formats are straightforward; the files will fit one of the following structures:

- A data file where each record is defined by multiple fields with varying data types and lengths. An example would be an address book where each record is defined by fields for the name, address, city, state, zip code, and phone number. This is the most common format on the AS/400.

- A data file where each record has a fixed length but does not have any defining field structure. This type of file is often used for text or is the result of copying spooled files.

On the PC, file formats are more complicated, because each vendor's application has its own file format. Microsoft Excel, for example, does not have the same file format as Borland's Paradox or Lotus Notes. Fortunately, most of these applications export and import data using a format that the data-transfer program can use. The common file formats used by the data transfer programs are

- *Comma Separated Variable (CSV) or BASIC Sequential.* Such files place commas between each field in the record and quote marks around character information. This format works well for transfers where the record structure contains multiple fields. Many PC applications, including Microsoft Excel and Lotus 1-2-3, import and export this file format. As an example, if the AS/400 record structure contained a numeric field for item number, a character field for description, a character field for image reference, and a salesperson ID, Figure 9.11 shows what the CSV file would look like after it was transferred from the AS/400.

Figure 9.11
CSV File Layout

```
803195,"Drill","K\IMAGES\DRILL.DXF",40000
785213,"AS/400","K:\IMAGES\IMAGE1.PCD",20000
785214,"PC Monitor","K:\IMAGES\MHMON.PCX",20000
```

- *Text or DOS.* These files are straight ASCII files without field delimiters. Records may be appended with a carriage return and line-feed character. These file formats are best suited for transferring source code, spooled file data, or word-processing text.

• *Binary Interchange File Format (BIFF) and Data Interchange Format (DIF).* These files are created from some spreadsheet and database applications. These file formats are best suited for applications that do not import and export comma-separated files.

Many reasons exist for transferring files from the AS/400 to the PC. Data may need to go to another company with a different type of computer that requires ASCII data. Or PC applications such as Microsoft Excel may be used to import data and prepare graphical presentations and reports. If the AS/400 is not equipped with fax or e-mail software, data may be transferred to the PC to accomplish these tasks.

Likewise, there are many reasons for transferring files from the PC to the AS/400. Many vendors provide information only in a PC format, so the data must be transferred and placed in an AS/400 database so applications can use the data. An example would be vendors who send their product information on a PC disk in CSV format and that information is transferred to your AS/400's purchase-order system.

Transfer Requests: AS/400 to PC

When creating a transfer request from the AS/400 to the PC, you have several options for how the data will be transferred. Figure 9.12 shows the two entry screens for creating a transfer request with Client Access for DOS. With the DOS versions, the RTOPC command is used to work with AS/400-to-PC transfers. With Windows, you access the file-transfer program by selecting the File Transfer icon, as shown in Figure 9.4. The Windows version looks different but operates on the same principles.

Figure 9.12
Transfer Request:
AS/400 to PC,
Screen 1

Figure 9.12

Transfer Request:
AS/400 to PC,
Screen 2

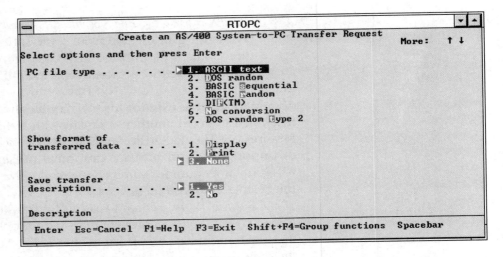

The FROM entry in Figure 9.12 is the name of the AS/400 file that is transferred. The SELECT entry indicates what fields from the AS/400 database file are transferred. An asterisk (*) indicates that all fields are transferred. If you need only certain fields, enter the fields' names, separated by a comma. Pressing F4 with the cursor in the SELECT entry displays a list of fields from the file. You can select fields from the list to build the SELECT entry. The WHERE entry indicates that records from the file are conditionally selected for transfer. As Figure 9.12 shows, only records where the field ITMSP is equal to 2000 are transferred. The ORDER BY entry indicates the sort order of the transferred records. If the entry is blank, records are transferred in the same order in which they are in the AS/400 file. If you need a sort order, enter field names separated by a comma. Pressing F4 with the cursor in the ORDER BY entry displays a list of fields from the file. If you are familiar with Structured Query Language (SQL), the format of the FROM, SELECT, WHERE, and ORDER BY entries follows SQL syntax.

The option to save the transfer description saves the AS/400 file-selection information into a file-definition file (FDF). The FDF can then be used by the program that transfers PC data to the AS/400 file. The FDF is different from the transfer-request file that is saved, and it is only used in the PC-to-AS/400 transfer process.

After the transfer information is entered, press F5 to run the transfer. If all the entries are valid, the records are transferred from the AS/400 file to the output device selected. If the output device is a file, the records are transferred to the PC file named in the "To . . ." entry. You can save the transfer request to a PC file and recall it later to run again or to modify the file. You also can use the transfer-request file in a DOS batch file to automate the file-transfer process.

Transfer Requests: PC to AS/400

When you create a transfer request from the PC to the AS/400, the options are simpler than those for the AS/400-to-PC transfer. Figure 9.13 shows the entry screen for creating a transfer request with Client Access for DOS. With the DOS versions, you use the RFROMPC command to work with PC-to-AS/400 transfers. With Windows, you use the same File Transfer program that you use to request file transfer from the AS/400 to the PC to transfer files from the PC to the AS/400. Again, you access the file-transfer program by selecting the File Transfer icon (shown in Figure 9.4).

Figure 9.13
Transfer Request:
PC to AS/400

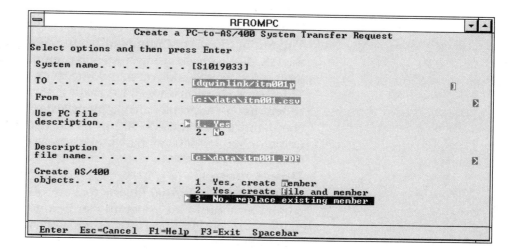

In Figure 9.13, the "Use PC file description" entry is the name of the file-definition file (FDF) saved with a previous AS/400-to-PC transfer; this file indicates the format that the PC data should be in when it is transferred to the AS/400. The information in the FDF file is compared to the record structure of the AS/400 file to make sure they are compatible.

After you have entered the transfer information, press F5 to run the transfer. If all the entries are valid, the records are transferred from the PC file to the AS/400 file. You can save the transfer request to a PC file and recall it later to run again or to modify it. You can also use the transfer-request file in a DOS batch file to automate the file-transfer process.

Other Features

Terminal and printer emulation, shared folders, and data transfer are common features used with PC Support and Client Access, but they are not the only features of the products. PC Support and Client Access offer several other features that some AS/400 shops use sparingly — and some AS/400 shops probably use every day.

Virtual Printer

For many years — and it's still the case in some companies — printers were few and people had to share the printer as a resource. If your company needs to share printer resources, the Virtual Printer feature of PC Support and Client Access can help. PCs can use an AS/400 printer as if it were attached directly to the PC via Virtual Printer Support. Because the AS/400 printer is not actually attached to the PC, it is called a virtual printer. When the PC prints a report, the report is routed to the LPT port assigned to the virtual printer. Virtual printers are best suited for text-based reports, where a company may want to take advantage of the high speeds that some AS/400 printers offer.

Submit Remote Command

The Submit Remote Command feature allows a PC to send a command to the AS/400 without using a terminal emulation session. The command is sent as a valid AS/400 command line, such as CALL PGM(QGPL/PROCA). This feature lends itself well to creating AS/400 objects or calling processing programs. For example, after a file transfer, you can use the Submit Remote command to call the AS/400 program that processes the transferred data into another AS/400 database and prints a report.

Data Queues

Data queues are AS/400 objects that are often used for program-to-program communications. One program can be on the AS/400 while the other program is on the PC. Data queues are similar to AS/400 physical files, in the respect that they have a defined length and contain entries similar to records. Entries can be placed on the data queue, retrieved from the data queue, and removed from the data queue by programs on the AS/400 or by using PC Support and Client Access commands.

ODBC for Microsoft Windows

Open Database Connectivity (ODBC) is a programming interface designed for Microsoft Windows that allows applications to work with a database regardless of where the database is or what type of database it is. With ODBC, for example, Microsoft Excel could open a database called MYDB and work with the records regardless of whether MYDB is an AS/400 database, a PC database, an Oracle database, or some other database. Client Access provides an ODBC driver for accessing AS/400 databases. The application on the PC must be able to work with the ODBC specifications for you to use the feature.

Client/Server Programming

Situations exist where the supplied programs you have aren't quite enough. In these cases, PC Support and Client Access allow you to develop your own client/server applications. Both versions supply you with documentation and samples showing how to write a program using the program's internally called functions, called Application Program Interfaces (APIs). You can use

PC programming languages such as BASIC, C, and Pascal to develop client applications. You might develop an application in Microsoft Visual Basic that prompts the user for an item number and then uses the Client Access file-transfer APIs to retrieve the item's sales history and load the history into Microsoft Word.

Additional References for PC Support and Client Access

The following table lists the books found on IBM's *Softcopy Library* CD, which is distributed with the AS/400's operating system. The books listed below focus on setup and on using the basic features. Other books also are available on CD to help with advanced topics such as Client/Server programming.

Book on CD	Description
QBKA6202	*AS/400 PC Support/400 User's Guide for DOS*
QBKA6302	*AS/400 PC Support/400 DOS Installation and Administration*
QBKAK001	*Client Access/400 for DOS Setup V3R1*
QBKAKW01	*Client Access/400 for DOS User Guide V3R1*
QBKAK401	*Client Access/400 for DOS Ext Memory - Getting Started*
QBKAKC03	*Client Access/400 for DOS Ext Memory Setup V3R1*
QBKAKD03	*Client Access/400 for DOS Ext Memory User Guide V3R1*
QBKAKM02	*Client Access/400 for Windows 3.1 - Getting Started*
QBKA6G01	*Client Access/400 for Windows 3.1 User Guide*
QBKA6J00	*Client Access Windows 3.1 Client for OS/400 ODBC User's Guide*
QBKAKB00	*Client Access/400 PC5250 User's Guide*

Key Terms

Client Access for OS/400
Data transfer
Downloading
File transfer
PC Support

RUMBA
Router
Terminate-and-Stay-Resident
   programs
Uploading

Workstation functions

Review Questions

1. The PC Support/400 and Client Access for OS/400 products provide what features for the AS/400 user?

2. Why is it important to create a backup of a PC's AUTOEXEC.BAT and CONFIG.SYS files before installing PC Support or Client Access for DOS on a PC?

3. What is the name of the batch file that starts PC Support for DOS ?

4. What is the adapter handler's function?

5. What is the advantage and disadvantage to using the Shared Folders function on the AS/400?

6. What reasons exist for transferring files from the AS/400 to a PC?

7. What is a PC file description in reference to the transfer function?

Exercises

1. Using the Windows File Manager, browse the folders available on your AS/400.

2. Transfer a file specified by and supplied from your instructor to a diskette on your PC.

Chapter 10

Accessing the AS/400 Database

Objectives

To understand the function of DB2/400 files

To be able to

- ✓ access Program Development Manager (PDM)
- ✓ create members using PDM
- ✓ enter records using Source Entry Utility (SEU)
- ✓ save a member with SEU
- ✓ compile a source member
- ✓ create and compile a logical file
- ✓ create a customized Data File Utility (DFU) program
- ✓ save a DFU program
- ✓ enter data using a DFU program
- ✓ create a Query for OS/400 program
- ✓ generate a Query for OS/400 spooled report

Overview

A company's business information must be handled efficiently, and employees must have access to up-to-date information. Database management system software frequently provides the most effective way to manage data files and the relationships between them.

The AS/400 is shipped with a database management system named DB2/400 as an integrated part of the OS/400 operating system. A database integrated into the operating system provides a consistent user interface, consistent security access, and more efficient system management. For example, a security officer can use the same CL security commands to maintain the database objects as (s)he uses for other AS/400 objects.

As system operator, you may be responsible for keeping an inventory of purchased and used hardware. Creating a database for reference and reports would be helpful for tracking such equipment. In this chapter, we will supply an example of the procedures required to create and access an inventory file such as you might use for equipment tracking. You can describe and create DB2/400 files in various ways on the AS/400. You can use an AS/400 licensed program such as SQL, COBOL, or RPG. You can use the Interactive Data Definition Utility (IDDU) to create database file descriptions, but IDDU is limited to describing only physical files. OS/400's data description specifications (DDS) provides a way to externally define physical and logical files. You must create a DDS source member using a source editor and then compile the program to create the *FILE object.

This chapter will give you the information you need to create and access DB2/400 files using the utilities provided with OS/400. In this chapter, you will use the Source Entry Utility (SEU) to enter DDS and create source members. You will use the Program Development Manager (PDM) to work with and manipulate the source members to compile and thus create objects. With the Data File Utility (DFU), you can quickly (but possibly without audit trails) create, update, or delete data within the physical file object. Then you will be able to create reports using Query for OS/400. This sequence will give you an overview of how to create a database, enter data into the object, and then create printed reports from the data.

Program Development Manager (PDM)

The first step in creating a database is to access the appropriate tools to make this a simple task. The operating system supplies the Program Development Manager (PDM) to work with objects and members. The PDM screens represent a user-friendly interface, including lists of objects, and members with options to process these objects.

To access the Work with Objects Using PDM screen,

Type	WRKOBJPDM	on the command line
Press	Enter	

The objects that exist in your library will be listed on this screen, shown in Figure 10.1. Source members must be created within a source type file with a PF-SRC attribute.

To access more options from this screen,

Press	F23	for "More options"
Type	12	in the SOURCE object option column or any object column with a Type of *FILE and an Attribute of PF-SRC on the Work with Objects Using PDM screen
Press	Enter	to access the Work with Members Using PDM screen

The Work with Members Using PDM display (Figure 10.2) is where you can see a list of all source files and work with them. You can edit, delete, display, print, and rename files (among other options) from this screen.

Figure 10.1
Work with Objects Using
PDM Screen

```
                        Work with Objects Using PDM

Library . . . . .    USRLIB          Position to . . . . . . . .
                                     Position to type  . . . . .

Type options, press Enter.
  2=Change        3=Copy         4=Delete        5=Display       7=Rename
8=Display description     9=Save          10=Restore      11=Move

Opt   Object      Type        Attribute    Text
__    USRID       *OUTQ                    User output queue
__    SOURCE      *FILE       PF-SRC       User source file
__    USRID       *JOBD                    User job description




                                                            Bottom
Parameters or command
====>_____

F3=Exit         F4=Prompt            F5=Refresh          F6=Create
F9=Retrieve     F10=Command entry    F23=More options    F24=More keys
```

Figure 10.2
Work with Members
Using PDM Screen

```
                        Work with Members Using PDM

File. . . . . . .    SOURCE
  Library . . . .    USRLIB                   Position to . . . . . . . .

Type options, press Enter.
  2=Edit         3=Copy         4=Delete        5=Display       6=Print
7=Rename       8=Display description  9=Save            13=Change text...

Opt   Member     Type        Text

   (No members in file)




                                                            Bottom
Parameters or command
====>_____
F3=Exit         F4=Prompt            F5=Refresh          F6=Create
F9=Retrieve     F10=Command entry    F23=More options    F24=More keys
```

Source Entry Utility (SEU)

SEU is the editor OS/400 provides for creating source members. SEU is a
full-screen editor that provides prompts for an easy user interface. SEU is a
programming editor, not a word processor; so word wrap is not available with
SEU. When entry errors are made, the SEU syntax checker will highlight the
line with the error.

To access the Start Source Entry Utility (STRSEU) screen, shown in Figure 10.3,

| **Type** | STRSEU | on the command line |
| **Press** | F4 | prompt function |

Figure 10.3
Start Source Entry Utility
(STRSEU) Screen

```
                      Start Source Entry Utility (STRSEU)

 Type choices, press Enter.

 Source file. . . . . . . . . > SOURCE        Name, *PRV
   Library. . . . . . . . . >   USERLIB       Name, *LIBL, *CURLIB, *PRV
 Source member. . . . . . . .  *PRV           Name, *PRV, *SELECT
 Source type. . . . . . . . .  *SAME          Name, *SAME, BAS, BASP, C...
 Text 'description' . . . . .  *BLANK_____




 F3=Exit   F4=Prompt   F12=Cancel    F13=How to use this display
 F24=More keys
```

Now let's work through an example in which you will enter DDS in SEU to create a physical data file specification. The Source file parameter in Figure 10.3 represents the file that will contain the members you create in the SEU session. The Source file Library parameter is the library that contains the source file. This Source member is the name of the member you are creating with the source entry utility. The *PRV default represents the previous member you have worked with using SEU; this provides a quick way to return to previous SEU sessions. The Source type entered will determine the prompt available for use within the SEU session. On the Start Source Entry Utility (STRSEU) screen,

Type	INVTRY	to replace the source member name
Type	PF	for the "Source type"
Type	Inventory file	for the "Text 'description'"
Press	Enter	

When the SEU Edit Screen first appears (Figure 10.4), the End-of-data line will be located at the bottom of the screen. This display is useful for advanced users and for making corrections. Your library name and source file name will be displayed in the upper right-hand corner. The cursor is located in the right-hand corner of your display screen. Pressing the Enter key will position the cursor at the beginning of the source code entry and compress the blank lines.

For experienced SEU users, free-form entry is available. The type of source code being created will determine the acceptable position or column location in which code can be entered. The prompt utility provides the user with easy-to-use, fill-in entries with headings, and it places the values in the proper position. The SEU command line (located near the top of the display) offers access to SEU commands, including SAVE, CANCEL, and CHANGE.

HINT

Press the Help key for instructions for SEU display commands and tools.

Figure 10.4
SEU Edit Screen

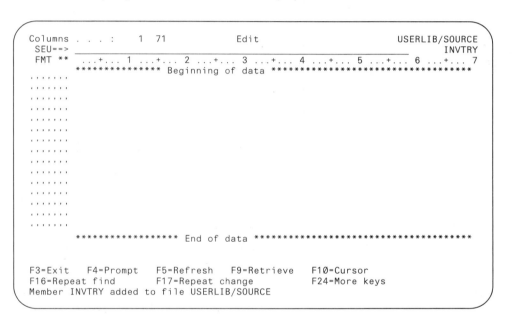

```
Columns . . . :    1  71            Edit                    USERLIB/SOURCE
  SEU==> _____        INVTRY
  FMT **   ...+... 1 ...+... 2 ...+... 3 ...+... 4 ...+... 5 ...+... 6 ...+... 7
           *************** Beginning of data *********************************
  .......
  .......
  .......
  .......
  .......
  .......
  .......
  .......
  .......
  .......
  .......
  .......
  .......
  .......

           ***************** End of data ***************************************


F3=Exit    F4=Prompt    F5=Refresh    F9=Retrieve    F10=Cursor
F16=Repeat find         F17=Repeat change            F24=More keys
Member INVTRY added to file USERLIB/SOURCE
```

Press   Enter   to delete blank lines

Type   IP   for the Insert and Prompt utility

Figure 10.5 represents the SEU Edit screen with blank lines deleted. You will use this screen as you work through the steps required to create files with DDS.

Figure 10.5
SEU Edit Screen,
Blank Lines Deleted

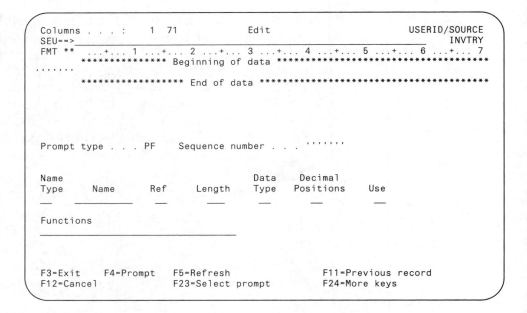

```
 Columns . . . :   1  71          Edit               USERID/SOURCE
 SEU==>_____    INVTRY
 FMT **   ...+... 1 ...+... 2 ...+... 3 ...+... 4 ...+... 5 ...+... 6 ...+... 7
........  *************** Beginning of data ***************************************

          ***************** End of data ****************************************


 Prompt type . . . PF   Sequence number . . . '''''''


 Name                                   Data   Decimal
 Type      Name      Ref     Length     Type   Positions     Use
 __     _____    __       ___       __      ____         __

 Functions
 _____


 F3=Exit    F4=Prompt   F5=Refresh              F11=Previous record
 F12=Cancel             F23=Select prompt       F24=More keys
```

On the above screen, the cursor should be located in the bottom half of
the screen, in the Name Type field. You should use the Field exit key to move
to the next field. If you make a mistake, move back to the previous field by
holding down the Shift key and pressing the Tab key. When all entries for the
record are correct, use the Enter key to complete the entry. For our example,

Type	R	for the "Name Type" parameter
Type	INVTRYR	for the "Name" parameter
Press	Enter	

For a data description specification, the first line entry always specifies
the name of the record being described. The R in the "Name Type" parameter identifies this as a record format statement. In our example, the name of
the record is INVTRYR. Enter the record's field descriptions as shown in the
following steps:

Press	Field Exit	to bypass the Name Type field parameter
Type	PRODID	in the Name parameter
Press	Field Exit	twice to bypass the Reference parameter
Type	6	for the Length parameter
Press	Field Exit	
Type	A	in the Data Type parameter
Press	Field Exit	to bypass the Decimal Positions parameter

Press	Field Exit				to bypass the "Use" parameter
Type	COLHDG('PRODUCT ID')				for the "Functions" parameter

The field PRODID is defined above as a six-character-long alphabetic field with the column heading of PRODUCT ID.

Using the following information, continue to enter the field descriptions for INVTRY. Remember that the first two lines have already been completed.

Name Type	Name	Fld Len	Data Type	Dec Pos	Functions
R	INVTRYR				
	PRODID	6	A		COLHDG('PRODUCT ID')
	SNUM	10	A		COLHDG('SERIAL #')
	DESC	13	A		COLHDG('DESCRIPTION')
	DEPTNO	3	A		COLHDG('DEPT NO')

Type	FILE	on the SEU command line to save the source member

You can use the FILE SEU command at any time within your SEU session to save the DDS description and then return to editing.

Press	F3	to exit SEU
Press	Enter	to return to the Work with Members Using PDM screen

Option 14 on the Work with Members Using PDM screen lets you compile a source member. When the source member's compilation is complete, the operating system will send a message related to the success or failure of the compile. From the Work with Members Using PDM screen,

Type	14	in the option column for member INVTRY
Press	Enter	
Type	DSPMSG	on a command line to determine whether the compilation was successful
Press	Enter	

The compilation message will inform you that the compile completed normally or abnormally. During compilation, the operating system sends a spooled file related to the compile to the output queue. This spooled file is valuable for correcting errors in the source code.

Press	F12	to exit the Display Message screen
Type	WRKSPLF	on the command line to view the spooled file
Press	Enter	
Type	5	to display the spooled output file created during compilation
Press	Enter	

If there are errors noted in the compilation listing, return to the WRKMBRPDM display and use option 2 to edit the member. If you prefer CL commands, type STRSEU on any command line and press Enter. To return to the previous source member edit session, leave the default *PRV and press Enter.

Logical Files

Unlike a physical file, a logical file does not contain data. A logical file provides an alternate access path to records stored in a physical file, perhaps by sorting the records differently or by including only selected data records. This alternative can be extremely helpful because it is very difficult to modify physical files once data has been included in the object. For our example, let's choose to access our physical file by department number, so we will create a logical view for our physical inventory file, INVTRY, with the department number as the key.

We will also use SEU to create the logical file member for the physical file, as shown in Figure 10.6. To access this screen,

| Type | STRSEU | on any command line |
| Press | F4 | to prompt |

Figure 10.6
Start Source Entry Utility
(STRSEU) Screen

```
                    Start Source Entry Utility (STRSEU)

Type choices, press Enter.

Source file  . . . . . . . . . . > SOURCE      Name, *PRV
   Library . . . . . . . . . . >   USRLIB      Name, *LIBL, *CURLIB, *PRV
Source member . . . . . . . . .   *PRV         Name, *PRV, *SELECT
Source type . . . . . . . . . .   *SAME        Name, *SAME, BAS, BASP, C...
Text 'description'. . . . . . .   *BLANK_____




 F3=Exit   F4=Prompt   F12=Cancel    F13=How to use this display
 F24=More keys
```

At this point,

Type	INVTRYL1	for the Source file name
Type	LF	for the Source type
Type	Logical inventory file	for the Text description

Press	Enter	
Press	Enter	to delete blank lines
Type	IP	for the Insert and Prompt utility

The SEU Edit screen is shown in Figure 10.7.

Figure 10.7
SEU Edit Screen

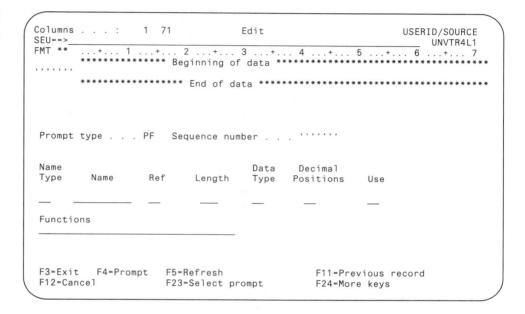

```
Columns . . . :    1  71              Edit                    USERID/SOURCE
SEU==>_____    UNVTR4L1
FMT **   ...+... 1 ...+... 2 ...+... 3 ...+... 4 ...+... 5 ..+... 6 ...+... 7
         *************** Beginning of data ***************************************
.......
         ***************** End of data ******************************************


Prompt type . . . PF   Sequence number . . . ''''''''


Name                                    Data   Decimal
Type       Name       Ref     Length    Type   Positions    Use

__      _____    __      ____      __     ___          __

Functions
_____



F3=Exit   F4=Prompt   F5=Refresh           F11=Previous record
F12=Cancel            F23=Select prompt    F24=More keys
```

The "Functions" parameter is used here to make the connection between the physical file and the logical file.

Type	R	for the "Name Type" parameter
Type	PFILE(INVTRY)	for the "Functions" parameter
Press	Enter	

Continue to enter the field descriptions for the INVTRYR record in the logical description, as follows:

Type	Name	
R	INVTRYR	PFILE(INVTRY)
	PRODID	
	DEPTNO	
	SNUM	
	DESC	
K	DEPTNO	

You do not need to enter the field length, data type, and functions again, because these attributes will be accessed and retrieved from the physical file.

Type	FILE	on the SEU command line to save the source member
Press	F3	to exit the SEU Edit screen
Type	14	in the option column for member INVTRYL1
Press	Enter	
Type	DSPMSG	on a command line to determine whether compilation was successful
Press	Enter	
Press	F12	to exit the Display Message screen
Type	WRKSPLF	on the command line to view the spooled file
Press	Enter	
Type	5	to display the spooled output file created during compilation
Press	Enter	

HINT

If there are errors noted in the compilation listing, return to the WRKMBRPDM display and use option 2 to edit.

Data File Utility (DFU)

You can use the Data File Utility (DFU) to add, update, or delete physical file records. Most installations purchase or create their own custom programs to update data files. These systems provide adequate protection via audit trail reports to reduce unauthorized data modification, and this method is preferred. At times, however, this approach is not feasible because of time constraints. For our example, DFU provides a quick method for creating update entry programs to enter actual data into the INVTRY file.

To start DFU,

Type	STRDFU	
Press	Enter	
Type	2	to "Create a DFU program"
Press	Enter	

To customize a DFU program, you can use either the Create a DFU Program screen (Figure 10.8) or the Create a Temporary DFU Program screen. The second option requires no programming, but it provides only the default specifications.

The Create a DFU Program screen prompts you for the name of the program to be created and the data file that will be used by the program. The default for the "Library" parameter should be your current library, *CURLIB.

Figure 10.8
Create a DFU
Program Screen

```
                            Create a DFU Program
Type choices, press Enter.

   Program . . . . . . . . . .    _____    Name, F4 for List
      Library . . . . . . . . .   *CURLIB        Name, *CURLIB
   Data file . . . . . . . . .    _____    Name, F4 for List
      Library . . . . . . . . .   *CURLIB        Name, *LIBL, *CURLIB




   F3=Exit    F4=Prompt    F12=Cancel
```

HINT

Press F4 (Prompt) to select the data file for your DFU Program.

In the example, the logical file INVTRYL1 will be used, allowing access to the file in departmental order.

For our purposes, we will name the DFU program INVNTPR. Therefore, all programs relating to the INVTRY file will have the same initial characters and can easily be identified as part of the inventory system.

Type	INVNTPR	for the "Program" parameter
Type	INVTRYL1	for the "Data file" parameter
Press	Enter	

The Define General Information/Indexed File screen, as shown in Figure 10.9, allows you as the operator to control the general characteristics of the program. You should assign a job title that the program can recognize later. The "Display format" parameter offers you four choices of display formats. Select 4 to be "row oriented."

This screen offers other customization options. For users accustomed to the System/36 environment, the "S/36 style" parameter is available. Additionally, you can edit numeric fields for format, and updates can be disallowed.

Figure 10.9
Define General
Information/Indexed
File Screen

```
              Define General Information/Indexed File

Type choices, press Enter.

  Job title . . . . . . . . . .  _____
  Display format  . . . . . . .  4      1=Single,  2=Multiple
                                        3=Maximum, 4=Row oriented

  Audit report  . . . . . . . .  Y      Y=Yes, N=No
  S/36 style  . . . . . . . . .  N      Y=Yes, N=No
  Suppress errors . . . . . . .  N      Y=Yes, N=No
  Edit numerics . . . . . . . .  N      Y=Yes, N=No
  Allow updates on roll . . . .  Y      Y=Yes, N=No
  Keys:
    Generate  . . . . . . . . .  N      Y=Yes, N=No
    Changes allowed . . . . . .  Y      Y=Yes, N=No




F3=Exit    F12=Cancel    F14=Display definition
```

On this screen,

Type	Inventory maintenance program	for the "Job title"
Type	4	for a "Row oriented" format
Press	Enter	

HINT

Press the F14 key for further display definition or the Help key for information about the display as a whole.

The "Audit report" parameter specifies whether an audit report should be spooled. You should specify a Y for this value. A new screen will appear for further definition of the Audit report.

Type	Y	for "Audit report"
Type	N	for "Edit numerics"
Press	Enter	

This will take you to the Define Audit Control screen. The Define Audit Control screen, shown in Figure 10.10, provides you with control over what type of updates will be included within the audit report. Always print additions, changes, and deletions to attempt to prevent unauthorized modifications. The printer options are available so you can define the paper size being used for the audit report.

Figure 10.10
Define Audit
Control Screen

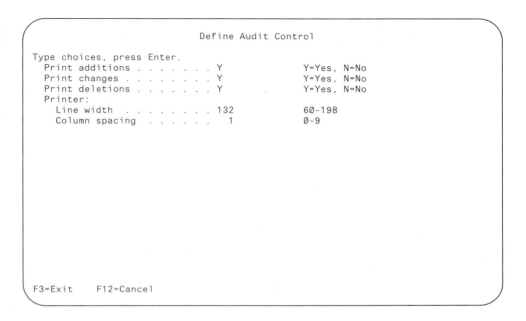

```
                            Define Audit Control
Type choices, press Enter.
   Print additions . . . . . . . Y              Y=Yes, N=No
   Print changes . . . . . . . . Y              Y=Yes, N=No
   Print deletions . . . . . . . Y              Y=Yes, N=No
   Printer:
     Line width  . . . . . . . 132              60-198
     Column spacing  . . . . . .   1            0-9




















F3=Exit      F12=Cancel
```

From this screen,

Type   the appropriate line width
             and column spacing

Press   Enter   to use the default values

The next screen you see, the Work with Record Formats screen, lists the record formats in the file specification. If a file specification has more than one record format, all formats will be listed. In our example, one record format, INVTRYR, should be listed, as shown in Figure 10.11.

You use the "Specify" option to select the record format. The "Multiple Records" specification allows multiple records to be entered on one screen.

Type   2   in the INVTRTYR option column

Type   Y   in the Multiple Records column

Press   Enter

You can customize data entry using the Select and Sequence Fields screen shown in Figure 10.12 to allow control over what fields can be viewed or accessed for update and in what order the fields will be displayed on the Update Entry screen.

Figure 10.11
Work with Record
Formats Screen

```
                        Work with Record Formats

File . . . :   INVTRYL1                        Library  . . . . :    USRLIB
Type options, press Enter. Press F21 to select all.
2=Specify    4=Delete
                        Multiple
Opt  Format        Records   Defined  Description
 _   INVTRTYR         N         N     Inventory Record













F3=Exit    F12=Cancel
```

Figure 10.12
Select and Sequence
Fields Screen

```
                        Select and Sequence Fields

    File  . . . . . . . . . :   INVTRYL1      Library  . . . . :    USRLIB
 Record format . . . . . . :   INVTRYR


 Select fields and their sequence or press F21 to select all; press Enter.
   Sequence   Field        Attr    Length   Type     Description
    1_____    PRODID                   6    CHAR     Product ID
    2_____    DEPTNO                   3    CHAR     Dept No
    3_____    SNUM                    10    CHAR     Serial #
    4_____    DESC                    13    CHAR     Description









                                                                    Bottom
 F3=Exit           F5=Refresh     F12=Cancel      F14=Display definition
 F20=Renumber      F21=Select all
```

You select and sequence fields by typing the preferred sequence in the "Sequence" column option field.

Type	2	in the PRODID option column
Type	1	in the DEPTNO option column
Type	4	in the SNUM option column
Type	3	in the DESC option column

Press   Enter

Press   Enter   to confirm choices

The Work with Fields screen, as shown in Figure 10.13, will appear with your selected fields displayed in the new order.

Figure 10.13

Work with Fields Screen

```
                              Work with Fields

File  . . . . . . . . . . :    INVTRYL1      Library . . . . :     USRLIB
Record format . . . . . . :    INVTRYR
Type options, press Enter. Press F21 to select all.
  2=Specify extended definition
  4=Delete extended definition


   Extended
Opt  Field        Definition     Heading
  _   DEPTNO           N          DEPT NO_____
  _   PRODID           N          PRODUCT ID_____
  _   DESC             N          DESCRIPTION_____
  _   SNUM             N          SERIAL #_____




                                                             Bottom
F3=Exit                      F5=Refresh              F12=Cancel
F14=Display definition       F21=Select all
```

You can access the Extended Field Definitions screen from this display using option 2. Extended field definitions may not be available if they were previously assigned within this display screen. Pressing the F21 key would specify that all fields can be designated for extended field definitions, thus leading you to an additional screen for each field. If extended definitions are not defined, the validation keywords from the DDS file description are assumed. To exit the Extended Field Definition display,

Press   Enter

The Exit DFU Program Definition screen lets you save, run, or save and then run, a newly defined DFU program. As shown in Figure 10.14, the INVNTPR program will be saved and the records can be added to the INVTRY physical file, via the INVTRYL1 logical file.

The F17=Fast path function key provides a direct way to execute the program. We will not cover other displays or optional screens in this discussion. To execute the program automatically,

Press   F17   for "Fast path," to execute the program automatically

Figure 10.14
Exit DFU Program
Definition Screen

```
                         Exit DFU Program Definition
Type choices, press Enter.
   Save program . . . . . . . . .    Y              Y=Yes, N=No
   Run program. . . . . . . . . .    Y              Y=Yes, N=No
      For choice Y=Yes:
         Type of run . . . . . . .   1              1=Change, 2=Display
   Modify program . . . . . . . .    N              Y=Yes, N=No
   Save DDS source . . . . . . . .   N              Y=Yes, N=No

   For Save program Y=Yes:
      Program . . . . . . . . .      INVNTPR        Name
         Library . . . . . . . . .   USRLIB         Name, *CURLIB, . . .
      Authority . . . . . . . . .    *LIBCRTAUT     Name, *LIBCRTAUT, . . .
      Text  . . . . . . . . . .      INVENTORY MAINTENANCE
   For Save DDS source Y=Yes:
      Source file . . . . . . . .                   Name
         Library . . . . . . . . .   *CURLIB        Name, *CURLIB, . . .
      Source member . . . . . . .    INVNTPR        Name




F3=Exit      F14=Display definition      F17=Fast path
```

You can enter multiple records on the Inventory Maintenance screen (this is the next screen you see), as shown in Figure 10.15 (the "Multiple Records" parameter was specified as Yes on the Work with Record Formats display).

The standard function keys are available on the Inventory Maintenance screen. You use the Field exit key to move from field to field.

Figure 10.15
Inventory Maintenance
Screen

```
INVENTORY MAINTENANCE                            Mode . . . . :   ENTRY
Format . . . . :   INVTRYR                        File . . . . :   INVTRYL1

   Dept no    Product ID    Description         Serial #
   ____       _____      _____        _____
   ____       _____      _____        _____
   ____       _____      _____        _____
   ____       _____      _____        _____
   ____       _____      _____        _____
   ____       _____      _____        _____
   ____       _____      _____        _____
   ____       _____      _____        _____
   ____       _____      _____        _____
   ____       _____      _____        _____



F3=Exit                  F5=Refresh                  F6=Select format
F9=Insert                F10=Entry                   F11=Change
```

Add the following six records to the record format on this screen:

Dept No.	Product ID	Description	Serial #
01	IBM	PC 300	1555999B0S
02	COMPAQ	PROLINEA/486	1555888C0S
01	NEC	POWERMATE	1555222J05
01	IBM	PC 300	1555111E0S
02	NEC	POWERMATE	1555333K0S

Press   Enter   to add the records and provide a blank screen

Press   F3   to exit the display

The End Data Entry screen will be displayed, revealing the number of records that have been added, changed, or deleted.

Press   Enter   to exit the program and end the session

The audit report will be spooled when the DFU session is ended. In these examples, we created a physical and logical file with DDS, and the data was entered into the physical file with a newly created DFU program.

Query for OS/400

As we mentioned at the beginning of this chapter, keeping track of inventory in a large company is sometimes difficult. Knowing what equipment was distributed to what department would be helpful. Query for OS/400 is an IBM licensed program that provides an easy method for creating reports by selecting and filtering data to provide useful information. Data does not become information until it is produced in an organized way to be useful to people. We will provide information here about building a basic Query report using either a physical file or a logical file. For more information about Query utilities, see IBM's *Query/400 User's Guide.*

To access the Work with Queries screen, shown in Figure 10.16,

Type   WRKQRY   on any command line

Press   Enter

The Work with Queries screen prompts the user for choices related to working with queries. From this screen a user can create a new query, run an existing query, or copy, delete, display, change, or print the definition of an existing query. A user can name the query definition within the Work with Queries display or later when (s)he is exiting from the Query utility.

Figure 10.16
Work with Queries Screen

```
                           Work with Queries

 Type choices, press Enter.


    Option  . . . . . .   __          1=Create, 2=Change, 3=Copy, 4=Delete
                                      5=Display, 6=Print definition
                                      8=Run in batch, 9=Run
    Query . . . . . . .  _____   Name, F4 for list
      Library . . . . .   USRLIB      Name, *LIBL, F4 for list









 F3=Exit       F4=Prompt      =F5=Refresh    F12=Cancel
```

On this screen,

Type	1	for the "Option" parameter to create a new Query report
Type	INVEN01	for the "Query" name parameter
Press	Enter	

You will see on the Define the Query screen, as Figure 10.17 indicates, that you can define and customize a Query report in many ways; the only required option for a Query report is to "Specify file selections."

Figure 10.17
Define the Query Screen

```
                          Define the Query
 Query . . . . . . :   INVEN01       Option . . . . . :   CREATE
   Library . . . . :   USRLIB        CCSID . . . . . . :   65535

 Type options, press Enter.  Press F21 to select all.
   1=Select

 Opt    Query Definition Option
   __       Specify file selections
   __       Define result fields
   __       Select and sequence fields
   __       Select records
   __       Select sort fields
   __       Select collating sequence
   __       Specify report column formatting
   __       Select report summary functions
   __       Define report breaks
   __       Select output type and output form
   __       Specify processing options


 F3=Exit        F5=Report       F12=Cancel
 F13=Layout     F18=Files       F21=Select all
```

Type   1   in the "Specify file selections" option column

Press   Enter

This will take you to the Specify File Selections Screen, shown in Figure 10.18.

Figure 10.18
Specify File
Selections Screen

```
                          Specify File Selections
   Type choices, press Enter.  Press F9 to specify an additional
     file selection.

     File . . . . . . . . .   _____     Name, F4 for list
       Library  . . . . . .   USRLIB        Name, *LIBL, F4 for list
     Member . . . . . . . .   *FIRST        Name, *FIRST, F4 for list
     Format . . . . . . . .   *FIRST        Name, *FIRST, F4 for list




   F3=Exit          F4=Prompt       F5=Report        F9=Add file
   F12=Cancel       F13=Layout      F24=More keys
```

On this screen, you must specify the "File" name parameter either by typing the file name or by prompting to view available files.

Type   INVTRY   for the "File" name parameter

Press   Enter

Press   Enter   to confirm

In this example, the physical file description is used to run the Query report; but the logical file's name could have been entered in the same way. A greater-than sign (>) will be visible next to the "Specify file selection" option, to inform you that a file selection has been completed. You could run the report by pressing F5; but if you do, the listing will be in record order.

To specify a sorted listing from the Define the Query screen, use the "Select sort fields" option on the Define the Query screen (Figure 10.17).

Type   1   in the "Select sort fields" option column on the Define the Query screen

Press   Enter

This will take you to the Select Sort Fields screen, shown in Figure 10.19.

Figure 10.19
Select Sort Fields Screen

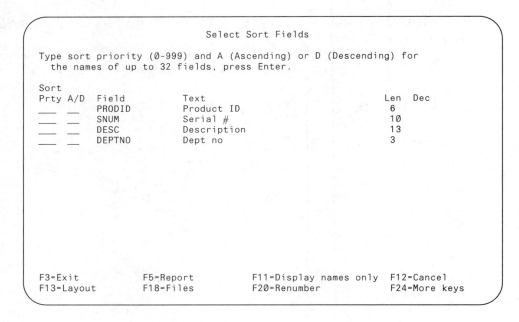

```
                              Select Sort Fields

Type sort priority (0-999) and A (Ascending) or D (Descending) for
  the names of up to 32 fields, press Enter.

Sort
Prty A/D  Field          Text                              Len  Dec
___  __   PRODID         Product ID                         6
___  __   SNUM           Serial #                          10
___  __   DESC           Description                       13
___  __   DEPTNO         Dept no                            3











F3=Exit            F5=Report          F11=Display names only  F12=Cancel
F13=Layout         F18=Files          F20=Renumber            F24=More keys
```

The fields included here are from the DDS for physical file INVTRY. The "Sort Priority" column defines how the database should be sorted. In this example, we wish to list our report with Department Number in ascending order, and Product ID in ascending order, to show what items are located in each department. To do this,

Type	2	in the "Sort Prty" option column for PRODID
Type	A	in the "A/D" option column for PRODID
Type	1	in the "Sort Prty" option column for DEPTNO
Type	A	in the "A/D" option column for DEPTNO
Press	Enter	
Press	Enter	again, to confirm choices

The query has now been defined using the physical file named INVTRY, and it will list the records in alphabetical order by product within ascending order by department number, as shown in Figure 10.20. To generate the Query report,

Press	F5	function key

Summary

Many methods exist to access DB2/400 files created on the AS/400. This chapter has stepped you through the process for creating a DB2/400 file and for printing a Query report. We used DFU to enter data. Following is a summary of the process we have used in this chapter to ultimately generate a spooled output report:

Figure 10.20
Display Report Screen

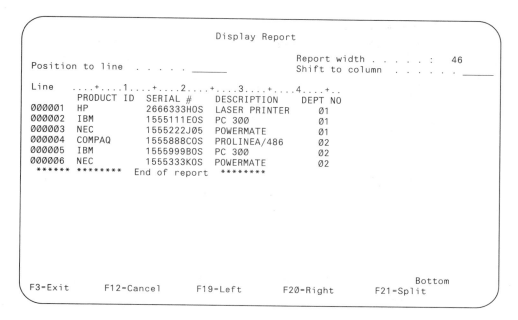

```
                            Display Report

                                    Report width . . . . . :    46
 Position to line  . . . . _____    Shift to column  . . . . . . _____

 Line     ....+....1....+....2....+....3....+....4....+..
          PRODUCT ID  SERIAL #    DESCRIPTION     DEPT NO
 000001   HP          2666333HOS  LASER PRINTER     01
 000002   IBM         1555111EOS  PC 300            01
 000003   NEC         1555222J05  POWERMATE         01
 000004   COMPAQ      1555888COS  PROLINEA/486      02
 000005   IBM         1555999BOS  PC 300            02
 000006   NEC         1555333KOS  POWERMATE         02
 ****** ********   End of report   ********

                                                              Bottom
 F3=Exit      F12=Cancel      F19=Left      F20=Right    F21=Split
```

1. Create the source member using SEU.

2. Compile the source member using option 14 on the Work with Members Using PDM screen. If the compile was successful, an object will be created with a file type *FILE and an attribute of PF-DTA.

3. Create a logical file using SEU.

4. Compile the logical file member using option 14 on the Work with Members Using PDM screen. If the compile was successful, an object will be created with a file type *FILE and an attribute of LF.

5. Create a DFU program to provide a customized data entry screen with multiple records that can be entered on the same display, to generate an audit trail report, and to resequence the fields to match the input forms. Then save the DFU program for future use.

6. Use the DFU program by pressing the F17=Fast path function key to enter the data records.

7. Generate a Query for OS/400 program to report on the data. Query requires the physical file or the logical file to be entered. Sort the report by department and then by product number. Save the Query program for future use.

8. Generate the Query for OS/400 report.

Key Terms

Data File Utility (DFU)   Query
DDS   Source Entry Utility (SEU)
Logical file description   Source file
PDM   Source member
Physical file description

Review Questions

1. What is DB2/400?

2. How does the AS/400 use DB2/400?

3. What do the initials SEU stand for? What function does SEU perform?

4. Why does SEU create a "member" within a source file?

5. Why does the member need to be compiled?

6. What do the initials DFU stand for? What function does DFU perform?

7. How can DFU be customized? How can a user access the "default" DFU program?

8. Using DFU, how would a user enter data?

9. What is the function of Query for OS/400?

10. How can Query for OS/400 use a logical file?

Exercises

1. Change the Query report to use the logical file. Run the report.

2. Change the Query report sort sequence to sort by description. Run the report.

3. Add the following records using DFU:

Dept No	Product ID	Description	Serial #
03	HP	DESK JET 560C	1666999ART
04	HP	DESK JET 560C	1666888ART
03	NEC	POWERMATE	134582DJ86
03	MINLTA	PC	1666593OPE
04	MINLTA	PC	1666492KEA
03	NEC	MONITOR 654	4568936JYE

4. Create a new logical file to key the report by serial number. Name the logical file INVTRYL2.

5. Print the report using the logical file INVTRYL2.

Appendix A

Commonly Used Commands

This appendix contains a summary of commands that the novice operator may be asked to use. We have found these generally helpful, and they may be the solution to problems that initially are not obvious. Frequently, the commands require Security Officer or System Administrator authority.

User-Related Activities
Activity: To delete all objects from a library.
To delete all objects from a library, use the CLRLIB (Clear Library) command. This command does not delete the library itself. If no current library exists or no current library is specified, then the library list in QGPL will be cleared. Therefore, we suggest that you always enter the library name when you use this command. These options require Security Officer or System Administrator authority.

Type	CLRLIB
Press	F4 to prompt
Enter	library name

Activity: To change an individual's object authority.
To change an individual's object authority, use the following commands: EDTOBJAUT (Edit Object Authority), GRTOBJAUT (Grant Object Authority), or RVKOBJAUT (Revoke Object Authority).

Activity: To change a password that has been forgotten or doesn't work any longer because it has expired.

Type	CHGUSRPRF
Press	Enter
Type	the User ID
Press	Enter
Change	the "Password" parameter to the same as the User ID
Change	the "Set password to expired" parameter to *YES
Press	Enter

Then have the user

Sign on	with the password that is now the same as his or her User ID
Type	CHGPWD

Press	Enter	
Follow instructions	on the Change Password screen	

Activity: To print a data file without having to do a screen dump.

To print a data file without having to do a screen dump, use the CPYF (Copy File) command. The spooled file will be placed in the output queue to which you are signed on.

Type	CPYF	
Press	F4	to prompt
Enter	name of file to print	(such as the "from file")
Enter	*PRINT	for the "to file" entry
Press	Enter	

Programmer-Related Activities

Activity: To look for backup objects from compiled programs.

To look for backup objects from compiled programs, use the WORKOBJOWN (Work with Object Owner) command. Any users, but generally programmers, might receive an error message indicating that they have exceeded the maximum storage for their user profiles. Each time a source member is compiled, a new object is created in the current library and in a library called QRPLOBJ. The system assigns the backup object a name that starts with a Q and ends with a number. To display the Q... object, execute the following command:

Type	WRKOBJOWN	(Work with Object Owner)
Press	Enter	

Look through the objects on the display. If this particular area has multiple Q... files, the backup objects could be causing the message. You can delete these objects without concern. System Administrator or Security Officer authority is required.

Activity: To delete all backup objects from the QRPLOBJ library.

To delete all backup objects from the QRPLOBJ library (generally created from source member compiles), use the CLRLIB (Clear Library) command. Use this command to delete all the Q... files. These options require Security Officer or System Administrator authority.

Type	CLRLIB	(Clear Library)
Press	F4	to prompt
Enter	QRPLOBJ	as the library name

The user must then sign off and then sign back on.

Activity: To end a program loop from a workstation.

A program generally loops during the development stage. If a program is looping, the Input Inhibit indicator stays lit on the workstation and the keyboard is locked. To end the program, the request to the system must be ended. Ensure that the programmer is notified of the program name and that the program was ended.

Hold down	the SHIFT key
Press	the SYSREQ key

An input line will appear across the bottom of the screen.

Press	Enter	
Choose	Option 2	to "End the previous request"

Software or Hardware Activities

Activity: To load an IBM licensed program.

If there is no version number listed in the right-hand column of the Installed Licensed Programs screen, then the licensed program has not yet been loaded.

Type	GO LICPGM	to access the Licensed Programs Options screen
Type	11	to access the Installed Licensed Programs screen
Press	Enter	

Activity: To change the device address.

After you move a device from one location to another, the device must be re-addressed. No two devices can have the same address at any time, whether the devices are varied on or off. As operator, you must assign a non-existent address to the old device, possibly the matching port number with a switch setting of 99. Next, change the new device to the appropriate port and switch settings.

VARY OFF	the old device	
Type	WRKCFGSTS	
Press	F4	to prompt for command parameters
Type	*DEV	for the "Type"w parameter
Press	Enter	to accept other parameter defaults

Then change the Port and switch settings for the old device:

Select	Option 8	to "Work with device description"
Select	Option 2	to "Change" on the Work with Device Description screen
Change	the Port Number and Switch Setting parameters	
Press	Enter	

Repeat the previous steps to change the port and switch setting for the new device. Then vary on the new device.

Activity: To test whether the modem is working before you use ECS for the Electronic Customer Support.

Type	SNDSRVRQS	on any command line
Press	F4	to prompt for command parameters
Enter	*TEST	for the appropriate parameter
Press	ENTER	

Activity: To access more information about the printer.
The AS/400 stores pieces of information concerning printing in five different objects. The system will move through the list until it has gathered enough information to print a given report. The following list shows the location and the order the AS/400 uses to find the information for printing output:

1. Printer device file
2. Job description
3. User profile
4. Work station description
5. Printer device description system value (QPRTDEV)

Some values for devices and output queues can cause this sequence to change. IBM's *Guide to Programming for Printing* (SC41-37133) has more specific information about these exceptions. The following table represents a summary of the information.

To change the Printer Device File	Change the DEV (Device) parameter value on the CHGPRTF (Change Printer File) command or on the OVRPRTF (Override Printer File) command.
To change the Job Description	Change the PRTDEV (Print device) and OUTQ (Output Queue) parameters on the CHGJOBD (Change Job Description) command.
To change the Work Station Description	Use the WRKDEVD (Work with Device Description) command; use option 2 (Change) for the device to change. Then change the PRTDEV (Print Device) and OUTQ (Output Queue) fields.
To change the User Profile	Use the PRTDEV (Print Device) and OUTQ (Output Queue) parameters on the CHGUSRPRF (Change User Profile) command.
To change the Default Printer	To change the default printer for the entire system, use the Default system printer field on the Change System Options display. To find this display, type GO SETUP on any command line and press the Enter key. Then select option 1 (Change system options).

Power On/Off Considerations

Activity: To implement the semi-emergency power-down AS/400 instructions.
The option to power off the system from the console can only be used if at least 40 minutes are available to complete the power down.

Type	GO POWER	
Press	Enter	
Select	Option 3	to "Power off immediately"

Activity: To power on the AS/400 after an emergency shutdown.

Turn on	the Operator's console
Turn the Key lock switch	to the Manual position
Turn the Unit Emergency switch	to On

When the Sign-On screen appears,

Sign on	as the system operator

You can answer most of the screens that will appear after sign-on by pressing the Enter key.

Appendix B

System Hardware Documentation Forms

As we discussed in Chapter 6, it is important to document your system hardware before you add new devices to the AS/400. To help you do this, we have included the following sample forms from the *AS/400 Device Configuration Guide*:

Form C1 Local Work Station Diagram (Twinaxial Cabling). Use to document your addresses and other information needed to configure displays, printers, and other devices.

Form E1 9406 Tape Controller and Tape Unit Diagram. Use to document your tape and tape controller information.

Form E2 9406 Diskette Unit Diagram; Form E3 9402 and 9404 Tape Unit and Diskette Unit Diagram. Use to document your diskette and diskette controller information.

C1 Local Work Station Diagram (Twinaxial Cabling)

System _____ Card Address _____

Service for Cabling _____ Work Station Controller Name _____

Telephone Number _____ Location of Twinaxial Work Station Attachment _____

Twinaxial Work Station Attachment Port Numbers

| 0 | 1 | 2 | 3 | 4 | 5 | 6 | 7 |

Device Name	
Device Type, Model	
Location	
Device Address	
Display ☐ Printer ☐	
Telephone Number	

Device Name	
Device Type, Model	
Location	
Device Address	
Display ☐ Printer ☐	
Telephone Number	

Device Name	
Device Type, Model	
Location	
Device Address	
Display ☐ Printer ☐	
Telephone Number	

Device Name	
Device Type, Model	
Location	
Device Address	
Display ☐ Printer ☐	
Telephone Number	

Device Name	
Device Type, Model	
Location	
Device Address	
Display ☐ Printer ☐	
Telephone Number	

Device Name	
Device Type, Model	
Location	
Device Address	
Display ☐ Printer ☐	
Telephone Number	

Device Name	
Device Type, Model	
Location	
Device Address	
Display ☐ Printer ☐	
Telephone Number	

Device Name	
Device Type, Model	
Location	
Device Address	
Display ☐ Printer ☐	
Telephone Number	

Note: A maximum of 7 work stations can be attached per port on the Twinaxial Work Station Attachment

Note: You may copy as necessary

E1   9406 Tape Controller and Tape Unit Diagram

System _____

Service Contact_____

Telephone Number _____

Tape Controller

Controller Name	
Controller Type, Model	

Tape Unit with Tape Controller

Controller Name	
Device Name	
Device Type, Model	
Switch Setting	

Tape Unit without Tape Controller

Device Name	
Device Type, Model	

Controller Name	
Controller Type, Model	

Controller Name	
Device Name	
Device Type, Model	
Switch Setting	

Device Name	
Device Type, Model	

Controller Name	
Controller Type, Model	

Controller Name	
Device Name	
Device Type, Model	
Switch Setting	

Device Name	
Device Type, Model	

Controller Name	
Controller Type, Model	

Controller Name	
Device Name	
Device Type, Model	
Switch Setting	

Device Name	
Device Type, Model	

Note: You may copy as necessary

E2   9406 Diskette Unit Diagram

System _____

Service Contact_____

Telephone Number _____

Device Name	
Device Type, Model	

Device Name	
Device Type, Model	

Device Name	
Device Type, Model	

Device Name	
Device Type, Model	

Device Name	
Device Type, Model	

Device Name	
Device Type, Model	

Device Name	
Device Type, Model	

Device Name	
Device Type, Model	

Note: You may copy as necessary

E3 9402 and 9404 Tape Unit and Diskette Unit Diagram

System _____

Service Contact _____

Telephone Number _____

Tape Unit

Device Name	
Device Type, Model	

Diskette Unit

Device Name	
Device Type, Model	

Tape Unit

Device Name	
Device Type, Model	

Diskette Unit

Device Name	
Device Type, Model	

Note: You may copy as necessary

New Books in the Duke Press Library

BUILDING AS/400 CLIENT/SERVER APPLICATIONS
Put ODBC and Client Access APIs to Work
By Mike Otey

Mike Otey, a leading client/server authority with extensive practical client/server application development experience, gives you the why, what, and how-to of AS/400 client/server computing, which matches the strengths of the AS/400 with the PC GUIs that users want. This book's clear and easy-to-understand style guides you through all the important aspects of AS/400 client/server applications. Mike covers APPC and TCP/IP communications, as well as the underlying architectures for each of the major AS/400 client/server APIs. CD with complete source code for several working applications included. 505 pages.

CONTROL LANGUAGE PROGRAMMING FOR THE AS/400, SECOND EDITION
By Bryan Meyers and Dan Riehl, NEWS/400 technical editors

This comprehensive CL programming textbook offers students up-to-the-minute knowledge of the skills they will need in today's MIS environment. Chapters progress methodically from CL basics to more complex processes and concepts, guiding students toward a professional grasp of CL programming techniques and style. In this second edition, the authors have updated the text to include discussion of the Integrated Language Environment (ILE) and the fundamental changes ILE introduces to the AS/400's execution model. 522 pages.

DEVELOPING YOUR AS/400 INTERNET STRATEGY
By Alan Arnold

This book addresses the issues unique to deploying your AS/400 on the Internet. It includes procedures for configuring AS/400 TCP/IP and information about which client and server technologies the AS/400 supports natively. This enterprise-class tutorial evaluates the AS/400 as an Internet server and teaches you how to design, program, and manage your Web home page. 248 pages.

INSIDE THE AS/400, SECOND EDITION
Featuring the AS/400e series
By Frank G. Soltis

Learn from the architect of the AS/400 about the new generation of AS/400e systems and servers, and about the latest system features and capabilities introduced in Version 4 of OS/400. Dr. Frank Soltis demystifies the system, shedding light on how it came to be, how it can do the things it does, and what its future may hold. 402 pages.

1001 SECRETS FOR WINDOWS NT REGISTRY
By Tim Daniels

Without expert guidance, meddling with the registry can be disastrous. But for the accomplished user, *1001 Secrets for Windows NT Registry* is the definitive reference for system customization and optimization. Organized into sections that cover networking, applications, system management, hardware, and performance, the book also has an exhaustive index to help you quickly find the registry information you need. The accompanying CD is packed with innovative registry monitoring and performance utilities, plus an Internet link to our Registry Secrets home page (www.registrysecrets.com) for registry updates and many interactive services for registry "spelunkers." 321 pages.

THE ADMINISTRATOR'S GUIDE TO MICROSOFT SQL SERVER 6.5
By Kevin Cox and William Jones

This book guides database managers and administrators into a thorough understanding of the client/server aspects of the SQL Server 6.5 product, and includes many useful tips for managing security, troubleshooting, and improving performance. 469 pages.

INTERNET SECURITY WITH WINDOWS NT
By Mark Joseph Edwards

Security expert and *Windows NT Magazine* news editor Mark Edwards provides the quintessential guide to Internet and intranet security from the Windows NT platform. Security is the number one concern of NT users, and this comprehensive book covers network security basics as well as IIS and MPS, and includes specific advice about selecting NT tools and security devices. The accompanying CD-ROM includes security-related utilities, tools, and software packages — firewalls, port scanners, network-monitoring software, and virus detection and prevention utilities. These tools, combined with the tips and techniques in the book, are powerful weapons in your security efforts. 520 pages.

THE MICROSOFT OUTLOOK E-MAIL AND FAX GUIDE
By Sue Mosher

Here's a book for Microsoft Outlook 97 end users and the administrators who support them. This easy to read volume will expand your knowledge of Outlook's e-mail functions and explain the real world tasks that you are likely to encounter. Sue Mosher explains the setup of individual e-mail services and components, e-mail options and when you might want to use them, and many time-saving techniques that take you beyond the basics. Users at all levels will learn from this comprehensive introduction to Microsoft's next generation of messaging software. The book includes coverage of the Internet Mail Enhancement Patch, Rules Wizard, and special features for Microsoft Exchange Server users. 500 pages

Also Published by Duke Press

DDS Programming for Display & Printer Files
By James Coolbaugh

Offers a thorough, straightforward explanation of how to use Data Description Specifications (DDS) to program display files and printer files. Covers basic to complex tasks using DDS functions. The author uses DDS programming examples for CL and RPG extensively throughout the book, and you can put these examples to use immediately. A complimentary diskette includes all the source code presented in the book. 444 pages.

Database Design and Programming for DB2/400
By Paul Conte

This textbook is the most complete guide to DB2/400 design and programming available anywhere. The author shows you everything you need to know about physical and logical file DDS, SQL/400, and RPG IV and COBOL/400 database programming. Clear explanations illustrated by a wealth of examples demonstrate efficient database programming and error handling with both DDS and SQL/400. 772 pages.

ILE: A First Look
By George Farr and Shailan Topiwala

This book begins by showing the differences between ILE and its predecessors, then goes on to explain the essentials of an ILE program — using concepts such as modules, binding, service programs, and binding directories. You'll discover how ILE program activation works and how ILE works with its predecessor environments. 183 pages.

Mastering the AS/400
A Practical, Hands-On Guide
By Jerry Fottral

This introductory textbook to AS/400 concepts and facilities has a utilitarian approach that stresses student participation. A natural prerequisite to programming and database management courses, it emphasizes mastery of system/user interface, member-object-library relationship, utilization of CL commands, and basic database and program development utilities. 484 pages.

The Microsoft Exchange Server Internet Mail Connector
By Spyros Sakellariadis

Achieve Internet connectivity using Exchange Server 4.0 and 5.0. This book presents four Internet connectivity models, shows how to set up the Internet Mail Connector with an Internet Service Provider, and illustrates how to monitor Internet traffic. It also includes troubleshooting and reference guides. 234 pages.

The Microsoft Exchange User's Handbook
By Sue Mosher

Microsoft Exchange is all about making connections — connections to a Microsoft Mail server, to Exchange Server, to a fax machine, or to online services. Here's the must-have, complete guide for users who need to know how to set up and use all the features of the Microsoft Exchange client product. Includes chapters about Microsoft Exchange Server 5.0 and Microsoft Outlook. 692 pages. CD included.

Migrating to Windows NT 4.0
By Sean Daily

This book is a comprehensive yet concise guide to the significant changes users will encounter as they make the move to Windows NT 4.0. The author, a Microsoft Certified Systems Engineer (MCSE), eases the transition with his enthusiastic presentation of a wealth of tips and techniques that give readers the sense they're receiving "insider information." 475 pages.

Powering Your Web Site with Windows NT Server
By Nik Simpson

Powering Your Web Site with Windows NT Server explores the tools necessary to establish a presence on the Internet or on an internal corporate intranet using Web technology and Windows NT Server. The author helps readers navigate the process of creating a new information infrastructure, from the basics of justifying the decision to management through the complete implementation cycle. 640 pages. CD included.

Programming in RPG IV, Revised Edition
By Judy Yaeger, Ph.D., a NEWS/400 *technical editor*

This textbook provides a strong foundation in the essentials of business programming, featuring the newest version of the RPG language: RPG IV. Focusing on real-world problems and down-to-earth solutions using the latest techniques and features of RPG, this book provides everything you need to know to write a well-designed RPG IV program. 435 pages.

Programming in RPG/400, Second Edition
By Judy Yaeger, Ph.D., a NEWS/400 *technical editor*

This second edition refines and extends the comprehensive instructional material contained in the original textbook and features a new section that introduces externally described printer files, a new chapter that highlights the fundamentals of RPG IV, and a new appendix that correlates the key concepts from each chapter with their RPG IV counterparts. 481 pages.

RPG IV Jump Start, Second Edition
Moving Ahead With the New RPG
By Bryan Meyers, a NEWS/400 *technical editor*

In this second edition of *RPG IV Jump Start*, Bryan Meyers has added coverage for new releases of the RPG IV compiler (V3R2, V3R6, and V3R7) and amplified the coverage of RPG IV's participation in the integrated language environment (ILE). As in the first edition, he covers RPG IV's changed and new specifications and data types. He presents the new RPG from the perspective of a programmer who already knows the old RPG, pointing out the differences between the two and demonstrating how to take advantage of the new syntax and function. 214 pages.

Starter Kit for the AS/400, Second Edition
An indispensable guide for novice to intermediate AS/400 programmers and system operators
By Wayne Madden, NEWS/400 *publisher and editor in chief,*
with contributions by Bryan Meyers, Andrew Smith, and Peter Rowley

This second edition contains updates of the material in the first edition and incorporates new material that focuses on installing a new release, working with PTFs, AS/400 message handling, working with and securing printed output, using operational assistant to manage disk space, job scheduling, save and restore basics, and more basic CL programming concepts. Optional diskette available. 429 pages.

TECHNICAL REFERENCE SERIES: DESKTOP GUIDES
Edited by Bryan Meyers, a NEWS/400 *technical editor*

Written by experts, these unique desktop guides put the latest AS/400 applications and techniques at your fingertips. These "just-do-it" books are priced so you can keep your personal set handy. Optional online Windows help diskette available for each book.

Desktop Guide to CL Programming
By Bryan Meyers, a NEWS/400 *technical editor*

This desktop guide is packed with easy-to-find notes, short explanations, practical tips, answers to most of your everyday questions about CL, and CL code segments you can use in your own CL programming. Complete "short reference" lists every command and explains the most-often-used ones. 230 pages.

Desktop Guide to OPNQRYF
By Mike Dawson and Mike Manto

The OPNQRYF command is the single most dynamic and versatile command on the AS/400. But unless you understand just what it is and what it does, it can seem mysterious. Our new desktop guide leads you through the details with lots of examples to bring you up to speed quickly. 147 pages.

Desktop Guide to SQL
By James Coolbaugh

The *Desktop Guide to SQL* is an invaluable reference guide for any programmer looking to gain a better understanding of SQL syntax and rules. For the novice SQL user, the book features plenty of introductory-level explanatory text and examples. More experienced users will appreciate the in-depth treatment of key SQL concepts. 217 pages.

The Technology Guide to Accounting Software
A Handbook for Evaluating Vendor Applications
By Stewart McKie

If you are involved in recommending or selecting financial software for your department or company, this book is must reading! It is designed to help managers evaluate accounting software, with an emphasis on the issues in a client/server environment. McKie provides a range of useful checklists for shortlisting products to evaluate in more detail. More than 50 vendors are profiled, and a resource guide and a glossary are included. 225 pages.

Using Query/400
By Patrice Gapen and Catherine Stoughton

This textbook, designed for any AS/400 user from student to professional with or without prior programming knowledge, presents Query as an easy and fast tool for creating reports and files from AS/400 databases. Topics are ordered from simple to complex and emphasize hands-on AS/400 use. 92 pages.

FOR A COMPLETE CATALOG OR TO PLACE AN ORDER, CONTACT

NEWS/400 and Duke Press
Duke Communications International
221 E. 29th Street • Loveland, CO 80538-2727
(800) 621-1544 • (970) 663-4700 • Fax: (970) 669-3016

OR SHOP OUR WEB SITE: **www.dukepress.com**